LANDMARK COLLECTOR'S LIBRARY

GLOSSO
REMEMBERED

NEVILLE T. SHARPE

Published by

Landmark Publishing Ltd
Ashbourne Hall, Cokayne Ave, Ashbourne, Derbyshire DE6 1EJ England
Tel: (01335) 347349 Fax: (01335) 347303
e-mail: landmark@clara.net
website: www.landmarkpublishing.co.uk

ISBN 1 84306 199 6

Print: Bath Press, Bath
Design: Mark Titterton
Cover: James Allsopp

Front cover: White Mill, Hadfield, an early cotton mill on the Padfield Brook.

page 3: Tram in Station Road, Hadfield.

Back cover top: The fire which destroyed the Jubilee Mill, September 1994.

Middle: P.C. Ralph Shaw giving a Road Safety Demonstration at St Andrew's School.

Bottom: After a blizzard near the Quiet Shepherd. Such winters seem to be a thing of the past.

LANDMARK COLLECTOR'S LIBRARY

GLOSSOP REMEMBERED

NEVILLE T. SHARPE

Landmark Publishing

ACKNOWLEDGEMENTS

This book would not have been possible without the help of numerous people, many whose names I never learned, but nevertheless put me on the track of some interesting facet of Glossop's history.

Others are well known to me and I must take the opportunity to thank Barrie Shaw for providing many photographs and giving so generously of his time to seek out those odd elusive facts. Also Sue Hickinson and Michael Brown at the rejuvenated Heritage Centre who have so often provided illustrations and information on topics such as the local Constabulary or discoveries during excavations at the Roman fort at Gamesley.

Kenneth Wright and Arthur Tomlinson have provided some fascinating insights into the past, particularly with regard to Old Glossop. Douglas Brereton and Lena Matthews have done the same for Charlesworth, and Frank Gee for Whitfield. Through them I was able to learn something of local coal mines, cotton mills, rope works, wartime incidents and a host of intriguing details. I have recognised the contributions of William Kinder and James Chatterton elsewhere in the book. Captain R.M. Turner, C.B.E., Doctor Milligan's grandson, kindly checked my notes and supplied further information concerning our former M.O.H.

The Library Service both in Derbyshire and Western Australia has as ever been a reliable source of information and always willing to assist.

CONTENTS

INTRODUCTION

Why write another history of Glossop? We already have *Glossop Dale, Manor and Borough*, published by the Glossop and District Historical Society over thirty years ago, and more recently, *The Book of Glossop*, by local historian Dennis Winterbottom, published in 1991. These books have relied to a great extent on the sterling work of Robert Hamnett, but the history of the town did not suddenly cease with his death in December 1914.

Previous histories have certainly covered much of what has happened in the past, but there are several areas which have received little or no attention, and there have been developments in the interim. The population of Glossop has doubled over recent years and there must be many who would like to know more of past events in their new home.

I can also add a few insights gained from personal experience. There is something inevitable in history being written from a personal point of view, especially with regard to recent events; I hope that I have managed to keep this tendency in check.

Winston Churchill stated that in writing history, one should always heed the dictates of chronology. I have tried to follow his dictum with the early chapters, but with later topics I have thought it better to start from the earliest dates once more.

For most of its existence the Glossop area has been a quiet, backward spot. When the Romans built their fort at Gamesley it must have seemed the most exciting thing that had ever happened, but once the Brigantes had been subdued, life for most locals would have returned to rearing cattle and sheep while many of the benefits of Roman civilisation passed them by.

Without written records we can only guess what happened when the Romans withdrew. As to battles between the remaining Britons and the invading Angles, we can only surmise that they would have taken place. Standing on the borders of the later kingdoms of Northumbria and Mercia, the inhabitants may have seen the armies of either kingdom marching through Longdendale.

Derbyshire was under the control of the Danes for a period, but the only reminder of those times is the number of local place names and words still in everyday use. Did William the Conqueror and his army sweep through Longdendale as part of the "Harrying of the North" in 1069–70? The statement that "all Longdendale is waste" in the Domesday Book suggests that he may have done so.

Under the early Norman kings the district was part of the Forest of the Peak which made the life of peasant farmers hard, but the Forest Laws were gradually relaxed and the building of small farms allowed. From this period onwards the district would remain an agricultural area slowly improving as more land was cleared for the raising of crops and grazing. There would be setbacks during the troubled times of Stephen and Matilda, but under the control of the Abbots of Basingwerke from 1157 onwards, life would return to the normal round of

Aerial view of the Roman fort at Gamesley showing sites of buildings and roads.

View of Longdendale with Redgate in the foreground.

toil on the land until Henry VIII changed the whole ownership of land by the Dissolution of the Monasteries in the 16th century.

The Wars of the Roses may have passed by without Glossopians being aware that anything was happening outside their neighbourhood, unless they were called upon by their Lords to take up arms and follow them to take a part in that dynastic struggle. Even the English Civil Wars left little impression on most of the population, apart from funds and supplies forcibly extracted from them by the contending forces.

We can trace the origins of Glossop back to the Roman station at Gamesley and unearth details of struggles between peasants and powerful landowners. The genealogy of the Lords of the Manor can be traced back for hundreds of years and some of the improvements they worked are still with us, but Glossop as a society really begins with the Industrial Revolution.

The peaceful rural existence was destined to change, slowly at first, but at ever increasing speed with the growth of the textile industry. Starting with the building of the first mills towards the end of the 18th century, a collection of agricultural hamlets had become a centre of industry by the middle of the 19th. It probably seemed that this rapid progress would continue into the foreseeable future and the idea that the thriving cotton industry would have disappeared completely and Glossop become a residential district would never have been considered for a moment.

Much of the history as it was taught in our schools was the history of the rich and powerful and the way they used their wealth and power. With the growing interest in social history people want to know more of the actual lives and working conditions of those who by their daily toil in field and factory created the country's wealth. What of their living standards, their hopes and ambitions for the future, their reactions to the rapidly changing world around them?

White Mill, Hadfield, an early cotton mill on the Padfield Brook.

The Howards improved local living standards and appear to have been benevolent employers. Certainly the cotton masters created work for thousands and later provided most of the local amenities. But what about the contributions of people like Dr Milligan to the health of the community, or Miss Jessie Rowbottom, a teacher at Whitfield School who got such wonderful results under extremely difficult conditions?

What also of the efforts of councillors in difficult times, both after the granting of the Borough Charter in 1866 and during the Depression of the 1920s and 30s, or those who started local businesses; the farmers who have striven to make a living on soil which is far from the most productive; the quarrymen who hewed the stone out of local hillsides; and the masons and other tradesmen who built the mills and houses?

I am frequently asked where I find the information that appears in my books. The sources are many and varied; some comes from Robert Hamnett's lecture notes, some from the pages of the *Manchester Guardian* and the *Times*. Information has also come from poring over ancient documents, but far more from putting on a pair of stout boots and getting out and about. This activity supplies information from two sources; actual observations, and interesting facts supplied by people I have met in my excursions.

This second source is a cause for wonder because I don't understand how I manage to meet the right people. Perhaps everybody has something to contribute. Whatever the true explanation I have been fortunate to get into conversation with some remarkably knowledgeable folk. William Kinder, who worked for Middleton's the builders for most of his life, was a mine of information on such topics as who built certain rows of houses and what they did for a living, where the stone came from, problems with seams of sand; all entwined with some entertaining stories about the people involved. Mr James Chatterton of Tintwistle, after spending a lifetime in the Longdendale valley, seems to know the answer to my every question on that district.

I listen carefully to what people have to say and, once we have gone our separate ways, make notes as fast as possible, trying not to miss out a detail while all is fresh in the memory, checking the accuracy later. Sometimes they are wide of the mark, but there is usually a sound basis for what they have told me. Sam Gregory, for instance, told me that his ancestors were at the Jumble when the Manor of Glossop came to the Howards as part of Alathea Talbot's dowry in 1606. He was right! Amongst many other things he remarked upon was that the valley containing Jumble Farm once supported eight families, and now there was only one left farming it, just one more detail showing the changes that have occurred in living memory.

I don't know the names of many of the folks who have put me on the track of some interesting detail, but they have included policemen, stonemasons, farmers, council workers, cotton operatives, nurses and millwrights, to mention but a few. Someone of an academic bent may unearth facts buried away in ancient documents, but you would be surprised what a building worker can turn up when renovating some old property, or a council worker cutting the grass at the side of the road with a scythe.

Some of the folks I meet say, "This sort of thing should be written down before it is forgotten." They are right and I do my best to comply, but that does not stop them from complaining when the topic eventually appears in print.

History is all around us; the older streets are often named after previous lords of the manor, or former cotton masters. Corn Street, Cross Cliffe, Townend Well and Toll Bar House – all have a story to tell. Redgate may well take its name from some ancient skirmish, and Monk's Road from when the Abbots of Basingwerke held the land. In fact, one can hardly step outside without coming across some reminder of the past.

There is something evocative about walking along some track which was once a packhorse way. It is not difficult to conjure up the long lines of ponies with their panniers loaded with salt, coal, or perhaps newspapers for the local gentry. The creak of their harness, the sound

Above: One of the Howard Lions in Howard Park.

Right: Peter Shaw (far right), the mason who carved the lions. (Supplied by Mr A.W. Tomlinson)

of the bells on the leading pony, the cries of the jaggers and the barking of dogs as the procession moves on. One has only to stand on the summit of Mouselow with its commanding views over all the possible approaches to understand why it was chosen as a castle site.

Other features which can still be made out from such vantage points include the lines once traversed by old tracks used long before modern roads were constructed; rectangular field marks which were once the sites of long vanished cottages; depressions in the ground which were small quarries or delphs from which the stone was obtained to build farmhouses and the dry stone walls.

One of my earliest memories is of being taken by the hand up Padfield Main Road by Mr Evans, a retired railwayman, to watch the steam engines pass under the bridge, belching smoke and steam. Now the steam engines are long gone and the line taken up. What changes will the next seventy years bring?

I can remember the smells of the cotton mills, the wagon loads of coal being delivered to feed the rows of Lancashire boilers, smoke pouring from mill chimneys, children shouting "T'mills loosing!" when the hooter sounded at Wood's Mill, and a great crowd rushing out, some making a clatter with their clogs on the cobbles; "Tiger" tractors towing loads of cut logs to Turn Lee Mill; A.B. Taylor's Foden steam lorries; farmers delivering milk door to door in a horse drawn float, or on a sledge in the worst blizzards; the erection of Belisha beacons in the town centre and their replacement with traffic lights shortly afterwards, something thought quite revolutionary at the time; Frank James as a soloist in Whitfield Church Choir singing "O for the Wings of a Dove"; "Skippy" May making baskets of every description in his workshop at the corner of Victoria and Derby Streets; boys kicking up sparks with their clog irons from the granite setts which used to fill the centre of the roads where the tram lines had run; Remembrance Day processions before World War II; the formation of the Territorials as it became obvious that the country was heading inexorably towards war; the arrival of the evacuees from Gorton and later from Lowestoft; the sky glowing red at night during the Manchester blitz; the Panhouse Explosion at Turn Lee; the devastating floods of 1944; and a host of other incidents.

What of the characteristics of local folks? They certainly liked to poke their noses into other people's business and could often rattle off a fair bit of someone's pedigree, or details of their past which they might prefer forgotten. At a lecture on the cotton masters, when the speaker informed his audience that Daniel Wood had never married, an old lady at the rear of the hall piped up, "Yes, but he didn't die without issue."

This interest could prove helpful; a girl from Ashton-under-Lyne obtained a post at Olive and Partington's in the office as her first job. She was apprehensive as she had never been to Glossop previously and discussed her worries with an older friend. She was soon put at her ease: "Don't worry at all. Ask the first person you meet when you walk out of the station and they will tell you how to get to Olive and Partington's. But don't be surprised if they know you are coming."

Another aspect of knowing the origins of others applies for some strange reason to folks born outside the district. Why it should be so important to be born in a particular place escapes me, but certainly it was regarded as a matter of status with older folks. "Yes I know 'e's ninety-three, but 'e werna born 'ere. Came from Hyde when 'e were a lad."

Coal trains in Longdendale.

Another distinctive feature which is fast disappearing is the local accent, probably due to the influx of people from outside the area and the effects of radio and TV. Just as well in many ways because a stranger asking directions years ago might have thought himself in a foreign country. Many words in everyday use could be described as Middle English; *sithee*, *getten*, and *bonk*, for example. Also *hoo* for she; and, best of all, *shus how* meaning anyhow, or "choose how". Chaucer would have had no problems talking to locals.

Finally, it should be pointed out that I have been surprised at the number of people who, when I mentioned the idea of writing a local history, said, "Write it as it was, Neville." That is exactly what I intend to do, although what emerges may upset a few. History doesn't have to be boring and it should be made clear that it belongs to all of us, not some self appointed elite.

Aftermath of the Panhouse Explosion.

Shirebrook, late 20th century housing.

Top o' Town. Early 19th century houses used in the film *Cure for Love*.

1

Prehistoric Glossop

The heavy boulder clay in the valley bottom was deposited by the glaciers during the Ice Ages as were the glacial boulders, such as the one in Howard Park. This is not the only example; when the Police Station was being erected in 1861, a glacial boulder was found. It was so large that it was decided to leave it in situ rather than go to the expense of moving it. Again, when the basement of Montague Burton's outfitters shop was being excavated on the site of Hawley's Dome in 1937, a glacial stone was found and can be seen in a garden in Fauvel Road. Such boulders are quite common, but most have been moved when fields were cleared and are now embedded in the bottoms of field walls. This topic will be revisited when the Township boundaries are described.

There was a cycle of ice ages interspersed with warmer interglacial periods between 150,000 and 12,000 years ago. As the ice retreated, the grasses and trees colonised the bare ground, taking hundreds of years to become established. With a food supply provided, herbivores moved north to graze the new pastures, the first being small creatures like shrews, but gradually animals such as hares, reindeer, horses, woolly rhinoceros and mammoths arrived. These in turn attracted carnivores such as cave lions and hyenas. As the ice sheet advanced or retreated the plants and animals were forced to respond to the climatic changes or die out.

Microscopic examination of the pollen found at archaeological sites tells us which plants were common at various stages of occupation. Calculating the number of each species gives a picture of the vegetation. There is a world of difference between arctic tundra, bare but for a few mosses and lichen, and semi-tropical savannah grasslands. The pollen record shows that these extremes occurred in England. It certainly suggests that after the last Ice Age, there was a warm period with tree cover on the moors. By 8,000 years ago oak trees had spread over most of Britain. Dead tree roots can still be found sticking out of the peat, and beside the Pennine Way between Mill Hill and Moss Castle, fossilised hazelnuts can be found.

The first men to enter the district came as family groups of hunter-gatherers, following the herds of wild animals. The primitive hunter-gatherers required a large hunting area to support them. These folk did not only live in caves; they would make tent shelters from hides and branches. Each camp might be perhaps a hundred or more miles from the next and they had to be prepared to move as the animals became scarce and the bushes and trees in a locality were stripped of nuts and berries.

Wolves were dangerous competitors, but once domesticated they became useful companions on the hunt. The men provided meat and fish with their hunting skills, but the women were equally important, collecting berries, edible roots, and herbs. Our forebears certainly ate foods we avoid today as unpalatable, or too much trouble to gather. Examination of neolithic and bronze age sites shows that acorns, blackberries, elderberries and crab apples were eaten.

The evidence for the existence of Stone Age man can be found in the shape of flint tools

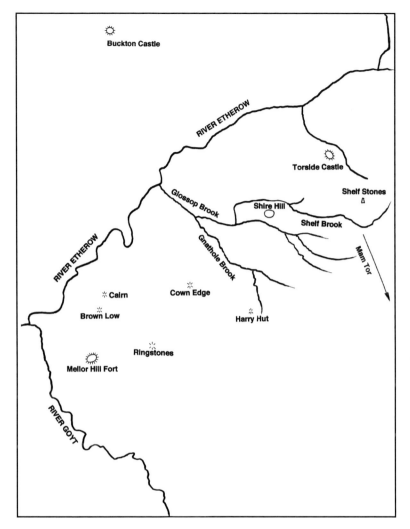

Map One: Prehistoric sites in the area.

and chips. Mr Jack Wrigley had a collection of over 1,800 flint pieces with their sites marked. Some were flint chippings, produced when a flint axe or knife was being fabricated, but others were microliths with sharp edges which could be put to a variety of uses. A flint microlith, perhaps 25 mm long, may not look an effective weapon, but used to bore a hole in the end of an arrow shaft and then embedded in place by melting resin it can produce a weapon capable of killing small game and inflicting a severe wound on a larger animal. Mr James Chatterton found a fine flint knife just below Shelf Rocks and a polished stone axe was found near Ringstones by Abner Froggatt.

The only materials to hand were wood, stone, animal skin and bone, bark strips and osiers to make into baskets. Tools were required to make other tools. Flints could be used to shape bone awls which in their turn could be used to make holes in skins so that they could be held together with strips of hide, to make clothing or boots. The wooden shafts of spears and hand axes could be scraped into shape with flint knives and flint points or axe heads bound into place with thongs of animal hide. Only the flint and bone survive; all the rest has rotted away.

The Stone Age can be divided into three main periods. The earliest is known as the

Fine example of a flint knife found below Shelf Stones by Mr James Chatterton.

Palaeolithic, which started with the emergence of men capable of making simple pebble tools and extended until the end of the last Ice Age. The Palaeolithic is further subdivided into the Lower Palaeolithic, starting millions of years ago and characterised by pebble tool and hand axe manufacture; Middle, associated with Neanderthal man; and Upper, beginning around 40,000 years ago and in Europe associated with Cro-Magnon Man and cave art.

The next period is known as the Mesolithic, which is generally characterised by the production of microliths, tiny flint tools which could be hafted into wooden or bone handles. This period intervened between the last ice age and the gradual evolution of farming communities. The dog was the only domesticated animal. The final division of the stone age was the Neolithic. Various dates have been suggested for the arrival of Neolithic farmers in Britain between 4,000 and 3,000 years ago. It would be later before their methods penetrated the Peak District. These farmers had domesticated cattle, sheep and pigs and grew cereals, and thus could support a far larger population. Whatever the timescale, the peoples with the more efficient technology would be successful and either oust the existing inhabitants or absorb them. This pattern would be repeated in the centuries before the Roman Invasion by the arrival of men with the knowledge of working in bronze and later iron.

Known flint chipping sites around Glossop are all located on the higher ground, typically at a saddle in the hills. There is a Mesolithic site at Harry Hut, and another even better one has been covered over by improvements to the Pennine Way at SK063902. The thick peat layer which covers much of the high moorland was laid down after the stone age and has preserved flint pieces in pristine condition.

Flint does not occur naturally in the Peak District and flints unearthed there may have come from Grimes Graves in Norfolk or the Lake District, so men must have valued this stone to carry it for great distances. There has been considerable loss of the peat cover in recent years, partly attributable to the peat-forming plants being killed by industrial pollution and partly due to severe moorland fires which have in many instances burnt right through the peat to leave the earth beneath exposed. One bonus from this loss of peat cover is that more flint chipping sites are being revealed. Flint chippings are usually found just under the peat where it has been eroded away, or a little lower down where it has been carried by the action of rain and the passage of walkers and sheep.

When you examine the flint chippings closely, you realise that they are not randomly shaped pieces of stone. Despite having been broken off thousands of years ago they still retain very sharp edges and sometimes signs of their edges having been worked can be discerned. The keen edges make them a very useful tool for scraping the inside of a pelt or for smoothing wood or bone.

Worked pieces of black chert occasionally turn up among the flint. Black chert can be found in the Wye valley, which is much closer to hand, but it does not hold a cutting edge as well as flint.

During excavations of old human habitations, pebbles with a crazed surface can be found. As there were no utensils capable of being stood over a fire, foodstuffs would be placed in a leather skin or crude earthenware pot filled with water and the contents heated by placing pebbles into a fire and, when hot enough, dropping them into the bowl. This method quickly brings the water to boiling point and the constant heating and quenching of the pebbles gives them a distinctive crazed appearance. Hence they are known as pot boilers.

More obvious are the mounds indicating burial sites. These may be marked as cairns or tumuli on maps. Burial mounds are not common in Glossopdale; within the boundaries of the township of Ludworth there is a tumulus in the plantation on Brown Low which is a well-known landmark. About a quarter of a mile away to the north-north-east is another on the line of the wall which delineates the boundary between Ludworth and Chisworth. On Cown Edge at SK021919 is a third tumulus. One reason for the dearth of tumuli in the area is that they have served as quarries when field walls were being built during the enclosure of waste land.

Torside Castle at SK076965 was on the 1926 list of old monuments prepared by the Commissioners of Works, but we shall have to wait for it to be excavated to determine if it is a natural feature or a man-made mound. If the mound is artificial then it is likely to be later than the stone age.

Just outside the limits of the Glossop townships, at Rowarth, are the remains of a stone circle which has given Ringstones Farm its name. Mr Thelwall wrote an account in which he describes a total of nine stones once having been on the site.

An interesting discovery was made in 1995 when Ann Hearle noted the manner in which the ground dried out on the hill where Mellor Church stands during the exceptional drought of that year. Her first impression was that it might indicate the foundations of medieval buildings, but later excavations revealed a defensive ditch. Perhaps the most surprising feature of the dig so far has been the discovery of items ranging from flint tools and cracked pebbles to coarse Iron Age pottery and even Roman pottery. Post holes from some wooden building have also been found. Thus the site must have been occupied since the Mesolithic period up to the Romano-British. The work at this site is ongoing so we can expect a few more surprises.

Anyone interested in prehistory should pay a visit to Cresswell Crags, close to the Nottinghamshire border.

Torside Castle. Natural feature or man-made?

2

CELTIC AND ROMAN PERIOD

The Mare's Back. Landslip or tumulus?

The Greeks and Romans regarded the Celts as barbarians. The Greeks called them Keltoi and the Romans referred to them as Gauls. Having left no written records, the Celts are something of a mystery, the details of whom are being slowly revealed by archaeology. From the artefacts they produced it appears that they had reached a high level of workmanship in metal and woodwork, and from the distribution of such artefacts that their culture had spread over much of Europe. Their southward spread brought them into contact with the Romans and in 390 BC Gaulish tribes sacked Rome.

Prior to the Roman invasion, Britain was occupied by tribes at various levels of civilisation. Those closest to the continent engaged in trading wine, slaves and hunting dogs and imitated the Roman lifestyle, while those more distant were still in the Bronze Age. Among them would be fugitives from Gallic tribes who had fled to Britain after being defeated by the Romans. They posed no threat to Rome but, having given support to Gallic tribes opposing Caesar and providing a refuge for Gallic chiefs, may have created a reason to invade.

Julius Caesar led military raids into southern Britain, the first in 55 BC and the second in 54 BC; these were of short duration and achieved little. According to Caesar's account he withdrew on both occasions because of damage to his ships caused by Channel storms.

In AD 43, Emperor Claudius despatched four legions to Britain with the intention of making a permanent conquest. The Romans landed at three points on the coast of Kent and, although there was fierce resistance by some tribes, within five years the Romans had conquered the south-east and advanced as far as the rivers Severn and Humber. The Britons were not united; some tribes were allied to Rome, others were fighting among themselves and the Romans were able to use this intertribal jealousy to their advantage. Resistance was piecemeal; some of the leaders of defeated southern tribes collaborated with the invaders, which was probably a sound policy under the circumstances.

The Romans laid out the Fosse Way in AD 47 to mark the frontier of their advance. It is a remarkable example of alignment and the name indicates that the boundary ditch was its main feature. The Fosse Way runs from Exeter to Lincoln via Axminster, Cirencester and Leicester, and once linked a line of forts spaced out at regular intervals. These forts were located to the north-west of the Fosse Way. Laid out over a distance of 200 miles, it deviates no more than eight miles from a straight line in this distance, only diverging to avoid the Somerset levels and similar difficult terrain.

It is possible that the Romans had no desire to conquer the whole island and would have settled for holding the economically productive south and Midlands, leaving the less fertile north and west to the barbarians. They had plenty to keep them occupied in Syria and along the Danube.

Beyond the tribes in the south-east were other tribes who at first took no part in resistance. Living amongst them would be members of the southern tribes who were not prepared to submit to Rome, eager to foment rebellion whenever the opportunity arose. Parts of the frontier would be in turmoil, a danger to the colony the Romans had established behind the Fosse Way.

The north of Derbyshire was inhabited by the Brigantes who were the largest tribe in Britain, dominating an area as far north as what is now the Scottish border. The Brigantes raised cattle, sheep and horses and hunted the deer and wild pigs. The Brigantes had their own coinage and examples found at Almondbury and Lightcliffe near Halifax are described in the *Victoria History of Yorkshire* as "remarkable for little save their low metallic standard, their rudeness of execution, and their lateness in point of time".

To deal with the problem the Romans applied the well-tried method of using client states as buffers on their boundaries while dealing with their enemies one at a time. There had been fighting between the Brigantes and the Romans previously, but Queen Cartimandua had made an alliance with Rome.

The Romans did not advance beyond the Fosse immediately as they foresaw the need to protect their western flank against the Silures of south Wales. This was achieved by constructing forts linked by a military road running north from Cirencester and building the fortified town of Viroconium near Shrewsbury. With the Silures contained, the Romans were free to attack the Ordovices in central and north Wales. The Ordovices were led by the British chief Caratacus who, after fighting the Romans in the south, had fled to Wales where he was leading a successful guerrilla campaign. Eventually Caratacus decided to take on the Romans in a major battle which led to his defeat, after which he fled to Queen Cartimandua of the Brigantes, hoping for support or at least refuge. Instead, Cartimandua thought it politic to stand by her alliance with Rome and had him put in chains and handed over to the Romans, who took him to Rome to parade in one of their victory processions. This act led to civil war north of the Trent and for the next few years the Romans were content to watch the Brigantes weaken themselves by internecine strife.

The Romans were working to a definite plan of campaign: having subdued the tribes in Wales they first consolidated their position before tackling the turbulent Brigantes to the north. The Romans may have pacified the south within five years, but to conquer the uplands was to take them another forty years and in this they were never completely successful. It is significant that there are no major Roman military fortifications of the period in lowland Britain but they begin once the Fosse Way is crossed and become more numerous in Wales, Lancashire, Yorkshire, Cumbria and Northumberland. The more civilised south must have adapted easily to a Roman lifestyle because this is where the majority of Roman villas are to be found. Throughout the Roman period, Britain remained a frontier province: apart from Syria it was the only province permanently garrisoned by three legions.

The Romans might have been content to leave the Brigantes in peace as long as they acted as a friendly state, but at some date prior to AD 57 Queen Cartimandua quarrelled with her consort Venutius, from whom she had been divorced. This quarrel destroyed the cohesion of Brigantia, which relied on marriage allegiances. Cartimandua took Venutius's relatives prisoner and he retaliated by invading her territory. Venutius was the leader of the anti-Roman faction of the tribe, so Cartimandua promptly called on her Roman allies for aid. Roman intervention made Cartimandua's position safe for the moment.

Venutius awaited his opportunity to pay off old scores and the chance came when the Roman world was riven by civil strife. Cartimandua, meanwhile, had married her former husband's armour bearer named Vellocatus. Venutius once more invaded Cartimandua's territory, and again the legions were obliged to intervene. They succeeded in rescuing Cartimandua but for the moment had to leave Brigantia under the control of Venutius. The Brigantes under Venutius were able to put a powerful army in the field which left the Romans with no alternative but to conquer the north if they were to have peace in the south.

Forts were set up at Templeborough (Sheffield), Brough, Gamesley and Manchester, with roads connecting them, during the period AD 78–84 when Agricola was Governor of Britain. These forts guarded the frontier with the Brigantes, and behind them roads linked Little Chester near Derby to Buxton and Manchester, Little Chester to Templeborough via Chesterfield, and Buxton to Brough and Gamesley. From these secure bases Agricola was able to advance until by AD 80 he had overrun all northern England and was securing his frontier with Scotland. The Romans went about the task methodically, advancing up each side of the Pennines building roads and forts as they progressed.

After their experiences against Caratacus, the Romans had no wish to provide the Brigantes with the opportunities to wage guerrilla warfare, where the heavily armed Romans would have been at a disadvantage. Instead they forced the Brigantes to face them on their own terms by attacking the Brigantian fortresses in succession. This type of warfare had much in common with the colonial wars of the 18th and 19th centuries. The Romans were equipped with powerful artillery in the shape of catapults and ballistas which could inflict carnage amongst enemies without the means to retaliate at long range. In addition to this advantage, the Romans used their ships to move supplies for their forces or to outflank the opposition. The Brigantes were eventually crushed between the arms of a pincer movement.

We know little about the battles between the Romans and the Brigantes, but James Butterworth, writing in 1827, was of the opinion that the mounds known as Mare's Back and Robin Hood's Shooting Butts were burial barrows for the fallen after such a battle. One has only to stand on Coombes Rocks and look down on these mounds to see that they are part of a large landslip and bear no resemblance to tumuli.

With the tribes occupying Wales and England defeated, the Romans placed their legions strategically to deal with any possible uprising. To overawe the Welsh tribes the fortress of the Second Legion was set up at Caerlon. The Sixth Legion was based in York so as to be able to control the north of England, and the Twentieth Legion was located at Chester where it could intervene in either area. In addition to the three legionary fortresses there were many smaller forts occupied by cohorts of auxiliary troops. Once established in Britain, the Romans recruited and trained auxiliaries from among the young men of the region, who were later sent abroad to defend other Imperial frontiers as far away as Palestine and Romania. In addition to augmenting the forces available to Rome, this method had the advantage of removing those likely to present a threat to Roman rule. These auxiliary troops were organised in cohorts of 1,000 or 500 men.

The campaign against the Brigantes led to a Roman presence in the Glossop valley. The fort at Gamesley was erected about this time, probably around AD 79–80. We have no certain written record of what the Roman name for this fort was, but it may have been known as Edrotalia from the nearby River Etherow, in the same manner as the Roman fort at Derventio took its name from the River Derwent. Ardotalia or Zerdotalia are other possible names. It certainly wasn't Melandra, despite the learned articles written on the subject. The main motive behind such articles was the opportunity to display knowledge of classic tongues.

The earliest fort at Gamesley was constructed with an earthen rampart topped with a wooden palisade. This fort lay within an outer defence system of which little sign now remains, and it may be that it was at first intended as a marching camp during the pacification of Brigantia. A Roman soldier was trained to put up fortifications and build bridges, culverts and roads, in addition to his fighting skills. When marching through unconquered country it was the practice to build a marching camp each evening as a precaution against attack.

Once the officer commanding decided to establish a fort it would be staked out to a regular pattern, with detachments set to dig out the trench to the required depth, while others would fell timber for palisades, huts for the troops, officers' quarters, and other buildings such as gatehouses. Sharp stakes would be cut to line the inner slope of the fosse.

This timber has disappeared under the later stone fort, but traces of the wooden palisade have been discovered buried in the rampart. A temporary marching camp could be quickly converted into a permanent fort and experiments using the equipment of the time suggest that a wooden fort could be constructed in approximately a month. There is no record of the unit of the Roman Army which built this wooden fort.

Later, the wooden palisades would be replaced with stone walls. The rounded corners of the fort and the absence of barbicans at the gates and intermediate towers are a feature of all early Roman forts. In later times, intermediate towers were erected between each gateway and the corner observation towers, plus a barbican on each side of each gateway.

The Emperor Trajan made the decision to have several forts in Britain rebuilt in stone to overawe the local tribes who were never truly pacified. Evidence found at the site shows that at least two cohorts of auxiliary troops were involved in the building of the stone fort; the 1st Cohort of Frisians, and the 3rd Cohort of Bracara. These troops also worked on the fort at Manchester.

The Centurial Stone of the 1st Cohort of Frisians was found by Sammy Cooper, who built it into the wall of his house. This stone is now in the Museum at Buxton; the inscription reads "C(o)ho(rs) 1 Frisiavo(num) (Centuria) Val(erii) Vitalis". Watson's translation was "Valerius Vitalis, commanding a century, or company of the first cohort of the Frisians, was stationed here."

The Frisians, being a 1st Cohort, would have roughly 1,000 men, including specialist craftsmen such as carpenters and stonemasons who could do the work of building, which explains why the centurial stone from the walls of the fort is that of the Frisians and not the Bracara.

The Cohort of Frisians was recruited from the area north of the Rhine, which had been in revolt in AD 96. It is probable that this cohort was raised around AD 98–100 and may have come to Britain early in the 2nd century as reinforcements in early Trajanic times.

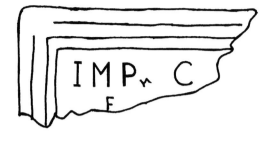

Centurial Stone from Edrotalia, now in
Buxton Museum.

Holyngworthe Stone from Edrotalia
(now lost).

The evidence for the presence of the 3rd Bracara takes the form of a tile stamped "C III Brac". The 3rd Cohort of the Bracara Augustani were raised from the colonies of Bracara Augustonorem in Portugal and were probably Iberian Celts. They were transferred from the legionary HQ on the Rhine to Caerleon in AD 89 and seem to have been attached to the XX Legion Valeria Victrix at Chester.

Rebuilding the fort in stone would be a lengthier process, involving clearing the site, realigning several buildings and rebuilding the walls, and it appears that this work was carried out around AD 108. Roman forts were usually built to a standard design, so that, if the general outline of a building can be made out during excavations, it is possible to make a fair estimate of the original appearance of the building from other examples which have survived in a more complete state.

Edrotalia is situated on slightly elevated ground where the junction of the Glossop Brook and the Etherow provide natural defence on two sides. The site was chosen because it enabled the Romans to control the entrances of two valleys giving access to the north Derbyshire hills and thus present an obstacle to any tribesmen intent on debouching into Cheshire or cutting the Roman roads supplying the legions.

Edrotalia was first identified as a Roman station by the Rev John Watson, Rector of Stockport, who visited the site in July 1771. Watson states that the local people called the interior the "Castle Yard", and eleven fields adjoining the "Castle Carrs". Watson was able to write that "The plough had not then defaced it, and its form could not be mistaken."

Various finds have occurred around the site over the centuries. In 1832 a portion of a larger inscribed stone was found and was purchased by Captain de Holyngworthe of Hollingworth Hall for 2s. 6d. The stone has since been lost but a sketch was made. This stone was almost certainly of importance, the letters "IMP" suggesting that the missing portions would reveal the name of the reigning Emperor. The rest of the Holyngworthe stone remains as yet undiscovered, but could be buried in some drystone wall.

In 1841, when Samuel Shepley was making a goyt for his mill at Brookfield, he discovered a stone coffin containing the remains of a Roman soldier. In the coffin was a silver coin of the Roman Emperor Domitian, AD 81–96.

Serious attempts to discover more about Edrotalia have occurred during two main periods. The first was at the end of the 19th and beginning of the 20th centuries. Robert Hamnett made a report on the discoveries made during the search of 1899–1900 and this appeared in the *Journal of the Derbyshire Archaeological Society*. The Manchester Classical Association made a report on the site around 1906 and Hamnett and his associates made further excavations in 1906–7.

Lord Howard and other gentlemen made contributions, but lack of cash was a major problem. One couldn't expect Victorian gentlemen to take off their jackets and set to with pick and shovel, so men used to manual labour were employed. Such men would be willing to earn a few extra shillings, but while they might be able to wield a spade expertly, they were hardly trained to carry out an archaeological excavation and some objects must surely have been damaged in the eagerness to get on with the job.

A wide variety of items was unearthed during the earlier dig: whetstones for sharpening tools with the wear marks evident; Roman bronze and lead weights; iron spearheads; a hatchet; lead dice and a soldier's iron signet ring. Many bronze and silver coins were also found. Those which were identifiable fell into two groups from their dates. One group bears dates between AD 69 and AD 135, while the second dates between AD 259 and AD 388. These give an indication of the length of time that the Romans were in occupation and also suggests two separate periods of occupation, the earlier in the first, and the later towards the close of the third century.

Coins were found at other sites; a Bronze denarius, of Emperor Posthumus, AD 259, was found in the Hague, and a silver denarius, Emperor Alexander Severus, AD 231–235, was found in Bank Street, Hadfield. Many coins of this Emperor and the Empress Julia were found in 1838 at Hooley Wood Quarry, Padfield. The location of Hooley Wood is something of a puzzle. In one article, Hamnett stated that it was just over a mile north-east of the fort in the township of Padfield. We would need to travel for 1.28 miles in this direction to reach the Padfield township boundary and a little further on at SK027963 there is a quarry beside the route of the former railway line. This may be significant because 1838 would be the time that the line was being constructed.

Another possible explanation comes from Jim Chatterton of Tintwistle, who used to shoot over an area known to him as Hooley Wood. This is the area on the Padfield side of Torside Reservoir just below Woodhead Dam. There is also no shortage of quarries along the road close by. Just which of these quarries the coins were found in is a question which may remain unanswered.

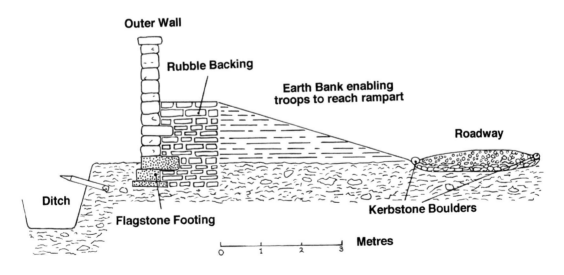

A section through the rampart of the Roman Fort.

The excavations showed that the foundations of the walls consisted of gritstone flags resting on boulders embedded in the clay. Above these flags was the first course of the wall, built from stones with the characteristic picked finish. The stone wall was narrower than the foundation, just as we would build today. The total height of the walls can only be estimated, but it would need to be at least shoulder height above the rampart and may have had castellations.

There was a tower at each corner with a rounded outer face, the entrance to the towers being from the rampart as no trace of an entrance from ground level was found. The lower rooms of the towers could thus be used as prisons or storerooms, with the sentries on the rampart being responsible for the safe custody of their contents.

The fort had double gateways, and there was an inscribed stone over the centre of the outer arch. The sentries stood in the recesses between the entrances and there was a small guardroom in one of the lower rooms. There was a gravelled road between the western and eastern entrances and some of the kerb stones lining the road were still in place in 1900. This road divided the fort roughly in half with the Principia, granary, offices and altars in the southern part. The northern section contained the soldiers huts and workshops. The floor of the granary was paved with square tiles. Floor tiles, wall tiles and fragments of hypocaust tiles were also found. Some of them have the letter R on them, some VV, which is an abbreviation of "Valiant and Victorious", the motto of the 20th Legion. Another find was the iron shoes of the south gate, which were found on the stone sockets of the gateway.

The eastern entrance was cleared to the foundations, which were found to be perfect, with a guard chamber on the left, and a small tower on the right, having their lower courses of stone still remaining. The gateway was a double arched one, and many of the arch stones were found in the debris which enabled a portion of one of the pillars of the arch to be restored with the original stones found at its base. A stone flagged conduit was uncovered for over sixty yards which was probably the main drain for the camp, and outside the station, near the west tower, was found a gravel road nine feet wide, leading to a plateau in an adjoining field which may have been a parade ground.

Since Rev Watson's day and for long before that date, local farmers and others used the site as a convenient quarry to supply ready dressed stone, which explains why there is little to be seen today. This re-used stone has been found at Woolley Bridge, Melandra Farm and in walls throughout the district. It is believed that considerable quantities of the stone were used in building Mottram Church, and large amounts of gravel were taken from roads on the site and used for the levelling of local roads in the 18th and 19th centuries.

Evidence was found that the fort had been destroyed by fire with signs that many of the stones had been subjected to intense heat, and charcoal was found near the inner walls of the rooms in the Praetorium and elsewhere. When the Romans abandoned a fort it was routine practice to remove the gates and burn them to prevent use by others, which would explain the charcoal. Alternatively it could have occurred in AD 367 when the Picts swept over Hadrian's Wall, looting, burning and slaying. This incursion was extremely serious, with the invaders capturing the Roman commander in the north and killing the Count of the Saxon Shore. Records of the time indicate that the cause of the breakthrough by the Picts was the treachery of the frontier scouts who were bought by promises of a share in the loot.

The date of the Roman withdrawal from the fort may have been in the mid-second century when other Derbyshire garrisons were withdrawn. However, this does not explain the coins dated for the last half of the third century.

Before leaving a fort, the Romans buried their altars. Robert Hamnett found the crown of the one at Edrotalia and it can be seen in the museum at Buxton. Hamnett also adds that the lead found was very pure, and must have been plentiful, for scraps had evidently been thrown away before the Romans would go to the trouble of remelting. The sheet lead showed the nail holes where it had been nailed to the roof. The Roman remains at Edrotalia were placed in the Glossop Museum which occupied part of the Victoria Hall. They were transferred to Buxton Museum during the 1930s.

After the enthusiasm for excavation at Edrotalia at the end of the 19th and beginning of the 20th centuries the work was not continued. Robert Hamnett, one of the driving forces, died in December 1914 and a few years later the Howards sold their Glossop Estates. With the decline in the cotton trade the descendants of the cotton masters had moved into other occupations elsewhere.

Further excavations started at the site in 1961, speeded up by talk of building an overspill estate. This work was led by Michael Brown and John Broadbent, plus friends, and continued to around 1965. They were convinced that the site was larger than the 3.5 acres occupied by the fort. Their investigations revealed sites well beyond the confines of the fort. Much of the material, such as leather shoes and boots with studs, cobblers' offcuts and wood, were taken to Manchester Museum, but the cost of the preservative polyethylene glycol treatment at the time meant that much was lost.

The prospect of building at Gamesley led Michael Brown and John Broadbent to approach Travis Collier, the Manchester Corporation official in charge of building the new estate, who happened to live in Simmondley. Thanks to his co-operation it was possible for the Ministry of Works to conduct several rescue digs in advance of building operations. These digs were run by the archaeologist P.V. Webster and the findings have been published in the *Derbyshire Archaeological Journal*.

Michael Brown was the site supervisor on most of the digs and made himself responsible for the recruitment of likely persons as diggers. On one occasion a busload of prisoners from Strangeways worked on the site. The original rescue digs were where the car park stands today, but due to further field work by Michael Brown in co-operation with Travis Collier, the area in which Roman remains were found soon spread. To the east, a large building, probably a Mansio or 'Posting Station', and the remains of the Civil Settlement were discovered, and a long ditch and rampart cutting off the fort from the rest of the spur. The only indications of most buildings were post holes but there were some large baulks of timber left in the holes. The Civil Settlement ditch was full of debris, which had the effect of sealing pottery and other organic material in good condition. Much of the Native Settlement is now hidden under the Gamesley estate.

In 1971 Michael Brown discovered traces of the bath house and later excavations showed that it was of the standard military type as at Vindolanda on Hadrian's Wall. It was also found that although the bath house had originally stood closer to the fort, it had gradually slipped down the bank towards the Glossop Brook due to the hill collapsing.

Assistance was given by local people, Anthony Ward, Patsy Rimmer, Joyce Powell and Norman Shuker to mention a few. This assistance took various forms, from giving talks to Historical Societies to raising money, writing newsletters and pamphlets, and to assisting with digs where they brought along friends and families. Archaeological students from Manchester University carried out a number of training digs on the site until 1998.

The interior of the fort held six barrack blocks for the garrison of around 500 officers and men; granaries, store sheds, officers' billets, the commanding officer's house and the Headquarters building. Only the foundations of the Headquarters can be made out; the other buildings were timber framed and have left little trace. Into the eastern rampart were built the camp ovens, situated so that the prevailing winds would carry smoke and sparks away. The only building within the fort constructed of stone was the Headquarters or Principia which contained a hall large enough to hold a full century of troops, plus various offices and the shrine. The room which appears to have been the Commanding Officer's, judging by the lines of nails found, once had a floor of wooden boards and a hearth in the centre.

The gateways were the obvious points for an attacker to make for since they were the places which could be assailed without crossing a ditch. To guard against this, they were

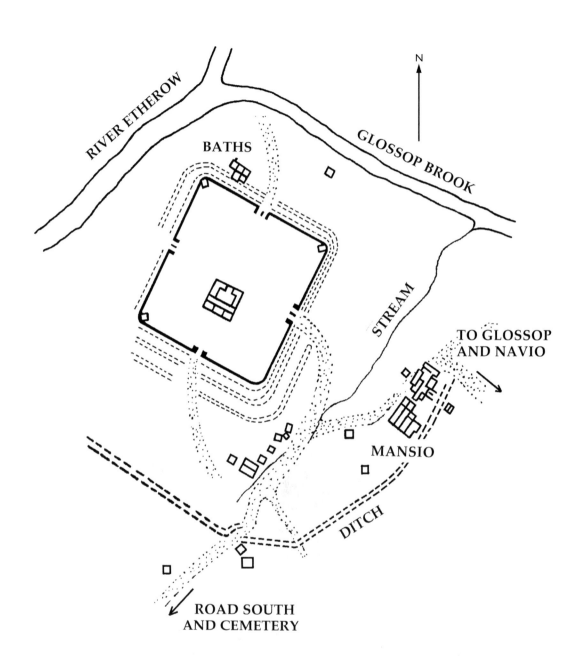

Map Two: Roman Fort and Civil Settlement.

built as strong defensive points from which missiles could cut down attackers with flanking and enfilading shots. To withstand battering rams the gates had to be of stout construction and the hinges were usually protected by the stone edges of the gateway. All the gateways at Gamesley had twin towers, but the south gateway was narrower with a single door.

What of the Britons in the area? Around all but the forts in the wildest parts of upland Britain there grew up military villages, or *vici*, which played a part in the economic development of northern Britain. Traders would gather in simple timber shacks and men could set up workshops to cater for the needs of the garrison. There would be skilled workmen, because the Britons had carts requiring skill in construction, and there would be blacksmiths capable of making weapons or horseshoes. It would form the centre for a local market and also provide for the recreation of the soldiers. Any such village near to Edrotalia would have disappeared when the fort was abandoned as no longer necessary for the pacification of the district.

In Brigantia the natives living in forests or in the fells would be tied to their sheep and cattle. The Roman presence meant that they were prevented from indulging in intertribal strife and their little farms would be able to grow and spread. But neither the way of life nor the economic level of such folk was conducive to an adoption of Roman ways. Their market needs were few and could be met at either tribal fairs or in the settlements for entertainment and trading which grew up round the forts. The small farmers would provide rents or taxes to support tribal and provincial government.

In a survey of Longdendale by the North West Water Authority, two earthworks were discovered. The first was a rectangular raised platform adjacent to Mottram Church, which may have been the site of a Roman signal station with wide views in all directions, which would have been invaluable to the garrison at Edrotalia in controlling the Longdendale Valley. Below Highstones Rocks on the 900 ft contour overlooking Torside Reservoir are what appear to be the remains of a Roman fortlet. The defences, which have not been thoroughly excavated, consist of a rampart, ten metres wide, and a V-shaped external ditch with a causewayed entrance facing south.

Crown of the Roman altar from Gamesley, now in Buxton Museum.

Roman Roads in the District

Other empires built roads but none have lasted so well. Some Roman roads were intended to be a permanent feature and these were carefully engineered. The topsoil was removed to a depth of about a metre and the foundation levelled. The road was made of small stones rammed down, and these were covered with larger stones fitted closely together. The Roman road system was one of their most useful weapons. The legions were often outnumbered but they had the advantage of being able to transport men and material rapidly to any danger spot. At intervals of one Roman mile along these major roads a cylindrical stone marker was erected giving the distance to Rome and commemorating the Emperor responsible. Lesser roads linking minor forts, which might well be abandoned once the area had been pacified, were built to lower standards, but have still left traces in many places.

In much of the south of England, Roman roads could follow a direct course, deviating no more than a quarter of a mile from a straight line over a distance of twenty miles. Between the extreme points of the road there are many pieces of straight road not quite in the same line. These occur where an obstacle such as an unnecessary crossing of a river, or a steep hill which need not be passed over, was met. Where steep-sided valleys had to be crossed, the road zigzagged up and down to make ascents and descents easier, but resumed the straight line on the other side. When we look at Roman roads today, we should remember we are looking at the ruins of a system whose systematic maintenance ceased over 1600 years ago.

The late Victorian Ordnance Survey map of Glossop to a scale of 1:2500 shows a Roman road running along the Top Sandhole with a further stretch across the field to the west of Lower Bank Farm. These two lengths of old track do not align with each other, and are most likely the remains of medieval ways leading from Simmondley towards the old centre of Glossop.

Roman forts were located at a distance equal to a day's march from each other, which enables us to make an estimate of where to look for the remains of a fort once the location of others in the area is known. Peter Wroe has written an account of his efforts to trace several of these roads in a book entitled *Roman Roads In The Peak District*. Wroe's work is of value because it is based on digging sections across the suspected line of Roman roads to check exactly which route they followed.

Hypocaust tile from the bath house (found during dig c.1971).   Black storage jar (found during dig.

Excavations at the east
end of the bath house
(*c.*1971).

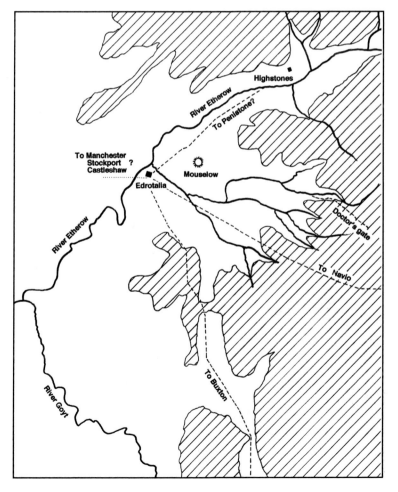

Map Three: Roman
roads from the Fort.

At one time it was stated that Doctor's Gate was of Roman origin and the paved portion over Coldharbour Moor cited as a classical example of Roman work. Wroe's efforts certainly cast doubts on this view and it seems more likely that Doctor's Gate is a medieval track. Weight is added to this view by the fact that the paved section has definitely deteriorated over the last sixty years.

Watson mentions a gravel road from Edrotalia pointing towards Stockport, and another road passing through the Hague and Mottram and on to where it joined the great military road from Manchester to York. The Victorian Ordnance Survey map and the 1910 map of the Roe Cross area both indicate a Roman road heading north from Gallows Clough in the direction of Castleshaw. Presumably after leaving Edrotalia and crossing the Etherow, this road made for the low point at Roe Cross farm between Shaw Moor and Harrop Edge, following the line of the Coach Road, and once this obstacle had been by-passed, turned north. Roads to Manchester and Stockport would set off in the same way and separate later. The 6 inch map of the Hattersley area of 100 years ago has the straight stretch of road passing through the estate marked as a Roman road, headed for Stockport.

Moving in a clockwise direction, the next road was the one heading for Penistone, of which little trace remains. Wroe suggests that the most likely line for this road would be north-eastwards from SK012951, just below the fort, to SK021960 on the crest of the hill shoulder and partway along Stanyforth Street, Hadfield. From that point a turn was made more easterly following existing roads as far as SK024961, where a north-easterly course was resumed. This turn was to avoid low ground immediately ahead. The next stretch is probably along the same line as the railway, which took the most obvious and level way through. After that the course is open to some speculation; it may have headed for the fortlet at Highstones, crossing the Etherow at around SK056983, or it may have followed the line of the railway up the valley, in which case the evidence will have been lost.

The route to Navio after leaving Edrotalia headed southeast above the Glossop Brook, passing along Adderley Place and continuing in the same direction until it was traced again by sections dug at Hob Hill and near Brownhill. After passing near the lodge at Moorfield House it continued up Bray Clough, where further sections revealed its presence beyond Wood's Cabin and close to where the enclosure road to the Whitfield Turf Pits emerges onto open moorland. From here it was estimated that it carried on over Moss Castle, where the road had been buried under the peat until it was traced again near to where Upper Gate Clough joins the River Ashop. The route continued down Ashop Clough, crossing Nether Gate Clough and Lady Shaw Clough before passing behind the Snake Inn, crossing Oyster Clough and then the Snake Road just short of Hayridge Farm. Beyond Hayridge Farm it continued in a fairly straight line until it passed the present site of the guide post known as Hope Cross and so on to Navio.

Wroe has traced the line of the road to Buxton and has dug sections at intervals to verify the methods of construction. After leaving the fort this road headed straight uphill until it met Monks Road, which it followed for a short distance. At the top of the hill above Plainsteads Farm it left the line of Monks Road, and under the right lighting conditions its course can sometimes be made out following a straight line for a short distance just after it has crossed the road heading for Rowarth, and then making a slight turn to the left and heading directly for the Abbot's Chair, where it makes yet another turn to get back to its original direction.

That the sudden deviation in the road should be marked by the Abbot's Chair, which is a medieval cross base, is interesting because it suggests that this road continued in use for many years after the Romans had departed. A further deviation in the same road occurs further south at the site of Martinside Cross. At one time it was possible to make out the line of the aggar or embankment of this road at SK024909, where it was crossed by the road leading to Rowarth or Cown Edge. The stones in the drystone wall followed the curve of the aggar quite clearly until around 1998–9 when the wall was expertly rebuilt with neat horizontal courses.

A stretch of the Roman Road from Navio (Brough) to Glossop. Note Hope Cross, an 18th century guide stoop.

The Abbot's Chair, a cross base sited where the Roman road makes an angular change of direction.

3
ANGLIAN AND DANISH TIMES

With the withdrawal of the legions we enter a period where it is far from clear what was happening in Britain; hence the term "Dark Ages".

With the legions fully occupied on the Continent, the Britons were left to see to their own defences. Roman Britain had long acted as a magnet to the tribes that lived to the north and west, the Picts and Scots. There were also Irish settlers in north-west and south-west Wales. At one stage the number of settlers from Ireland may have been greater than those invaders who came from the north-west corner of Europe.

The Angles first appear in the Baltic area of Germany, to the south of Jutland. The Saxons occupied north-west Germany, on the North Sea near the mouth of the Weser. The Frisians had been known since the 1st century, but the Jutes were a more obscure people, and are not recorded until the end of the 3rd century.

These raiders possessed the skills in shipbuilding and navigation to make long journeys, but what were the reasons behind this sudden upsurge of peoples prepared to embark on maritime expeditions? Pressure from the east by the Huns, a non-Germanic people, was one reason for the westward movements. Young warriors seeing little prospect of fame and wealth at home would gather a band of like-minded companions and set out in search of plunder in the form of treasure or slaves. Once settled on new land, the invaders would start to farm in order to support themselves, and it may be that it was the pressure to find fresh land that impelled them to set out in the first place.

In the early 6th century Britain was still dominated by British kingdoms. At that time the Anglo-Saxon population had been present for less than a century. By AD 500 Kent had become a German-ruled kingdom and there were considerable settlements in East Anglia, Hampshire, Lincolnshire and Yorkshire. Other bands were beginning to penetrate the Midlands, moving along the rivers.

There were battles in which the owners of the land were defeated and killed or driven westwards, but it may be nearer the truth to think of it as a violent takeover with the original Romano-British leaders being replaced by new Anglo-Saxon ones and the peasants being enslaved and continuing to work the land under new masters. The outcome was that by the end of the 6th century the Anglo-Saxons occupied or controlled a large part of Britain.

For information on these turbulent times we can turn to the Anglo-Saxon Chronicles, written several centuries after the earliest events. These were times when few could read or write and history was passed down orally. Such stories may have been embellished, but were based on actual events. It is probable that the Chronicles had their origins towards the end of the 9th century, and King Alfred could be the instigator, since he was at the centre of a movement to produce works in English rather than Latin because he wished them to be more widely understood. The Anglo-Saxon Chronicles are a remarkable record of the first continuous national history of any western people in their own language.

The Chronicles report the arrival of the Anglo-Saxons in England:

> AD 443. "Here the Britons sent to Rome and asked them for help against the Picts, but they had none because they were campaigning against Attila, king of Huns; and then they sent to the Angles and made the same request to the princes of the Angle race."
>
> A.D. 449. "Here Mauricius and Valentinian succeeded to the kingdom and ruled seven years. And in their days Hengest and Horsa, invited by Vortigern, king of the Britons, sought out Britain in the landing place which is named Ebba's Creek, at first to help the Britons, but later they fought against them. The king ordered them to fight against the Picts, and they did so and had victory wheresoever they came. They then sent to Angeln and ordered them to send more help, and tell them of the worthlessness of the Britons and of the excellence of the land. They then sent them more help. These men came from three tribes of Germany: from the Old Saxons, from the Angles, from the Jutes. From the Jutes came the Cantware and the Wihtware – that is the tribe which now lives on Wight – and that race in Wessex which they still call the race of Jutes. From the Old Saxons came the East Saxons and South Saxons and West Saxons. From Angeln, which has stood waste ever since between the Jutes and the Saxons, came the East Angles, Middle Angles, Mercians, and all the Northumbrians."

The success of these adventurers led to a stream of settlers from northern Germany who crossed the North Sea by the shipload, bringing their families and livestock with them. They advanced westward up rivers like the Thames and Humber and their tributaries and, after defeating the Britons, set up their own little kingdoms. The statement that Angeln stood waste after the Angles migrated suggests that the whole tribe moved. It is possible that, after the Pictish raids, much of the north-east and eastern England was depopulated and the Angles had little opposition when they first arrived.

In AD 495 Cerdic landed with five ships and within six years had driven out the Britons from the West Saxon kingdom. Further north the Angles were engaged in a struggle with the Britons of Strathclyde. In AD 547 Ida succeeded to the kingdom of Northumbria and built Bamburgh Castle, but it was not until the time of his grandson Æthelfrith that Northumbria became a powerful kingdom.

The early leaders of war bands set themselves up as kings of the areas they had conquered, and to validate their claims to kingship listed noble forebears going back in Germany to Woden. At one time these petty kings were numerous, but once the Britons were no longer a threat they fought each other to establish larger territories. We know little about these kings other than their names and the dates of some of the battles they were engaged in, but with the passage of the centuries, kings emerged who left their mark on English history, men such as Æthelbert, Offa, and Alfred.

Early in the 6th century, the Britons were able to regain land from the Saxons when they found a leader who led them in a series of battles. According to Bede in his *Ecclesiastical History of the English People*, this leader was Ambrosius Aurelianus, the sole survivor of Roman race from the catastrophe. Under his leadership the Britons took up arms and with God's help defeated the Angles. Thenceforward victory swung first to one side and then to the other, until the battle of Badon Hill when the Britons made a considerable slaughter of the invaders. The feats of Ambrosius are probably the basis of the tales of the legendary Arthur. Some of the Saxons returned to mainland Europe, but the success of the Britons was not to last, and by the late 6th century the Anglo-Saxons had reconquered all they had lost and gained supremacy over the remainder of England.

The Angles occupied the north and Midlands where the kingdoms of Northumbria, Mercia and East Anglia gradually emerged; the Saxons the south and west where their presence is recorded in such names as Essex, Sussex, Middlesex and Wessex. The little kingdoms were absorbed until prior to 800 there were seven – Northumbria, Mercia, East Anglia, Essex, Kent, Sussex and Wessex. At different times the Anglo-Saxon kingdoms had their periods of supremacy, the most important being Northumbria which was powerful in the seventh century, Mercia which supplanted it during the 8th century and finally Wessex which emerged as the leader in the 9th.

Glossopdale and Longdendale stood in the north of Mercia, on the border of Northumbria. The name Mersey is derived from the Old English words *mære* and *ea* which meant boundary and river respectively.

The ancient tribute list of the Mercian kings known as the Tribal Hidage gives the names of peoples owing allegiance to Mercia. To the north of the Mercians of the Trent valley, a folk of 1,200 households, known as the Pecsætan, was distributed sparsely over the Peak District of what later became Derbyshire, and parts of neighbouring Staffordshire and Cheshire. The Pecsætan, or people of the pec, are generally held to be the origin of the name Peak District, but the word *pec* is of unknown origin and could even be the original British name for the region. Derbyshire might easily have been named Pecset, like Somerset or Dorset.

Dr Nick Higham of the Department of Anglo-Saxon Studies at Manchester has shown that the Tribal Hidage was compiled under King Edwin of Northumbria *c*. AD 625, based on an earlier Mercian list under King Cearl *c*.600. Edwin's first wife was Coenburg, daughter of King Cearl, who was the first Mercian king to annex the Peak. Before the Mercian invasion the Pecsætan would have been British and had a Celtic name.

The Rev J.C. Cox was of the opinion that for about 150 years after the first coming of the English, the Peakland was retained by the Welsh, in the same fashion as they held the districts of Elmet and Loidis around Leeds. The homestead names of north Derbyshire are still strongly Celtic, whilst there is not a river that does not bear a Welsh name. Even the dialect spoken in the upper dales contains words of Cymric origin which can be detected by etymologists.

It would be natural for the conquering Angles to claim the best land for themselves and retain Britons to work the land, in which case British place names would have been passed on. The word "tor" for a rocky prominence, which is probably of Celtic origin, is found in many places within the Peak. The hamlet of Bretton could have got its name because it was once a place inhabited by Britons. The name Britland Edge at SE106025 might be a reminder of the boundary of an area once occupied by Britons. It is possible that the High Peak was never overrun by a military force, but that the small British population was gradually absorbed by the surrounding English.

The routes by which Angles reached the Peak District could have been via the Trent and Derwent valleys, or from Cheshire following the Mersey, Goyt and Etherow. Most of the Anglo-Saxon archaeological finds are to the south of the Peak, which suggests that the majority came by the southerly route. The place name endings for hamlets in the region are all English: *worth*, *field*, *ley*, *sop* and *wistle*. We have Celtic names for many rivers and hills, but *nase* for a protrusion and *comb* for the crest of a hill are of English origin, as in Peaknase and Coombes Rocks. *Clough* means a narrow valley. A *hop* or *sop* means a secondary valley off a main valley, hence Glossop, Hope and Ashop.

The pagan English cremated their dead and interred them in barrows, but after the introduction of Christianity they buried in graves. A typical Saxon warrior grave would contain an iron knife, an iron spear, and occasionally a sword and shield boss, while women were buried with amber necklaces, and silver rings or earrings. Why are there so few archaeological finds from the Anglo-Saxon period in Glossopdale? The answer may be that the area never had landowners with the wealth and inclination of the Batemans to do the spadework before the traces disappeared under roads, railways and buildings.

The only mention in the Anglo-Saxon Chronicles that might have relevance to the Peak is the entry for 605 which reads: "Here Æthelfrith led his army to Chester and there killed a countless number of Welsh; and thus fulfilled Augustine's prophecy which he spoke: 'If the

Welsh do not want peace with us, they shall perish at the hands of the Saxons.'" This raises the possibility that Æthelfrith marched down the Longdendale valley on his way to Chester.

Kings built their reputations by overawing their neighbours by success in battle and raiding their lands. Folks living on the border of Mercia would have been familiar with sheep and cattle raids, hence the need for "worths" to enclose their animals. On occasion they would make their contribution to Mercian armies raiding in the opposite direction.

One of the most important events in Anglo-Saxon history occurred when Pope Gregory sent Augustine on a mission to convert the heathen English to Christianity. The party landed in Thanet in early 597 and were fortunate in that the Kentish king, Æthelberht, had married Bertha, daughter of Charibert, the Frankish king. Presumably Christian practices were already followed within the king's household before Augustine's arrival, since the Frankish Bishop Liudhard had accompanied the queen to Britain. Æthelberht, convinced of their honesty, supplied Augustine and his companions with food and gave them a dwelling place in Canterbury, and allowed them to preach their religion. To convert the whole nation to Christianity was to take many years and there were times when pagan kings overthrew the new religion and their followers reverted to the old ways. Nevertheless, by the time of the Venerable Bede in the 8th century, the English Church had become one of the centres of western civilisation with English missionaries carrying the message of Christianity to the Old Saxons on the continent.

With the introduction of Christianity came the erection of crosses of a type known as a Mercian Pillar Cross, of which we have two examples locally in the shaft of Whitfield Cross and Robin Hood's Picking Rods. Whitfield Cross shaft closely resembles the Bow Stones near Lyme Hall and several other Mercian pillar crosses. These all have a collar at the top of a plain cylindrical section and are capped with a rectangular carved section and head. The interesting aspect of the seventeen known crosses of this type, is that sixteen of them are confined to the north and west of Derbyshire, east Cheshire and north Staffordshire, the area occupied by the Pecsætan.

The introduction of Christianity had many benefits; in addition to moderating the violent and often immoral behaviour of kings, literate monks provided a civil service to the state, being able to prepare charters and other records.

This more settled way of life was interrupted when in 789, according to the Anglo-Saxon Chronicles, "There came for the first time three ships; and then the reeve rode there and wanted to compel them to go to the king's town, because he did not know what they were, and they killed him. Those were the first ships of the Danish men which sought out the land of the English race. Again in 793 on 8th January the raiding of heathen men devastated God's church in Lindisfarne Island by looting and slaughter."

Despite this threat, English kingdoms were still fighting among themselves. The Viking raiders at this stage attacked undefended sites such as monasteries on or near the coast. In their opinion, wherever a priest put down his foot in England, silver sprang from the ground. Many of these raids were driven off with heavy losses to the Vikings, but the difficulty was in assembling a sufficient force to give battle before the raiders could make off with their loot. Soon the size of the invading fleets increased and in 836 King Egbert fought against 35 shiploads at Carhampton.

Viking successes encouraged them to greater enterprises and in 865 a Viking army stayed in Thanet and made peace with the inhabitants of Kent, who promised them money in exchange for peace. Thus encouraged, the Vikings were able to raid at will across the land and soon the only English kingdom which had not submitted to them was Wessex under King Alfred, and even he was driven for a time into the swamp fastness of Athelney.

In 878 King Alfred left Athelney and was reinforced by the men of Somerset, Wiltshire and part of Hampshire. He routed the Danes at Edington and so great was the victory that the Danes granted him hostages and made oaths that they would leave the kingdom. This was not the end of the Danes, because they were settled over much of England, which became

Robin Hood's Picking Rods. An ancient twin cross base used later to mark township boundaries.

known as the Danelaw. While this struggle was occurring, folks in the Peak were probably getting on with farming, often unaware of what was happening nationally.

The heart of the Danelaw was the Five Boroughs of Derby, Lincoln, Nottingham, Leicester and Stamford. Town and village place names of Danish origin are not common in north-east Derbyshire, which suggests that their numbers were few, but we have a number of place names of Danish derivation still in use in the region. *Warth* was old Norse for a ford or a flat meadow close to a stream. We have at least two "warths" locally; the wharf in Old Glossop and another by the Etherow in Hadfield. *Nab* is old Norse for a knob or knoll, and *gate* meant a path or road, as in Upper and Nethergate Cloughs in the Ashop Valley. *Carr, slack*, and *seat* are a few more words derived from Old Norse.

King Alfred's son Edward carried on the work of bringing England back under English control, settling burghs to consolidate English rule after each victory. In 907, Chester was regained, and in 913 Æthelflæd, Lady of the Mercians, built strongholds at Tamworth and Stafford. In 917 Æthelflæd took possession of the stronghold of Derby. The following year, King Edward went to Nottingham with an army and ordered a stronghold to be made opposite the other on the south side of the river, and from there went to Bakewell and ordered a stronghold to be built and manned.

With the death of Edward in 925, his son Athelstan succeeded to the kingdom and carried forward its unification. Athelstan took his armies north and for the first time established the rule of the southern English over the whole of England. Having established his authority throughout the north of England he turned his attention to Wales and forced their kings to acknowledge his overlordship. Next it was the turn of the West Welsh of Cornwall to learn of his power. In a few years he had brought the whole of England into submission.

Eventually an alliance of Welsh, Dublin Vikings and Scots established themselves in Northumbria from where they intended to strike south into the former Danelaw. Athelstan gathered an army to meet the challenge and late in 937 he overwhelmed the combined force at the battle of Brunanburgh.

King Athelstan died in 940 and his brother Edmund succeeded to the kingdom. The various factions who had sworn allegiance to Athelstan took this opportunity to seize their independence and in 941 the Northumbrians broke their pledges and chose Olaf from Ireland as their king. Edmund reacted; in 942 he captured the five boroughs, and in 944 brought the whole of Northumbria into his domain.

English successes came to an end due to a series of murders and revolts. These started when King Edmund was stabbed by the robber Liofa in 946 and continued until Æthelred came to the throne. He has come down to us as Æthelred the Unready; certainly his reign turned out to be a disaster. Once more the Viking raids became a menace. In 980 Southampton was ravaged by a raiding ship-army, and in the same year Cheshire was raided.

By 1013 the Danish king Swein had dispossessed Æthelred, but in 1014 Swein died and by 1016 his younger son Canute was established as king with the support of both his English and Danish subjects and so was the first king of the united kingdom of England.

On the death of Canute in 1035, the throne was taken by his illegitimate son Harold, who ruled until 1040 when Hardicanute, the son of Canute, who had been ruling in Denmark, was sent for.

On Hardicanute's death in 1042 the kingdom reverted to the native English line of Edward the Confessor. Edward's death in 1066 was to bring about the most famous crisis in English history. He was succeeded by his brother-in-law Harold II.

The English language is perhaps the most lasting testimony we have of the period. The languages spoken by the Anglo-Saxons and by the Danes and other Norse folk had common roots and they would have been able to converse without too much difficulty, but at the same time the language which would develop would needs be simplified, and perhaps this is why English seems able to absorb words from any culture which it comes in contact with.

Most of our shire and parish boundaries were set out by the Saxons in the years before the Norman Conquest and many of them still have the same ancient boundaries, or these boundaries can still be traced. In the 10th century the kingdom of Mercia was divided into shires, Derbyshire being the most northerly.

4
THE MEDIEVAL PERIOD

Arguments about who had the greatest right to the throne of England could fill volumes, but the indisputable fact is that William won at Hastings and seized the throne.

This was by no means the end of the struggle and for years afterwards William was engaged in suppressing revolts. The revolt which has relevance to the High Peak occurred after William sent an army into the north-east only to have it utterly destroyed. William's answer was the "Harrying of the North" in the years 1069–70, when he marched through the north laying waste to the lands between the Humber and the Tees. To stamp out the possibility of further resistance he slaughtered men and beasts, burned crops and buildings, and destroyed farming implements. When he had completed the devastation of the Vale of York he took his army over the Pennines into Cheshire, destroying everything in his path.

William replaced the English landed men who had fought against him at Hastings with his followers who had come from France in the hope of gaining land as a reward, and over the next few years those who rebelled were also replaced until the whole country had a Norman aristocracy. By the time the Domesday Survey was taken, 20 years after the conquest, only two out of 1,400 tenants-in-chief holding land directly from the king were English, and only eight per cent of the land was in English hands. The Domesday Book is a remarkable document which names villages; who held them on 4th January 1066 when Edward the Confessor was king; to whom they had been granted under William; and who held them in 1086. It lists how many hides or carucates the holding had contained and how many it still contained; how much woodland, pasture, meadow land, etc; how many mills, lead mines, salt works, churches and priests; how many free men, villagers, smallholders, ploughmen and slaves, what was the value of the village at the death of Edward and what was its present value? Armed with this information, William was in a position to exact the maximum income from taxation.

At the time of the Survey, Longdendale included land in Cheshire and Derbyshire. Tintwistle, Hollingworth, Thornsett, Ludworth, Charlesworth, Chisworth, Chunal, Hadfield, Padfield, Dinting, Hayfield, Whitfield, Glossop and Kinder would all be considered as part of it. The Domesday entries for these villages have been repeated often enough, but the information that "All Longdendale is waste. There is woodland, unpastured, fit for hunting. The whole eight leagues long and four leagues wide. Before 1066 worth 40 shillings", suggests that it was one of the districts laid waste.

Both Saxon and Norman kings regarded the Forest of Peak as a hunting ground. After the Conquest the forest laws were more stringently applied and English law defined the forest as those parts of the land exclusively reserved for the king's own hunting. In those days kings would travel the land to see to the administration of justice. Their retinues needed feeding, and local landowners would supply them from their estates. Hunting would provide much of

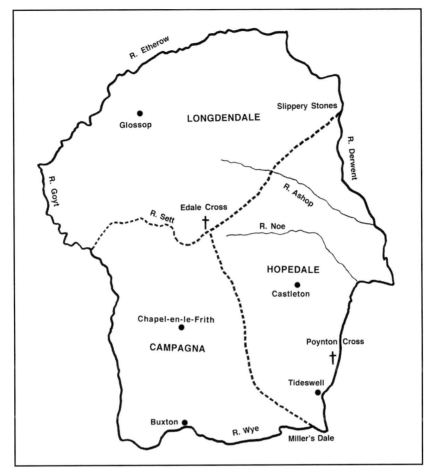

Map Four: The Royal Forest of Peak.

the meat required and also serve to keep his followers used to action in the field when they were not engaged in fighting.

The boundary of the ancient Forest of Peak followed the course of the River Etherow from its meeting with the Goyt at Watermeeting, to the point where Far Small Clough joins it just to the west of Saltersbrook. The boundary followed Far Small Clough and continued south, until it reached the head waters of the River Derwent. The boundary then followed the course of the Derwent as far as Mytham Bridge near Bamford. From Mytham Bridge it followed the River Noe until it reached the point where the Bradwell Brook joined it. The Bradwell Brook was followed upstream to Hazelbadge and on to Poynton Cross, and thence to the Tideswell Brook until it joined the River Wye. From there it followed the Wye to Buxton and on to the source of the Wye, then down to the River Goyt until it met the Etherow. The forest was divided into three parts; Longdendale, Hopedale, and the Campagna. The three parts met at Edale Cross, which stands at the summit of the old way from Hayfield to Edale.

William's illegitimate son, William de Peveril, was granted the Manor of the Peak and acted as the king's head steward, responsible for ensuring the forest laws were upheld. Peasants living within the bounds of the Forest of Peak would have to contend with foraging deer eating their crops and they were strictly forbidden to drive off the deer or kill them. In the

Left: Edale Cross, sited at the point where the three wards of the forest met and also at the highest point on the way from Hayfield to Edale.

Above: Arch in Buxton Museum constructed from stones found on Mouselow.

Below: Remains of the earthworks at Mouselow Castle.

Upper Derwent Valley there are the remains of ditches and banks designed to let the deer out of the forest, but prevent the peasants' cattle from straying within.

At certain times of the year peasants were allowed to graze their animals in parts of the forest on payment of a rent. From this it was a small step for foresters to build cottages and fence off gardens within the forest bounds. Such an offence could lead to the confiscation of the encroacher's land, but often the offence was merely noted and a rent levied. In this way the original purpose of the Forest was whittled away.

William I was not a believer in the death penalty since this would deprive him of manpower needed to work the land or serve in his armies. Instead, the penalty was often mutilation, such as cutting off an offender's ears. However, this usually seems to have been commuted into a heavy fine since no one drew benefit from cutting off a peasant's nose.

In the Civil War between Stephen and Matilda (1135–54), Peveril's son or grandson became involved when he supported the cause of Stephen. When in 1152 he was reputed to have poisoned Ranulf of Chester, Peveril fled to a French monastery when he was attainted by the new King Henry II. This meant that his estates were forfeit and he could neither inherit nor transmit by descent.

Mouselow is in an ideal position to place a castle with its commanding views in all directions. It could have been used in Celtic times, and later to protect the Earl of Chester's salt route into Yorkshire. There is also the possibility it was used as the site for a small castle during the struggles between Stephen and Matilda. Dennis Winterbottom, the Glossop historian, suggested that Mouselow was fortified by Ranulf II or his agents. Strength is given to this theory as the *Victoria County History* describes it as a motte with traces of a bailey. It goes on to say that there are fairly obvious traces of a double rampart and on the east a triple rampart, and also indicates that there may have been traces of a settlement and fortification prior to the period of the motte and bailey.

The motte and bailey was a feature of Norman castles and the site of Mouselow Castle was described by the Rev John Watson of Stockport, in 1775 as follows:

"On the top of the hill there was a strong fort surrounded by a wall, the whole encompassed by three large ditches. The ascent being small towards the south-west, the strongest works were raised on that side, on all other parts the hill is exceedingly high and steep. The earth on the top of the hill is exceedingly irregular, and has been robbed of most of its stone to build houses, and make fence walls."

J. Aiken, in 1795, states that "about 15 years since Mouselow was pastured to the top, on which it was plain to see that a building had stood, there being deep holes and a quantity of stones." Carved stones were found on Mouselow by the Rev George Marsden in 1846, whilst digging for stone to build himself a house. He built these stones into the gable end of a house near to the Spinners Arms from where they were removed by the Lord of the Manor. Edward Bernard Howard gave Mouselow the name of Castle Hill.

Why is there so little trace of a castle at Mouselow today? When Henry II came to the throne most of the unlicensed castles were pulled down, and if Henry said a castle had to be demolished, then demolished it was. Henry visited the Forest of Peak in 1158 and 1164, when he stayed at Peveril Castle and hunted in the forest.

In 1157 Henry II was campaigning in North Wales, and when his army marched through a gorge in the Forest of Coleshill he was ambushed by the Welsh leader, Owen Gwynedd, and Henry's army suffered heavy losses. As Henry retreated to Chester he came to the Cistercian Abbey of Basingwerke, on the Welsh bank of the Dee. It was about this time that Henry gave the Manor of Glossop to the Abbots of Basingwerke, and it could be that this was to give thanks for his escape from the Forest of Coleshill and the aid given to his followers by the monks. Henry II's charter states, "In free and perpetual alms ten pounds value of land in

Peveril Castle, Castleton.

Longdendale namely Glossop with the church that is there and with all lands and things relating to it just as William Peveril had it in the time of Henry my grandfather."

The Manor of Glossop was in the possession of the Roman Catholic Church for 380 years until they were dispossessed by Henry VIII. The monks would make improvements, building up flocks of sheep, and keeping fences and buildings in repair.

To the question, what was happening in Glossopdale at this time, probably the most accurate answer is, not a lot. We are, however, indebted to Mr C.H. Chambers, a former Headmaster at the Grammar School, for his painstaking research through old documents which revealed many interesting facts. For example, in 1222 a grant of wood was made for melting lead. Was the wood required for melting lead in the White Peak, or was the lead ore brought to Glossop to be made into lead for church roofs?

In 1251, the Vicar of Glossop and Abbot of Basingwerke were fined for taking a hind. So much for the harsh Forest Laws!

The following events show that progress was being made. 1275: Basingwerke has assize of bread, ale and gallows at Glossop. 1285: Abbot of Basingwerke charged with £50 damage to wood of Longdendale by building house 100 ft by 15 ft. The Abbot was present in court, and declared that he ought not to be amerced nor blamed for this; that the pasturage of the wood in leaves and herbage was his; and moreover that this wood was out of the limits of the Regard. It appears that the Abbot was successful because in the same year all the Basingwerke charters were examined and confirmed. 1289: Grant to Basingwerke of market and fair at Glossop. This grant gives also a weekly market at Glossop on Wednesday and three day fair at St Barnabas, afterwards changed to Monday and St Mary Magdalene. This could well be the date on which the Market Cross was erected.

Between 1293 and 1360, the Abbey of Basingwerke acquired lands in Charlesworth, Chisworth, Chunal, and Simmondley. In 1329, Basingwerke was granted a market at

Charlesworth. During this period the Chapel of St Mary Magdalene at Charlesworth, and Hayfield and Mellor Churches would be built, as they were all within the Ancient Parish of Glossop. The Abbots would lease land to others and in 1292–3 a post mortem on Thomas le Ragged mentions lands in Whitfield, Kynder, Buggesworthe, Berde and Ferniley. Again in 1309, Richard le Ragged, bailiff of the forest, has messuage and 40 acres in Chisworth.

The lives of ordinary folks in medieval times have been described as short, nasty and brutish. Certainly life expectancy was much shorter than today and personal hygiene of a low order. Leprosy appeared in Britain in the 6th century, and in the 14th the Black Death carried off thousands and was to return again and again.

Housing was very primitive. The more prosperous husbandman might have a timber house built on the cruck principle, with the spaces in the walls filled with lath and plaster, or kneaded clay mixed with chopped straw. The floor would be tramped earth, often used as a urinal. Sleeping space would be under the thatched roof, reached by a ladder. A hob of clay would serve as a fireplace and the smoke allowed to escape through a hole in the roof as chimneys were unknown. The smoke hole would have to be of a substantial size or the inmates would have been smoked like kippers. The peasant's home would be even cruder, built with posts wattled and daubed with mud or clay. Mud was used in building until relatively recent times. Lime for mortar had to be carried for a distance and to cheapen the work, mud was used inside the wall and lime mortar on the outside.

What did medieval people subsist on? Wheat would not be grown in Glossopdale due to the climate, but each peasant would have a patch of land to grow oats and barley for porridge, oat cakes, and brewing small beer. Potatoes and turnips were unknown, but beans had been grown for centuries. The weeds, Fat Hen and its tastier relation, Good King Henry, would be eaten. In hard times, other plants would be eaten, even beech mast and acorns. The local streams still have trout and before the rivers were polluted, salmon came up to spawn. With a much smaller population, the supply of fish should have been ample. The occasional hare and rabbit would end up in the pot. Glossop was formerly surrounded by vast commons on which the peasants could graze their animals and geese, the latter supplying eggs and a good source of meat. This advantage would be lost as land was gradually enclosed. Enclosure of land had taken place, as we have seen in the case of assarts in the king's forest, and with population growth more land in cultivation was required. At harvest time, medieval Glossopians would go to southern England to work in the same way that people from Ireland came to England and Scotland more recently.

Enclosure of arable, meadow, and waste land took place in England from the 13th century up to the middle of the 19th century, and two Statutes of the Realm – the Statute of Merton in 1235 and the Statute of Westminster in 1285 – laid it down that any enclosures of "lands, wastes, woods, and pastures" of a manor should not reduce the common pasturage necessary for the use of the free tenants of the manor concerned and neighbouring manors below their needs in husbandry.

Despite these statutes, enclosure carried on and was accelerated by the changeover in agriculture to sheep farming during the late 15th and throughout the 16th and early 17th centuries. During the 16th century, some lords of the manor turned to sheep farming, and to gain greater profit, evicted their tenants, fenced in their common land, and pulled down their houses. We have no record of such evictions in Glossopdale, but it is certain that common land was enclosed by the Talbots and the Howards. The fact that there was very little freehold land in Glossop, other than in Whitfield, certainly suggests that previous lords of the manor had steadily enclosed without an Act of Parliament.

When the Glossop Estates were being broken up in the mid-1920s, by an unfortunate mistake the bulk of the estate documents were taken away in two lorries and destroyed. A very strange mistake! If these papers had been preserved it would be possible to fill in many gaps in the history of Glossop, among them being details of past enclosures.

We have information on Abbots and Verderers, but for knowledge of the bulk of folks who worked the land we have to turn to tax lists. On the Lay Subsidy Roll for Derbyshire in 1327–8 the following Glossop men appear. Derbyshire at that date was not a wealthy county, with little commerce apart from the lead of Wirksworth and High Peak Hundreds.

Rob de Deywysnape
Hugo de Padfield
Jurdan de Gamelesley
Hugo Brouneson
Wills Godard
Adam de Thorp
Wills del Bothe
Wills de Holberode
Johes de Merpell
Rob del Heth
Wills Waynsulofwoll
Wills Aumson
Wills fil Rog
Ric fil Wills

Bailiff's House, Church Street. Note window built up to avoid window tax.

Several facts stand out straight away on this list: firstly, very few have a surname; secondly, many take their name from where they lived; thirdly, there is not a single surname based on a trade or occupation, which suggests that Glossop was not very prosperous in 1327; and finally, that names like Goddard, Thorp and Booth have been in the area for well over 600 years and doubtless longer. Dewsnap is a surname once only known in the Peak and takes its name from the farm of that name. The Norman French can be ignored: ordinary folk spoke English. The list for the rest of Derbyshire gives plenty of trade names such as Baker, Brewer, Chapman, Fowler, Mason and Salter.

Later, the Abbots of Basingwerke leased out their lands in Glossop to the Talbot family. From the records it appears that in 1435–6 the Manor was in the hands of Sir Christopher Talbot, and in 1447–8 it had been granted to Sir John Talbot. In 1484 the lessee was Sir Humphrey Talbot, and around 1494 John Pole and Geoffrey Talbot presented John Talbot as Vicar of Glossop by leave of the Abbot of Basingwerke.

With Henry VIII's Dispossession of the Monasteries, the Manor of Glossop passed in 1538 into the hands of George Talbot, Count of Shrewsbury & Waterford. The Manor stayed in the possession of the Talbots until 1607, when Lady Althea Talbot, the heiress of Gilbert, Earl of Shrewsbury, married Thomas Howard, Earl of Arundel and Surrey. From that date it remained with the Howards until recent times.

At Easter, tenants had to pay their Easter dues and tithes. Several of the lists have survived including one for 1433, written by Thomas Wagstaff who was the bailiff of the day.

Tithes were established for the support and maintenance of the clergy, churches and other religious establishments. In the Middle Ages, the church played a larger part in the lives of people than it does today. The church would be the only large stone building and serve as a meeting place for both religious and secular purposes. One duty which had always been performed by the church was the distribution of alms to the poor, and some portion of the tithe would be used for this purpose. The tithes were divided into the great tithe and the small tithe, the former going to the landlord and the latter to the vicar. After the suppression of the monasteries and the handing over of their estates to the nobles, with the right to collect tithes and dues from the people, a radical change occurred. The great tithe went to the Talbots instead of the Abbey of Basingwerke and the tenants were making a contribution to the maintenance of the gentry.

After nearly 400 years in the possession of the Abbey of Basingwerke, the change in ownership meant drastic changes for those farming the land. The new owners were determined to increase their income from the properties recently acquired. On the death of George Talbot in 1538, his son Francis held the Manor until 1560 and granted leases, some of which expired in 1563 and the remainder in 1579. The tenants whose leases had expired remained tenants at will until the expiry of the remainder, though they seem to have been warned by the Earl's officers that the new terms would differ from the old. The rent for a 20 acre farm was to be increased from four shillings to £14, a 70-fold increase.

Amongst them were men old enough to remember the conditions when the Abbey owned the lands. The new terms caused bitter resentment, but the demand that they should pay tithes otherwise than in kind and perform certain services may have further exacerbated the ill will.

The dispute had been developing for some time, and in 1579 a group of Glossop men decided to defy George, Earl of Shrewsbury by appealing to the Privy Council, and furthermore to arm themselves to defend what they considered their rights.

The Earl had problem enough with safeguarding the Queen of Scots as his prisoner at Sheffield, and the track from his Sheffield seat by way of the Woodlands and Doctor's Gate was not a route he would want to travel too often. This is probably why he only visited Glossop once between 1579 and 1581. Robert Dudley, Earl of Leicester, says that the tenants did not complain about the conduct of the Earl, but of his officers William Dickynson and

George Skargell. He was probably giving the true cause of the objection to the new duties, on one side overbearing officers, and on the other stubborn peasantry.

The four ringleaders were Botham, Booth, Jackson and Mellor, and the Earl decided to replace them with some of his own servants. The four responded by persuading 48 other tenants to join them, swearing that none would accept a tenancy unless the four were allowed to remain on their holdings.

The tenants sent two deputations to see the Earl at Sheffield. After the second interview they sent one of their number back to Glossop to "fetch all the rest", and go to London to the Privy Council. So many went that the Council put them all in the Marshalsea and heard only a selected few: Henry Botham, William Boley, Thomas Booth, William Booth, William Dawson and Oliver Smith. The tenants were to lose in the end, being compelled to make terms with their Lord, but they certainly kept up the struggle for as long as they were able, persisting in spite of imprisonment.

It would be interesting to know more about the dispute between Harry Botham and company and the Earl of Shrewsbury. The records tell us more about the earl than the tenants; what a pity that the Glossop Parish Registers don't go back another fifty years so that we could learn more about Harry Botham. However, one thing that emerges clearly is that the Bothams did not immediately leave the area. Between 1620 and 1737, the Parish Registers record 33 births, 46 deaths, and 29 marriages involving members of the Botham clan, who lived mainly in the Charlesworth and Simmondley townships. Oddly there are no Botham births recorded between 1737 and 1800 and no deaths between 1766 and 1800. Furthermore, the Index of Probate Documents for the Ancient Parish of Glossop lists 10 Botham wills between 1595 and 1774, but none after that date. Whatever became of them? The 1851 Census for Glossop shows not a single person of that surname. One thing is certain; they were once so numerous that if they were determined to resist by force of arms the Earl would have needed a considerable force to overcome them.

The revolt of the men of Glossop against their Lord was only part of a much larger struggle. The attitude of the nobility to the peasantry is at the root of the class system which has done so much to retard progress in Britain. The struggle to overcome the system is behind such diverse events as the spread of Lollardism, the Peasants' Revolt, the English Civil Wars, emigration to the New World, Luddism, and the American War of Independence.

From the list of Alehouses in Derbyshire for 1577 comes the following extract:

Glossopp: Robert Bothe, Thomas Bothe, Roger Bray, Robert Seele, Thomas Hutchclyff, Edwarde Wagstaff, Henry Wagstaff, Henry Hadfield, Henry Hadfield (sic), Charlys Wagstaff, Uxor Dowson, William Stafford, Vidua Willielmi Ratclyff. Alehowsis xiij. (These thirteen alehouses would be spread over the ten townships.)

Heyfelde: Roger Hadfeld, William Hadfeld senior, Ottewell Bowdon, Robert Bowdon, Peter Buresfed, William Hadfeld Junior, Thomas Bowden, Alehowsis vij.

When compared with the Lay Subsidy Roll of 1327–8, 250 years earlier, the most obvious difference is that everybody had a surname. Many of the foregoing names are still common.

It would be interesting to know the location of these alehouses. They would be of wooden construction, probably located in the centres of the old townships. Perhaps one stood where the Beehive stands today in Whitfield, or the Anchor in Hadfield. The old centres of Charlesworth, Chisworth and Padfield would have need of an alehouse. Chunal, standing on an old packhorse route, would have one as well, perhaps on the site of the Horseshoe Inn. The Bull's Head in Old Glossop is reputed to be the oldest public house and has a stone lintel over the back door which bears the date 1607, but it is likely that an alehouse stood on the same site long before that date.

Another method of taxation was by the Oxgang. An oxgang was a variable measure depending on the quality of the soil. It was originally the amount of land which could be cultivated in a year using one ox. Once again a tax gives us the names of those taxed and in

Glossop in 1603, shortly before the manor passed into the hands of the Howards, we find:

George Ratcliffe and Elizabeth Ratcliffe, his mother in land	4s.
Elizabeth Stafford, wydoe, in land	5s. 4d.
John Stafford, in land	16d.
John Hadfield, in land	16d.
Thomas Bowre, in goods	5s.
Thomas Hollingworth, in goods	4s.
William Dewsnoppe, in goods	3s.
Hugh Shirt, in goods	3s.

Summa 27 shillings

Note the appearance of Ratcliffes, Hadfields and Dewsnaps once more. I wonder where the Booths, Coopers and Wagstaffes were. Perhaps they were in the forefront of tax avoidance.

Some idea of the relative affluence of Glossop when compared with other villages in the Peak can be gathered from the tax levied on the following places.

Baslow	31 shillings and 4 pence
Yeolgrave	30 shillings
Tyddeswell	14 shillings

The Dispossession of the Monasteries was to start a revolution that was surely unforeseen at the time. A dissatisfied tenant might move to farm elsewhere at a lower rent, but with such a huge change in land ownership this would be difficult, with the new owners determined to maximise their income. In general, the tenants would have to increase their income to pay the increased rents and to do this many of them took to spinning and weaving in their own homes. This in turn led to the emergence of men calling themselves clothiers, who supplied raw wool to the spinners and collected the finished cloth from the weavers and took it to market. Here we have a seed of the Industrial Revolution because many of the clothiers accumulated considerable wealth, which later they were able to invest in the textile industry and become woollen and cotton masters.

The Index of Probate Documents for the Ancient Parish of Glossop gives remarkable insight into the changes that were taking place as the Medieval period came to an end and the first stirrings of the Industrial Revolution got under way. Most people never left a will, but from those who did and listed their occupation we find that in the 15th and 16th centuries the commonest occupation listed is that of husbandman. During the period 1472 to 1650 there were 186 probate documents left by people who styled themselves as husbandmen, but by the period 1841 to 1860 there were none. In their stead were farmers.

The first will of a clothier is that of Oliver Dearneley of Blackshawe, dated 1638, but their numbers grew until the years from 1776 to 1820 when 21 claimed that occupation. Over the next 20 years, their numbers declined as they were replaced by textile mills. William Shepley, Cotton Manufacturer, Whitfield left a will in 1797, and the following year Thomas Shuttleworth, a Fustian Manufacturer of Mellor, did likewise.

The Parish of Glossop would be largely self supporting and we find wills left by blacksmiths, coopers, carpenters, tanners and masons in early records. Wallers became more numerous in the 17th century, probably to build the drystone walls as common land was enclosed.

From the list of alehouses of 1577, we know there were innkeepers at an early date, but the first to earn a mention in the Probate Records was John Taylor of New Mills, in 1715. The first man to list himself as a shopkeeper was Robert Thorneley of Padfield in 1782. For the period from 1841 to 1860 the number had risen to 22.

The White House, Chunal.

Joseph Hague's grave, Old Glossop churchyard.

This list is not exhaustive; someone must have had the skills to make shoes, construct spinning wheels and looms, build carts and fabricate harnesses for horses. The slow and sometimes imperceptible changes of the Middle Ages were coming to an end and the first stirrings of the Industrial Revolution were becoming evident.

Despite the class system people were able to move both up and down the social scale so that an industrious husbandman might come to style himself a yeoman and perhaps his son own sufficient land to be a member of the minor gentry. The alternative to working on the land was to engage in trade, and some entrepreneurs made fortunes. Our local representative of a successful businessman was Joseph Hague. He was born in 1695 in a house in Chunal which was demolished long ago, and has come down to us as a boy born into poverty who made a huge fortune through perseverance and hard work. His name has been incorrectly linked with the White House: the White House, with its minstrels' gallery, would have been regarded as a substantial dwelling at the time, hardly the home of paupers.

Joseph is reputed to have started as a boy buying and selling small articles which he carried in a basket. When the basket became too small to carry his wares, he purchased an ass. In 1716 he went to London and invested his entrepreneurial skills and small capital in the textile trade. Nothing is known of his activities until 1751 when he appeared before a Parliamentary Committee, where it emerged Hague had built up a monopoly over the import of raw cotton into England. It was further revealed that some of the cotton was woven into "anabasses", which were blue and white striped loincloths. These cloths were popular with West African tribes and were exchanged for slaves brought from the interior to be carried to the West Indies and America. It would appear that some of his profits flowed from this inhuman trade.

In the late 1770s he purchased Park Hall at Little Hayfield and lived the life of a country gentleman. His fortune was distributed among his relations during his lifetime. Joseph Hague is best remembered locally for endowing the Charity School at Whitfield, and for his charitable donations leaving the annual interest of £1,000 towards the clothing of twelve poor men and twelve poor women out of the ten townships of Glossopdale for ever. He died at Park Hall, on 12th March 1786, aged 90 years. Joseph Hague's grave is in Old Glossop churchyard and his marble bust in Hayfield Church.

5

THE TEXTILE INDUSTRY AND ITS IMPACT ON GLOSSOPDALE

The prosperity of medieval England depended upon sheep, a reminder being the Woolsack, on which the Lord Chancellor sits when acting as Speaker in the House of Lords. Originally the trade was in fleeces exported and made into cloth by the weavers of Flanders.

Much of the wealth of the monasteries came from the rearing of large flocks of sheep. The Cistercian monks were leaders in the field of estate management and it is likely that much of the land around Glossop and Longdendale was developed into sheep runs when the Cistercian Abbots of Basingwerke held the land.

England was backward in cloth finishing, especially the dyeing process. The Wiltshire broadcloths were sold white to drapers in the Low Countries and North Germany, where fast dyeing techniques had been mastered before 1500. The real profits in the woollen trade were to be made from the finishing processes.

Troubles in Europe worked to England's advantage, when victims of persecution fled. In 1564 Elizabeth I granted a charter to Dutch and Flemish weavers who set up in business in Norwich. The revocation of the Edict of Nantes in 1685, which renewed the persecution of French Protestants, caused many to move to England, settling in Norwich and the Spitalfields area of London. The skills brought into England led to significant changes, and towards the the end of the 16th century Britain was making so much cloth that she became as important for the export of woollen textiles as she had once been of raw wool.

The main centres of wool production were in the Cotswolds and East Anglia. Lancashire and Yorkshire had plentiful supplies of soft water flowing off the millstone grit, but the local sheep yielded inferior wool composed of short thick fibres and fabrics made from it were of lower quality. However, this northern district had the advantage of being unhampered by the restrictive practices of the guilds and, assisted by the skills of settlers from the Low Countries, the woollen trade expanded steadily.

Under what has become known as the domestic system, women and children would wash, card and spin the thread, while men would weave at the loom. The handloom weavers working on the top floor of a three-storeyed cottage were able to make a good living when sufficient yarn was available. By the middle of the 18th century a study of the baptismal registers for the Manchester area shows that over half the fathers were employed in some branch of the textile industry, and in Saddleworth this figure reached 85%.

The real profits were made by the clothiers, who acted as middlemen supplying raw wool, and later linen and cotton to spinners and weavers using local agents. When the cloth had been woven the agent would collect it and take it to market towns such as Halifax and Stockport.

Cotton had been grown and made into fabric in the east for centuries. Cotton was introduced into Britain around 1640 but was used only in the making of fustian, a cloth which consisted

Three-storey weaver's cottage, Hague Street.

of a linen warp and a cotton weft. The linen would be grown in Ireland and the cotton imported from the Levant. By the end of the 16th century, the manufacture of fustian had reached Lancashire and began to oust the woollen industry.

Colonists planted cotton in the New World. Brazil and the West Indies had become world centres of cotton production by the 18th century. Cotton plantations had also been established in Virginia as early as 1650.

The reasons for the cotton trade being Lancashire-based were many – the existence of labour already skilled in the manufacture of woollens and fustians; the port of Liverpool had established a trade with the West Indies and Southern States of America; much of this trade consisted of exchanging brightly coloured cloths for slaves in West Africa, who were transported to work on the cotton and sugar plantations. The ships could then carry bales of raw cotton to Liverpool.

Dutch settlers introduced the Dutch engine loom early in the 17th century and by 1750 there were around 1,500 of these Dutch looms in use in Manchester. These machines could make several linen or cotton tapes simultaneously, and the Dutch loom workshops were a step towards the introduction of the factory system. An industry established in London was the printing of bright coloured designs on fustian. Later this industry moved to the north-west because of the ample water supply and to be near the place of fustian manufacture.

A stream of technical developments laid the foundation for the expansion of the cotton industry. John Kay invented the flying shuttle in 1733 and a machine for carding wool had been introduced in 1748 and was later adapted for cotton. Hand spinners could not produce yarn quickly enough for the weavers, and around 1764 James Hargreaves invented the spinning jenny, a machine with which several threads could be spun simultaneously. The first spinning jenny was a hand-cranked machine with eight spindles, but later models had up to 120 spindles and needed to be power driven.

The next major invention was Richard Arkwright's water frame which supplanted the jenny as the stronger threads it produced could be used as warp in weaving cotton. Large water driven mills were built to house the new machines, many of them by Arkwright himself. In 1779, Samuel Crompton perfected the spinning mule. The mechanisation of weaving was the next leap forward. In 1786 Edmund Cartwright succeeded in making a steam powered loom. Within a few years, Cartwright's power loom and Crompton's mule were increasing the output of cotton textiles. In 1793 Eli Whitney invented his saw-gin, which separated seeds from the raw cotton and further increased the supply of cotton reaching Lancashire. In 1822 Roberts' power loom was invented, and as the power loom was introduced into factories on a considerable scale during the 1820s and 1840s it led to a steady displacement of handloom weavers.

The Longdendale and Glossop valleys were ideal for the setting up of water powered factories. The main problem was the transport of the raw cotton from Liverpool and the finished cloth to Manchester and Stockport. With the early mills, coal was only required to provide steam for heating and increasing the humidity and the local deposits were sufficient for this purpose.

The power for cotton mills was still mainly provided by water power until after 1820 because the early steam engines cost far more and had running costs in excess of a waterwheel on a reliable stream. As the steam engine became more efficient, and with the development of the Lancashire and Yorkshire coalfields, it became the main power source in every cotton town in the north-west except in such Pennine centres as Glossop. The first steam engine to be used in a Glossop mill was installed in Whitfield Mill, worked by William, John and James Kershaw, around 1825.

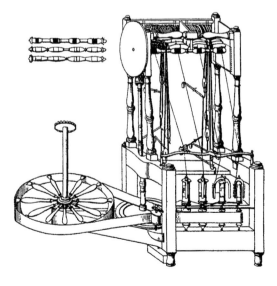

Arkwright's Water Frame.

Ring Spinning Machine at Cromford.

The changes wrought in Glossopdale must have seemed amazing to the inhabitants of a backward rural district. In the course of a lifetime they were to see mills spring up, turnpike roads constructed, the coming of the railway, and the population growing from an estimated 2,000 in 1780 to 3,625 by the time of the first census in 1801, and to 21,200 in 1861.

Glover writes of places "where in the year 1780 there were only a few hovels and here and there a farmstead where there are now establishments for woollen cloth spinning, weaving, and dressing, muslin, cambric and fustian weaving, bleaching and dyeing."

To cater for these changes, houses, public houses, schools, breweries, churches and chapels were springing up. Brass and iron foundries were established to supply the needs of the new industries. As the centre of progress moved from Old Glossop to Howardtown, shops providing a whole series of goods from fishmongers and greengrocers to cloggers and butchers gradually spread along the High Street. The town must have looked impressive with all the new buildings before they were blackened by the smoke belching from the factory chimneys.

The Howards, through their agents in Glossopdale, soon realised the potential for improving the income from their estate. Land could be leased for mills, coal mines and quarries, and ground rents levied on all the new buildings.

Map Five, based on sections of Burdett's maps of Derbyshire and Cheshire of 1763–67, shows only four mills in the district – the Lord's corn mill in Milltown; a mill at Brookside on the Etherow, which may have been a fulling mill – if so it was probably the first textile mill to be built in the area; Woolley Mill at Tintwistle; and a further corn mill on the brook which runs down from Mill Brow to Marple Bridge. By 1846 there were well over 60 cotton mills in Glossop parish alone.

Early mills, both woollen and cotton, were built along the River Etherow and the Glossop Brook and on any other stream that fed them which could supply sufficient head of water to turn a waterwheel. No mills were erected on the Shelf Brook where it flowed through the grounds of Glossop Hall.

Some of the earliest mills were built in Old Glossop. Shepley Mill, Warth Mill, Thread Mill, Old Water Mill, Barrack Mill and the New Water Mill were built between 1784 and 1815. These mills utilised water drawn from the Shelf Brook and the Blackshaw Clough Brook.

There were five mills along the stream which divides Charlesworth and Chisworth and a further six on the stream which delineates the boundary between Ludworth and Mellor. On the Padfield Brook there were at one time seven mills.

The builders of the early mills seem to have been local folk, if their surnames are a reliable guide. Among them we find Thornleys, Sheppards, Bennetts, Kershaws, Lees, Shepleys, Robinsons and Hadfields. The brothers John and Robert Thornley were involved in various local concerns from the 1780s. John Thornley, 1747–90, a fustian maker, was one of four partners in the Bridge End Fulling Mill on the Glossop Brook. His brother Robert by 1795 occupied Charles Hadfield's mill on the Gnathole Brook.

These early manufacturers produced mainly for the Manchester market where they attended regularly on Tuesdays and many had warehouses in Manchester. The commercial links of the area were very much with Manchester and Stockport, and like the neighbouring parts of Cheshire it was an extension of the Lancashire textile area. The first local mill masters met with varying degrees of success, but the real expansion of the cotton industry in Glossop came with the building of Wren Nest Mill by the Ellisons and the arrival of John Wood.

Wren Nest started as a small mill built in 1815 by the Howard agent, Matthew Ellison. Francis Sumner went to work for his uncle, Thomas Ellison, and later he purchased the mill from his uncle out of the proceeds of his father's estate. When he started in business in December 1827, the mill was assessed at £91, on 7,000 spindles, and worked by a waterwheel. He soon replaced the waterwheel with a steam engine, erecting his first engine house in 1829. In 1831 he began weaving with 57 looms and by 1836 Mr Sumner had 380 looms and 14,000 spindles.

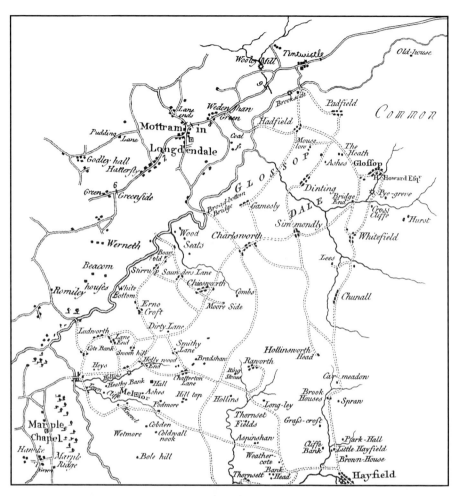

Map Five: Glossop and Longdendale in the 18th century based on Burdett's maps for Derbyshire and Cheshire.

John Wood was born in Marsden, Yorkshire in 1785. Before coming to Glossop he had worked in Liverpool and Manchester where he learned the skills of the cotton trade. He also had the necessary capital to start up in business and the ability to raise the money for the rapid expansion of his enterprises.

After arriving in Glossop in 1815 he worked the Water Mill and the Higher Water Mill on the Shelf Brook. Mr Wood changed the name of the Water Mill to Waterloo. Four years later, in March 1819, Mr Wood purchased the Bridge End Mill for £1,900. Mr Wood changed the name to the Howardtown Mill. He soon had his new acquisition in full working order, and during the coming years he took out further leases on adjoining pieces of land and erected further buildings. An impression of his rapid progress can be gained from the facts that in 1823 he had 143 looms and 5,580 spindles working.

The small size of early mills was a considerable handicap as new machinery developed. The later buildings were designed to accommodate mules and ring spinning machinery with the cast iron pillars spaced ten feet apart and the bays 20 feet wide. These mills were intended to be driven by steam engines which were installed at one end of the building and drove line shafts on each floor by means of cotton rope belts. The lines of pillars were cast with provision for the mounting of bearings to support the long line shafts. The problem with this arrangement was that if the engine stopped, the whole production of the mill was brought to a halt with it.

While the cotton trade was expanding, the former woollen mills were converting to cotton or going out of business, and by 1846 only two woollen mills remained those at Gnathole and Warp Mill at Hayfield.

Wood's Mill *c.*1850. Note the weirs in connection with the waterwheels.

Gnathole Mill today.

6
INDUSTRIAL STRUGGLES IN THE 19TH CENTURY

Bottoms Mill c.1860.

William Cobbett wrote, "I defy you to get a man to riot on a full stomach." If he was correct, then there must have been many hungry people around during the 19th century.

The Industrial Revolution inevitably led to dissatisfaction. Spinners and weavers, used to working in their own homes at a speed and time that suited them, were forced to work in factories for long hours at the speed of the machinery. No longer could they leave their work at the drop of a hat and go chasing after a hare.

The depressed state of the working classes was the reason behind the Luddite outrages and a series of riots and demonstrations throughout the 19th century. Much of this has been played down, but should be recorded in any attempt to portray the events of the time.

Robert Hamnett was too deferential to leading citizens, especially mill owners, which was probably a sound policy at the time. He does tell us that some were fined for breaches of the

Factories Acts. Writing in 1910, he would not have needed to check the archives. One could be excused for thinking that the cotton masters were a set of philanthropists from current local histories. A check of the Quarter Sessions reports reveals some of their other qualities.

It would be simple to judge the employers as a self-interested group whose only concern was in maximising profits, and allow one's sympathies to be entirely with the operatives, but the situation was more complex. The cotton trade was subject to boom and bust, the cotton masters had large amounts of capital tied up in their factories, there were constant improvements in textile machinery which left existing equipment uneconomic to run, foreign competition was growing and an employer who kept to the provisions of the Factory Acts could find himself at a disadvantage when compared with unscrupulous competitors. In times of boom an employer could agree to wage rises, but when the market for cotton fell, he could be heading for bankruptcy.

Workers were prevented from forming trade unions by the General Combination Acts of 1799 and 1800 due to fear of radical movements on the part of government. Theoretically, masters could be convicted for combination, but none were. The Combination Acts were repealed in 1824, which led to the formation of unions by spinners and other textile workers.

Despite the troubles besetting industry there was a steady improvement in wages and conditions as the century progressed. There were to be peaks and troughs due to trade cycles and the impact of the American Civil War, but the prosperity of all those employed in the textile trade was to grow due to a number of factors – the formation of Trade Unions and Friendly Societies; Savings Banks and Building Societies; and the passing of the Factory Acts being the most prominent.

Towards the end of 1830 trouble started to manifest itself in several branches of industry and agriculture. In parts of England there was an outbreak of rick burning and smashing of agricultural machinery. In the industrial areas there were turnouts by colliers, silk, woollen and cotton workers. For much of the information about events at this time we have to rely on the *Manchester Guardian*, which was biased in favour of the employers and usually described the turnouts as being misguided at best.

Relations between employers and workforce were on a knife edge. The spinners had ordered a complete turnout throughout the district, but according to the *Guardian* it was only in Glossop and Longdendale that this occurred. On the Monday, 13th December 1830, a body amounting to between 1,500 and 2,000 people went round nearly all the factories in the neighbourhood where the hands continued at work and compelled them to leave their employment without committing any acts of violence.

In late December and early January there were incidents of a serious nature including riots in Dukinfield, an attempted murder of a mill owner in his counting house at Stalybridge, and the murder of Thomas Ashton of Gee Cross on his way to Apethorn Mill.

One of the mills which turned out on 13th December was that of Ridgway and Thornton near Hayfield, but after a few days the hands returned to work when they found that the strike was not supported outside the district and they were not receiving assistance from the General Trades Union. When news of this reached Ashton-under-Lyne, a party of from 60 to 80 men were despatched with the intention of "turning the knobsticks out".

These men arrived near Ridgway and Thornton's factory in the evening while the hands were all at work. The manager ordered all the hands out and he had just got the factory cleared when the turnouts arrived. On seeing the manager, one of them presented a pistol to his breast and compelled him to open the door, and a strong guard being posted outside, the remainder entered the factory and searched every part of it. Finding no one within, they beat the manager severely but did not injure the machinery or the work in progress. On leaving they set up a shout of triumph and set off home discharging pistols as they went.

On Saturday 18th there was a tumultuous demonstration in Glossop which led to the magistrates drawing up the following notice:

"Whereas a large number of operative cotton spinners and others assembled and paraded through the township of Glossop, on Saturday the 18th of December instant, with a band of music and flags or banners; some of the said persons being armed with bludgeons, and others bearing firearms, which they occasionally discharged, and having otherwise illegally conducted themselves by intimidating the peaceable inhabitants of the said township.

And whereas it has been stated to us to be the intention of the operative cotton spinners to assemble at or near Glossop, on Monday the 27th instant, we do entreat all such persons strictly to abstain from a repetition of any of the aforesaid illegal acts, or any other breach of the peace whatsoever. Whilst we refrain, as magistrates, from any interference between the workmen and their employers with regard to the price of their labour, we are determined to enforce the law for the preservation of the peace throughout the district confided to our charge."

Given under our hands at Glossop, the 25th day of December, 1830.

Despite this notice, on 27th December a body of men, chiefly from Glossop and Longdendale, assembled near the Junction Inn, and then proceeded in regular array towards Hayfield, accompanied by a band. Mr White was in Glossop at the time and, on learning of what was afoot, accompanied by a troop of the 10th Hussars under the command of Captain William Osborne, followed the procession and caught up with it about a quarter of a mile from Ridgway and Thornton's factory.

Mr White rode to the head of the procession and stated that the magistrates of that district had announced that they would not allow it to be disturbed by processions of the character which he saw before him and after the occurrences which had recently taken place, he could not allow them to proceed. He therefore required that they should instantly turn back. The procession stopped when Mr White spoke to them, but as they did not seem at all inclined to obey his order to turn back, he directed the military to take into custody all the persons who composed the band, as well as two others who appeared active in marshalling the procession. The men then returned to Glossop, followed by the military, where they dispersed.

The prisoners were escorted to Glossop and confined in the prison at the old Town Hall, opposite the Queen's Arms, under a guard of the 4th infantry. On the following Wednesday morning the prisoners were brought before Mr White and G.W. Newton of Taxal. Their occupations were as follows:

Thomas Howard,	Spinner,	Glossop.
Robert Wood,	Spinner,	Glossop.
Henry Beard,	Spinner,	Glossop.
John Waterhouse,	Dresser,	Glossop.
Levi Robinson,	Spinner,	Glossop.
Aston Howard,	Spinner,	Glossop
James Bradley,	Spinner,	Hollingworth.
James Howard,	Spinner,	Hollingworth.
John Dewsnap,	Spinner,	Whitfield.
Robert Robinson,	Spinner,	Cock Brook, Near Ashton.
Joseph Dewsnap,	Spinner,	Glossop.

The two last named were those who had marshalled the procession. The others were bandsmen. Mr David Foulkes, of Manchester, appeared for the prisoners, and was assisted and instructed by Mr Downes, secretary to the Glossop Union of Operative Spinners.

The band claimed that they were going to New Mills as they were out of work due to the strike. The band involved was the old Volunteer Band which had been started around 1803 in connection with the Volunteer Corps. The band may have been on their way to New Mills, but in view of the notice posted by the magistrates they were certainly unwise to march there accompanied by a large group of turnouts.

Mr Thomas Ellison was called as a witness against the prisoners. He stated that a considerable number of the persons in the procession carried sticks, some of a large size, and the assemblage was in his opinion calculated to inspire terror in the peaceable inhabitants of the neighbourhood. Mr Ellison was cross-examined at some length by Mr D. Foulkes, and in the course of his cross-examination stated the persons assembled were not guilty of any violence that he knew of, and that the prisoners offered no resistance when they were apprehended. The sticks they carried were generally common walking sticks, though there were a few of large size. The witness did believe, after what occurred previously, that the procession was going to Ridgway and Thornton's factory.

This being the evidence against the prisoners, Mr Foulkes submitted to the magistrates that there was no case against his clients.

Mr Newton said he was of the opinion that there was a strong case against them for joining a riotous assembly; Mr White expressed his full concurrence. Mr Newton said the prisoners must all be committed for trial at the Derby Assizes. The offence, however, was bailable, and the magistrates would take their own recognisances in £40, with two competent sureties in £20 each.

Mr Foulkes again urged on the magistrates that the evidence did not make out a charge of riot; it was proved that they had been quiet, and that they had used no violence.

Mr White said that might be, but they had assembled in a manner calculated to strike terror into persons who were desirous of following their lawful employment, and, after what had occurred in the neighbourhood, it was the determination of the magistrates not to allow any processions or tumultuous assemblages in that district. It was their duty to keep the peace, and they would do their utmost to discharge that duty.

All the defendants found bail. The terms of the recognisances were that the defendants should appear at the next assizes for the county of Derby, to answer any indictments that might be found against them for a riot and tumultuous assembly. The sureties were, with one exception, turnout spinners, and it was stated by the magistrates that several of them were worth five or six hundred pounds each.

Fortunately for the defendants, before the trial their patrons exerted themselves on their behalf. Mr Thomas Ellison and others attended the trial and gave evidence in their favour. They all pleaded guilty and pleaded for mercy. Baron Vaughan reprimanded and then dismissed them. But for Mr Ellison they might have got transported.

On 8th August 1831, silver plate was presented to John White, Esq., J.P., G.W. Newton, Esq., J.P. and Mr Thomas Ellison by the gentry for their services in connection with the 4s. 2d., or swing turnout.

The *Manchester Guardian* of Saturday, 29th January 1831 carried the following report:

"On Saturday morning persons who attacked Ridgway and Thornton's mill were taken into custody by Mr Standrin, deputy constable of Ashton. The prisoners were conveyed to the lock up at Ashton from whence they were taken to Glossop and on Monday brought before the magistrates, John White and G.W. Newton. They were all committed to Derby gaol on the capital charge and were removed from Glossop on Tuesday morning under an escort of the 10th Hussars. Two of the men came from Stalybridge, one from Dukinfield and the other six from Ashton."

The first Factory Act of 1819 applied only to cotton mills and prohibited the employment of children under nine years of age. It also limited the hours of workers under sixteen to nine hours a day, exclusive of meals. This Act was largely ignored by unscrupulous cotton masters.

Althorpe's Factory Act of 1833, which was applicable to textile mills, laid down the maximum number of hours permitted each day for children aged 9–12 to 9 hours with a maximum of 48 hours a week. For those aged 13–18 the maximum was 12 hours a day and 69 hours a week. It also laid down that children were to have two hours of schooling each day and, perhaps most important of all, the first Factory Inspectors were appointed. They were few in number and the number of cotton mills large, but slowly they began to have an impact, although the courts were more lenient in dealing with the transgressions of the masters as compared with the workers.

Convictions Under the Factory Act. *Guardian* 4th July 1835

Cases involving the infraction of the provisions of the Factory Act, came for hearing on Thursday last at the petit sessions at Low Leighton, before George W. Newton, Esq., Richard Simpson, Esq., John White, Esq., magistrates for that county, and Robert Rickards, Esq., the Factory Inspector for this district. The first was one preferred against Mr John Wood, of Howard Town, by Mr James Bates, and Mr Rickards superintendent for that district, and it charged Mr Wood with having on the 27th May last worked Harriet Dawson and two other persons under 18 years of age being respectively 15, 16, and 15 years old, more than 12 hours on that day, and more than 69 hours in the preceding week. There was another complaint against Mr Wood for working the same persons between the hours of half past eight in the evening and half past five in the morning of the said day.

The first case was that of Harriet Dawson, and witnesses were called, who proved that she did work more than 12 hours on the day in question, and that she was at work at half past four o'clock on the same morning.

A printed notice was put in, published in July 1834 by Mr Rickards, which, on the ground that some mill clocks in that neighbourhood were sometimes as much as 50 minutes in advance of the correct time, required all the mill clocks in Glossop Dale to be kept to the regular time of the day. It was stated that one of these printed notices was put up in the mill of Mr Wood; despite this, Mr Bates found that the clock in the mill was about three quarters of an hour in advance, so that hands under 18 years of age, commenced working before half past five in the morning.

Mr Bates then stated that the girl had been certified to be eighteen years of age, and proceeded to show from entries in Mr Wood's certificate book that she was only fifteen. On reference to the book, it appeared that on the 27th February 1834 she was certified to be 13 years of age; and she had this year obtained another certificate, which was inserted in the same book, dated February 16th 1835, stating her to be 18.

The girl underwent an examination, in which she stated that she had gone to the surgeon for the latter certificate, and that he had asked her no questions as to her age. The magistrates examined the certificate book, and found that it contained 66 different cases where children of 12, 13, 14, and 15 years, and so certified in 1834, had in 1835 been all certified as 18 years of age.

The magistrates expressed surprise to find that all these false certificates set forth the age of the party as 18 years, and Mr White said that it was evident that the certificates had been obtained for some collusive purpose.

Mr Vaughan, of Stockport, who appeared for Mr Wood, said that his client had always been anxious to conform to the law, and that he was unaware that he had infringed its provisions. If he had done so, it must have been from ignorance, and not from any intention on his part.

The magistrates declared that it was evident that, though the surgeon who gave the certificates was principally to blame, it was impossible for Mr Wood to be exculpated from the charge of breaking the provisions of the 28th clause, in having "given currency to false certificates knowing the same to be untrue", which offence was punishable, with imprisonment not exceeding two months.

After conversation between the magistrates, and Mr Vaughan and Mr Wood, it was proposed on the part of Mr Wood that he should submit to a penalty of £10, and costs, in each of the two cases before the court, if Mr Bates would abandon the other informations. Mr Rickards said that he had preferred these cases with regret against Mr Wood, and that he had no wish to proceed with unnecessary rigour; and whatever the decision of the magistrates, he would concur in it. Mr Wood immediately paid the fines, £20 into court, together with £3 9s. 6d. costs, and promised that in future he would conform to all provisions of the Act. The £20 was left in the hands of the magistrates, for distribution among charities in Glossop district.

John Wood does not come out of this court case as the model citizen usually portrayed, however, the situation was obviously much more complex. For such widespread evasion of the provisions of the Factory Act to have occurred there must have been collusion between parents, the children concerned, the surgeon, and some sections of mill management. With the number of employees in Wood's Mill it is unlikely that John Wood knew individual young workers.

The parents would certainly know the ages of their offspring and that, if they worked longer hours and claimed to be older, their pay would be enhanced. The overlookers must also have had a good idea of what was going on, but turned a blind eye as long as production flowed smoothly. The surgeon's part in the deception is not so clear. As for the deliberate alteration of the works clock, then John Wood must have known.

Hayfield Petit Sessions, 8th October 1835
Convictions under the Factory Act

Several manufacturers in the parish of Glossop appeared to answer informations laid by Messrs Heathcote and Trimmer, Superintendents of Factories, for offences against the Act.

Mr Henry Lees of Woolley Bridge admitted the charges of working young persons under 18 years of age for more than 12 hours per day, and for neglecting to keep time book No 3. Mr Lees was fined £20, and costs on the first information, it being his second conviction for overworking, and £1 and costs for neglecting to keep time book No 3.

John and Joseph Bennett, of Turn Lee, Glossop, admitted similar offences, and were fined £10 and costs on first information, and £5 and costs for not keeping time books.

Moses Cooper, and two other operative spinners in the employ of Messrs Bennett of Turn Lee not appearing upon notice, summonses were taken out against them for having employed their piecers more than twelve hours a day, Moses Cooper having also been exceedingly insolent when the superintendents visited the mill.

Despite Mr Wood's previous assurances to the court, in April 1836 he was fined once more for failing to enter the name of Anne Howard, aged under 18, in his time book. Joseph Bottoms, overlooker, employed by John Wood, was also fined for failing to keep time books and making false entries. At the same court we find:

William Barber; cotton manufacturer, of Padfield Brook, employing children for more than 12 hours a day. Fined £3 and 16s. 6d. costs.

William Platt and George Platt; Hadfield Lodge, failing to keep time books and employing for more than 12 hours per day.

An indication of the robust state of the politics of the day is given by this account which appeared in the *Manchester Guardian* when in August 1837 George Arkwright, great grandson of Sir Richard, stood as the Tory candidate for North Derbyshire. The Liberal (or Reform) candidates were the Hon. G.H. Cavendish and William Evans, of Derby. George Arkwright had majorities in Chesterfield and Alfreton, but Cavendish and Evans came first and second in the poll:

> "We regret to state that a disturbance took place at Glossop, originating in the giving of liquor by Mr Arkwright's partisans. A number of drunken men, opposite the Howard Arms, the Tory Headquarters, committed an assault upon a young gentleman wearing the colours of Cavendish and Evans, which were torn from him and he was roughly treated. This circumstance coming to the knowledge of the crowd near the Norfolk Arms, an attack was made upon a carriage loaded with Tory voters, who were severely pelted with stones; and Captain White, the magistrate, coming to the spot, was accused by someone present of having struck one of the reform party; when he was immediately knocked down, and, if some of the leading reformers had not interfered he would have been severely ill-treated. Shortly afterwards a dog cart belonging to Mr White, conveying a voter, was driven furiously over the narrow bridge leading towards Hayfield, when it knocked down a man ninety years of age, from New Mills, who had come to vote for the reformers, and the wheels passing over his head inflicted injuries which it is feared will prove mortal. All these circumstances produced a strong feeling of irritation in the people of Glossop, who were in favour of the reformers; and a good deal of rioting took place."

Newspapers of the day record incidents indicative of serious dissatisfaction among a section of the population. In December 1838 a spinner by the name of Garlick, living in Padfield, called at a house in Tintwistle and asked if he could leave his walking stick as he was going to Mr Wilkinson's mill at Crowden, and would call for it later. Another visitor to the house noticed the peculiarities of the walking stick, and decided to examine it. When he tugged at a wire ring on the stick it went off with a loud report and the contents of the device hit the chair on which the lady of the house was sitting, but without injuring her. A closer examination revealed a gun about a yard long, encased with wood.

The spinner called for his stick afterwards and the gun was returned to him. Apparently similar implements could be had at the house of a Stephenite beer seller in Glossop, at which place firearms were regularly raffled for by the operatives employed in factories there.

This period became known as the "Hungry Forties" due to the depressed state of the cotton industry. Many mills were only working four days a week. Emigration and enlisting for soldiers seem to have been the only courses left for the labouring population. Upwards of twenty persons, principally heads of families, left Glossop for America. Upwards of thirty left Hyde, and 26 took their departure from Stalybridge. Quite apart from cycles in trade leading to widespread unemployment, the living conditions in the industrial cities which had sprung up without thought to sanitation or decent water supplies were enough to encourage folks to leave.

The following events were known as the "Plug Drawing Turnout" because the object of the strikers was to close the mill by removing the boiler plugs to extinguish the fires and make the steam engines inoperable. In August 1842 a group of disgruntled cotton workers from Ashton and Stalybridge marched to Glossopdale and claimed to have stopped every mill there. "Masters thought to stop us; got knocked down," was their boast.

Soon afterwards three mills recommenced working: Mr Samuel Shepley of Brookfield; Mr Joseph Cooper, of Holehouse Mill; and Platts, of Hadfield Lodge. On the Wednesday an attack was made by a mob upon Mr Cooper's mill, and the hands driven out. A similar attack was planned for the Friday on the Brookfield Mill and a mob consisting of men, women and children from Glossop, whose numbers were estimated as being from 600 to 700, marched upon the mill, but were repelled by Mr Shepley and some of his operatives who had been sworn in as Special Constables. A second attack was made by a still larger number of turnouts, but they were again baffled, and as the people engaged in these lawless proceedings came from the neighbourhood, four were identified and committed to prison.

The Glossop turnouts, having learned the danger of committing attacks where they were known, invited a mob from Stalybridge and Hyde to attack the mill, and on the following Tuesday morning at about 11 o'clock this mob came opposite Mr Shepley's mill, shouting, throwing stones and using violent language; some of them crying out, when they saw Mr Shepley, "Damn him, murder him." The windows in Mr Shepley's house and warehouse were smashed by the mob, who next attempted to force their way into the factory, the door of which was guarded by Mr Shepley and some of his Special Constables.

Mr Shepley, when examined, stated:

> "About 5 o'clock that morning, as men passed the mill, they said they should have company that day from Hyde and Stalybridge, who would level the mill. I sent one of my hands to scout at the top of the neighbouring hills and about 10 o'clock he returned and said there was a mob coming from Ashton and Stalybridge. I then sent off my son to Glossop for the military. During the whole of the forenoon crowds had been passing the mill, and used very abusive language. One of them said I would be attacked, on which I showed them that I was armed with a pair of pistols, and told them that I was prepared to defend myself. On turning round I saw a large mob about a half mile off coming towards the factory.
>
> I stopped the engine, collected 15 of my hands who were sworn in as Special Police Constables, and I stood in front of the road in front of the mill. The mob had then crossed over Woolley Bridge and they commenced running and making the most terrifying noise. I told them several times if they came I would assuredly fire upon them. Some stones were then thrown from the back of the mob. I then retreated into the warehouse, previous to which I had been struck on the head and body, as had some of the Special Constables.
>
> The door was then open about 16 or 18 inches, being held there by a crowbar. I pointed a gun at the crowd several times. Stones were thrown into the warehouse and the door was beaten against by some heavy instrument. I am satisfied that the mill would have been destroyed and I believe our lives were in danger.
>
> The first gun failed to fire. Another gun was given to me and I pointed that twice before I pulled the trigger. After I had fired the first barrel two or three hands seized the gun and tried to pull it out of my hands. I then took a pistol out of my pocket and fired it, and fired also the other barrel of the gun. A short time afterwards when I opened the door I found the mob retreating. James Jackson, one of the Special Constables, had two of his teeth knocked out."

Mr Shepley's defence of the mill may have given the rioters pause, but it was the sight of the 58th Infantry marching rapidly down the turnpike road from Glossop that sent them fleeing across the fields. Four men were wounded during the assault on the mill, three from Stalybridge and one from Hyde. Afterwards 20 men belonging to the 58th regiment were quartered in Mr Shepley's house and a County Magistrate, John Cheetham, also moved into the house.

Three of the wounded men, named Thomas Winterbottom, Oliver Fry and Thomas Smith, all from Stalybridge, were caught and placed in the New Bailey House of Correction in Manchester. Later they were transported by railway to Godley and were escorted thence by a party of the 11th Hussars to the Silk Mill, to be examined by the magistrates, who committed them for trial at the next Chester Assizes for rioting and beginning to demolish the premises. At Chester the prisoners received comparatively light sentences, the judge taking into consideration their sufferings from their wounds.

As a result of the turning out of his hands at Holehouse, Mr Cooper and two of his sons gave evidence before the magistrates against several of the rioters, who were committed to Derby Gaol for trial. On their way home Mr Cooper, his friends and two of his sons were attacked by a furious mob and severely beaten, and one of Mr Cooper's sons left in a state of insensibility. In connection with this attack a youth named Howard, aged about 18 years, was also committed to Derby to be tried on a charge of wounding with intent to murder Joseph Cooper junior.

Firm action by the courts and military seems to have restored order quickly because by 5th November 1842 the detachment of the 11th Hussars, which had been stationed at Glossop during the disturbances, had left on the previous Wednesday en route for Burnley.

Glossopians were involved in the Luddite troubles, the Radical movements at the time of the Peterloo Massacre, the Reform Bill and Chartist agitation. It is interesting to note that despite the participants in these demands being given a bad press at the time and since, most of their demands have come to pass. The only one of the Chartists' demands that has not been met is the one for annual parliamentary elections.

Robert Owen started the agitation for the ten hours working day and the Rev Joseph Rayner Stephens continued the struggle locally. It was to take 33 years before the Ten Hours Bill was passed on 8th June 1847 and came into force on 1st May in the following year. This Bill only applied to children, so the agitation continued to obtain the same conditions for all operatives. In Glossop, meetings were held on waste land on what is now Howard Street and the spot was known afterwards as "The Ten Hours Ground". The shorter working hours resulted in improved health for the operatives and caused the employers to look for more efficient methods to maintain their profits.

The next step in the struggle for better conditions was the agitation for "Straight up and down time". On Monday, 6th June 1853, there was an invasion of Glossopdale. Thousands arrived by the trainload, with bands and banners, from Manchester and nearby cotton towns to encourage this movement and to denounce the system of fines used in the cotton mills. Resolutions were passed pledging the operatives in Glossop not to commence work before six in the morning and to leave off at six in the evening. The operatives stuck to this resolution, and by 21st June the *Times* reported: "At Glossop the hands have been successful in compelling the mill owners to work short time."

The operatives may have won on this occasion but at a time of recession the masters were in a strong position. By November 1853 the masters gave notice to the weavers that the recent 10% advance in pay was to be taken off and the operatives, under the advice of their leaders, submitted for the moment. The textile unions intended to tackle problems in Preston first, the tactics being to take on one group of employers at a time using subscriptions from the rest of the cotton districts to support those on strike. The employers in their turn retaliated by introducing short time working so as to cut the wages of those supporting the strikers.

As the century progressed more Factory Acts were passed, limiting the number of hours worked and introducing part-time schooling. There was also legislation for the provision of fans to extract fumes and gases from factories; nevertheless it proved an uphill struggle.

Mr Leonard Horner, Inspector of Factories, in his report for the half year ended 31st October 1851, stated:

"In the greater part of my district, the mill owners close their factories at the expiration of 10.5 hours of work; but in Ashton, Dukinfield, Stalybridge, Oldham and Glossopdale a majority continue to work 12 hours, sometimes more with male persons over 18 years of age, assisted by the afternoon set of children, under 13 years of age, to the detriment of the latter, by their being kept from their homes to so late an hour."

These struggles coincided with a downturn in trade and on Saturday, 2nd January 1858 the *Times* reported that, "At Glossop and Hadfield the distress has been very great, but private benevolence has been exerted to relieve it. On Wednesday from 400 to 600 loaves, with tea, flour, etc. were distributed by Lord Edward Howard."

In 1861 new looms were introduced, which enabled the weaver to get more money, but their wages were brought down to their former level by a reduction of 25%. In March there was a turnout of weavers in the Ashton and Glossop district in consequence of the reduction in wages. This turnout led to the stoppage of 50,000 looms.

The struggle between the cotton masters and their employees was overtaken by an event which had tragic consequences for both parties and all the shopkeepers, publicans, coal merchants, landlords and others who depended on their earnings. On 12th April 1861 the American Civil War commenced and the supply of raw cotton was cut off by the Northern blockade and the neglect of plantations. The stocks of American cotton in England shot up in price from 6s. 5d. per lb in 1860 to 27s. 5d. per lb in 1864, as the supply fell from 2,421,000 bales in 1860 to 72,000 in 1862. Soon the mills were working short time and many closed. Wood's Mill closed on 24th June 1862.

The first meeting of the Glossop Relief Committee was held on 16th July 1862 with the Rev J. Teague as chairman. The Rev T. Atkin of Littlemoor Independent Chapel had drawn up a report explaining the distress and this was sent to the Lord Mayor of London. Application was also made to the Mayor of Manchester. The Rev T. Atkin stated that half of the population of Glossop were receiving Parish Relief. Messrs Wood's gave £1,000, Edmund Potter £1,000, Francis Sumner £1,000, and Lord Howard £500 and £10 weekly, and also made an offer to employ labour in cultivating land to the extent of £2,000 in wages.

On 21st May 1863 a soup kitchen was opened, and 500 quarts of soup were delivered out in over one hour. In June some men were working on the roads for 1s. per day, and had to walk 7.5 miles there and back. On 7th June relief was given on the following scale: single man 3s. 6d., man and wife 5s. 6d., every child 2s. per week, half of it in kind.

In November 1862, Henry Lees, of Woolley Bridge, put up cooking apparatus. On Mondays, tenants and others were allowed one herring and 2 lbs of bread per head per family; Wednesdays, a pint of soup; Fridays, a plate of potato pie.

The town was divided into seven districts by the Relief Committee, who did not relieve those who were receiving Parish Relief. All unmarried women receiving aid had to attend half of each day at the sewing class, the other half at school for reading and writing. All youths, from 13 to 21, were attending school five hours a day. The Market Hall was used, with 260 attending. The stoves, desks and forms were provided by Lord Howard. The schools were intended to keep the young hands occupied and the sewing classes helped to clothe folks who had no money to spare when food was the priority.

The Times, Friday, 30th January 1863: "The Ladies Committee at Leeds have this week sent the remainder of the clothing to Mrs Wood of Glossop. A special appeal which they have just issued states that funds are nearly exhausted. It appears that supplies for the sewing schools are most needed."

In 1861 the assessment for Poor Rate was seven and three-quarter pence per pound, in November 1862 12s. 8$^{1}/_{2}$d. per pound. It was estimated that over £20,000 of rent was remitted by landlords.

A comparison of the total number of persons relieved by the Guardians in the month of November gives us an idea of the amount of distress. In 1861, 221 were relieved; in November, 1862, 7,605; 1863, 6,752; 1864, 3,263; 1865, 195.

The Guardians expended in outdoor and indoor relief for the year 1861, £1,089; 1862, £1,439; 1863, £23,300; 1864, £44,269; 1865, £17,285. The Guardians obtained loans as follows: 18th September 1863, £3,500; 25th June 1864, £5,092; 8th December, £5,150; 22nd December, £7,500. The loans were expended on the water supply, road and street improvements, land drainage, and other agricultural works.

The distress was so severe throughout the cotton manufacturing districts that a national response was required. In London the Mansion House Fund was set up and in Manchester the Central Relief Fund.

The effects of the Cotton Famine were so severe in Charlesworth that the cotton industry there never recovered. On 17th May 1862, an application by the Rev Goodwin Purcell on behalf of the Charlesworth operatives was read at a meeting of the Mansion House Fund. He stated that the distress there was unprecedented and the fortitude and resignation of the people wonderful. One mill at Broadbottom, in the parish of Mottram, which employed nearly 1,600 people, had ceased to work since 1st January. These, he added, with those dependent upon them, were wasting from starvation, some had died, others were too far gone to recover by relief. The fear of depriving persons in greater need forbade him to beg for his own parishioners, but in that case he did so believing that no people in the neighbourhood of Manchester were in such distress. Mr Sidebottom, owner of the mill at Broadbottom, had been giving as many as came food twice a week in a schoolroom, and Mrs Chapman, wife of the member for Grimsby, had fed about 130 twice a week.

The following extracts from the Log Book of Whitfield School for 1862 tell of the hardships of children during the Cotton Famine:

September 29th 1862: Children left school before time to line up for soup.

February 13th 1863: The Market School commences late, therefore Whitfield children are late. Fifteen left to go to the Market School because they had a free tea. A great many children suffering from smallpox.

June 19th: Some of the relief children away from want of clogs, when they absent themselves to go to the depot for them.

The amount of pauperism in Glossop grew from 100 in November 1862 to over 400 in January 1864. These figures would have been worse if many people had not left to find work in the woollen industry, which benefited from the closure of the cotton mills. Many people decided to emigrate to Canada and the USA and the Central Relief Fund received applications for grants towards the cost. On 27th June 1864 sixty persons left Glossop for America.

Although the cotton operatives were starving, they supported the Northern States in the American Civil War. In consequence, barrels of flour were sent from America, but when an attempt was made to auction them on 2nd March 1863, the public rioted, rolled three barrels away, smashed them open and made off with the contents. Mr Sumner attempted to read the Riot Act, but Mr Williams, the Superintendent of Police, stopped him. The idea behind the auction would be to raise money to distribute to the distressed, but hungry folks were not prepared to wait when faced with barrels of flour.

In the *Ashton Reporter* for 20th August 1864 appeared the following welcome item of news. "A few days ago the first load of cotton for Woolley Bridge came to Hadfield Station; a procession was formed, two old women rode on top of the bales of cotton. A tea party was held to celebrate the event."

In three years the employers of labour paid nearly £30,000 in local rates, for which they received little benefit owing to short time and stoppage of their works.

On Thursday, 4th June 1863 there was a riot at the workhouse which resulted in the arrest and trial of seven men on a charge of riotously assembling and disturbing the peace. This event was a direct result of the hardships of the Cotton Famine. The immediate cause was a decision by the Board of Guardians to alter the conditions of the Labour Test which in some cases meant that the recipients were working longer hours for less money.

The seven accused appeared before the Glossop magistrates, John Wood and Francis Sumner,

Reading the Riot Act.

on Monday, 8th June. The case was conducted on the part of the Guardians by Mr Johnson, and the prisoners were defended by Mr Roberts, of Manchester. The anxiety of the ratepayers and others to witness the proceedings was shown by hundreds crowding the doors of the justice room which could not contain one tenth of those anxious to witness the case.

Mr Johnson stated that a deputation of men employed on the Labour Test waited upon the Board of Guardians, requesting them to reconsider the alteration they had made in their mode of payment. Their request was refused. The deputation then presented themselves a second time, and were again refused. A disturbance then ensued. The door of the boardroom was broken open, and the lock forced. Sixty persons entered the room and occupied it, causing business to be suspended for one hour. The police were sent for, and on the Guardians leaving the room they were followed by a mob of persons, hooting and shouting. The Guardians were public servants, and were entitled to protection. They strove to do the best they could for the ratepayers, and to promote their interests.

John Wood Bowden, when examined by Mr Johnson, said:

> "I am the Relieving Officer, and was at the workhouse when a deputation of three men came to boardroom. None of the prisoners were of the deputation. Their object was to request the Guardians to make an alteration to the amount of relief and the time of work system. On Tuesday last some of the men said that 'Some of the Guardians wanted killing, and would very likely get it.' This was about 11 o'clock."

Cross-examined:

> "The new system is received kindly by some, but not by others. It lessened the work of some. Under the old system the work for single and married men was alike, but it is not so now. None of the Guardians have been killed. I did not think the men meant it. They said, 'They were not going to sit down by the new system.'"

Mr Daniel Wood was called, and said:

"I am a Guardian. I was at the boardroom on the 4th and I was alarmed. I expected something more than the breaking of the lock; it was not safe without the police. I fear if this is not stopped we shall have a recurrence of like disorder."

When cross-examined, Mr Daniel Wood said:

"I am one of the new Guardians. I shall not answer your questions. There was no personal violence, but I was afraid. I never saw so riotous a crowd in my life."

From this point the witness refused to answer any questions. Mr Roberts then rose and addressed the bench:

"When I came here I knew nothing of this case and may have shown some excitement as its facts have been brought out in the evidence. I may have been excited as these men were, when they committed the offence they are charged with. But you gentlemen, as just and humane men, will allow for me, as for them; you will not strain the law, nor deem a loud word to be a threat. You as magistrates stand between the poor and the ratepayers. Yours is the highest position, and the most important function that men can fulfil, that of allaying the ill-feeling produced by imprisonment, illegal manacles, suffering, and torture. They do not desire to resent these, but they feel them.

We do not complain of these things, but these men feel them as a disgrace, and as an illegality unnecessary for the consummation of justice. The men were living among you and could have been found when required. All the highest legal authorities in our country support me in my protest against needless imprisonment before trial. But though we cannot alter the case, all inquiry into the truth does good. In this case the facts have been proved. We cannot by evidence alter the position, and these men bear the consequences patiently.

The working men have been accustomed to bear both suffering and wrong. They are praised for their patience, are lauded as the most patient nation on earth. But they must still bear, they must not use means to amend their condition. If they request, they are denied; if they remonstrate, they are insulted; and if, as at Stalybridge, their wrongs drive them to violence, the law takes hold of them; and they have still to bear with indignation a punishment which they feel to be undeserved. These men feel themselves to be innocent, and so do all in this court. There is not a man here, but owns their innocence. Yourselves also, gentlemen, in your hearts you know that there is no guilt in their going in a body to ask the Guardians to reconsider a decision which was giving to them an increase of work and less of pay.

If there are any clergymen here, I will give them a text to preach from, and if Mr Wood attends in his place, his face will be whiter than it is now. The word of God declares; 'Cursed is he that grinds the face of the poor.' The parties in this conflict are unequal, wealth against poverty, but I will do my duty to these poor men, these women and babes. You may strain this case into a riot, but I defy you to find a riot in the facts. I do not complain of anything my friend has elicited. These men came asking civilly for the old system, and were met with a stern refusal. Some men look upon the poor with a kindness, and some speak to them snarlingly. The work these men are put to is not such that they can work at it for ten hours a day. Their bodily health will not allow it. Not only does their usual employment unfit them for outdoor labourers, but the starvation they have so long endured has disabled them.

Look at these men and see in their shrunken forms the effect of the gradual application of the starvation system, which system the Guardians of the Poor wish to make you, the gentlemen of England, their tools in further pressing upon their victims. Consider what must be the feelings which will result from this conduct towards honest and industrious, but poor men. The only protectors of England are the magistrates of England, and will not you acquit yourselves of this responsibility? I do not know Mr Wood, but I do know that he is no high class man, because no high class man would refuse, in the witness box, to answer the questions necessary to bring out the truth, and I do know that the social tendency of a tyrannous execution of power is to provoke the very evils it pretends to prevent. It is said that these men hooted and shouted, but is that a violation of the law? As to the words used, the only ones of a definite character were 'We want bread!'; but is this the cry of starving men rioting?

It is said they came in numbers, but numbers do not make a riot; it is the purpose for which they act which constitutes the crime. How are starving men to act? They ask civilly, but are refused; they remonstrate, and you call it a riot, or try to make it a riot. There is not a horse in your stable which does not eat more than a whole family of these poor men, who have produced all your wealth. And yet they patiently endure, and in the extremity of their distress they shrink from a violation of the law, for it is given in evidence that they said, 'We do not want a Stalybridge row, but the Guardians make it.'"

John Wood's Whitfield House.

The magistrates decided to bind the accused over, each in his own recognisances, for £5, with one surety each for £5, to keep the peace for six months. Mr Roberts volunteered to be security for them all. The magistrates ungraciously accepted his generous offer. Mr Roberts further pleaded the utter poverty of the men, and requested the remission of his usual fees. This was also granted, and the prisoners were discharged. This court case serves to illustrate the changes in treatment meted out to working men when compared with the early years of the century.

The following report is from the *Times* of 16th November 1892, and illustrates how the struggle between masters and operatives was still continuing at the end of the century:

"The Employers Federation are making strenuous efforts to induce employers in other districts to adopt short time, thus making it impossible for the hands to help by large levies their comrades who are 'out'. Two important meetings were held in Manchester yesterday afternoon. In the first instance the North and North-east Lancs. Manufacturers Association met and resolved: '(1) That in the opinion of this meeting, it is desirable that all spinners in the North and North-east Lancashire district should run three days a week, on condition that two-thirds of the trade assent thereto; (2) that the local secretaries be instructed to ascertain the opinion of the trade and report to a future meeting; (3) that the general secretary be instructed to ask for a conference with the male spinners' and card room operatives' representatives with reference to a reduction of 5% in wages.' At another meeting a deputation from the Master Cotton Spinners had an interview at the federation offices with a number of influential manufacturers in the Hyde and Glossop district with a view to the adoption of short time. At the conclusion of the deliberations, Mr Tattersall, the secretary of the federation, stated that most of the largest concerns in the districts represented had signified their determination to at once commence running short time. Those few firms who have not yet decided to fall in with the movement will be communicated with immediately."

7
TECHNICAL PROGRESS
IN VARIOUS FIELDS

Technical advances in the textile industry were paralleled in other fields, including water power, transport, gas and electricity.

Water has played an important part in Glossop's history and warrants a closer study. For the early textile entrepreneurs it provided a cheap form of power to drive their spinning machinery and the clean water required in cloth finishing processes. Later, with population growth and the need for a wholesome drinking water supply, the building of reservoirs to supply water for domestic purposes became the priority.

The first major project in connection with water for industrial processes occurred in 1795 when Robert Thornley leased the Torside Goit from Bernard Edward Howard, to supply water to his mill. The Torside Goit draws water from Torside Clough and follows the contours of the hillside via Ogden Clough along the south side of the Longdendale valley and feeds reservoirs in Padfield.

Some notion of the number of mills which had waterwheels can be gleaned from the details of those on the Glossop Brook in 1847.

John Wood and Brothers, 30 horsepower, 14 feet 5.75 inches fall;
Abraham Jackson and Co. occupying one fifth of Shepley Mill, 20 horsepower, 14 feet 0.5 inches fall;
Francis Sumner, Wren Nest Mills, 30 horsepower, 19 feet 9 inches fall;
Samuel Oliver, Dinting Mill, 20 horsepower, 13 feet 7.5 inches fall;
Dinting Vale Printworks, 25 horsepower, 20 feet 6.5 inches fall;
John & William Shepley, Brookfield Mill, 25 horsepower, 19 feet 3 inches fall.

All the above mills had millponds fed by the Glossop Brook. At the same date there were water powered mills on the Gnathole, Shelf, and Hurst Brooks, and the River Etherow.

Despite the ample rainfall of the district, in times of drought the shortage of water caused factory stoppages and loss of wages. To solve this problem, the Glossop Commissioners, consisting mainly of mill owners, obtained an Act of Parliament in 1837 empowering them to construct the reservoirs which were intended to provide power for their water wheels. The intention was to build three reservoirs to be called Chunal Wood Reservoir, Shelf Reservoir and Hurst Reservoir, but the rapid development of the steam engine was making water power redundant and only the Hurst Reservoir was constructed in 1838.

The Duke of Norfolk, as the major landowner, had an interest in the scheme. The more prosperous the mill occupiers, the greater the value of his estates. The engineer was Thomas Ashworth and his surveyor was 28-year-old John Frederick Bateman whose name is usually linked to the building of the chain of reservoirs in Longdendale.

Hurst Reservoir, built to supply water to the mill waterwheels.

Artificial course of the Glossop Brook alongside Wood's Mill. (Supplied by Mr J.B. Shaw)

The contract for the work on Hurst Reservoir was advertised for tender in the *Manchester Guardian* at the end of May 1838. The contractor for the building of Hurst Reservoir was Samuel Taylor, who later obtained the contracts for building Arnfield and Hollingworth Reservoirs.

Many of the first mills were built along the Wharf in Old Glossop and they required a whole series of weirs, millponds and goits. Near Mossy Lea bridge is a weir where water is taken off to feed Mossy Lea Reservoir which was constructed in 1840 by the Duke of Norfolk to find work for local men during the "Hungry Forties". From this reservoir a goit conveys the water down the valley of the Shelf Brook, crossing the brook and Shittern Clough before passing behind the Tanyard and delivering water into a series of reservoirs. Below the Cote Lodge on the Blackshaw Stream was a further lodge which supplied water to Hawkshead Mill.

There was once a whole system of interconnected reservoirs in this area, much of which has disappeared with dams breached and mill ponds emptied. The reservoirs were arranged at different altitudes and as the water left one mill it was diverted into the next lodge where it worked a waterwheel until it finally entered Bottom Lodge which was directly behind the long row of cottages which stood along the Wharf. The water from Bottom Lodge powered the machinery in Lord Howard's Saw Mill. The water was then returned to the Shelf Brook and flowed through Manor Park until it met the weir just above the park lake. At this point some of the water was taken off by a goit which ran along the west side of the fish pond and fed into a lodge which provided the head of water to operate the Lord's Corn Mill in Corn Street.

The streams in spate carry down amounts of stone and gravel, which in time raises the level of the water course and is one of the causes of flooding. The Duke of Norfolk employed men to clear out the brook courses and cart the stone to the Union Workhouse where it could be broken up and used for road mending. One old gentleman told me, "In the Duke's day you could have driven a horse and cart under any of these bridges."

There is other evidence of engineering works to be seen. One has only to stand at the bridge over the Glossop Brook at the bottom of Cross Cliffe and look downstream to see that the river follows an artificial course. A similar straight length can also be seen from the bridge which leads to the Tesco supermarket and looking upstream past what remains of Wren Nest Mill. These artificial lengths are the result of work carried out around 1838 by Bateman in connection with the water supply to the waterwheels at Howardtown and Wren Nest Mills.

If you lean over the parapet where the Glossop Brook re-emerges after passing under the Market Ground and look downstream and to your right you will see the weir and the valve gear for the sluices that once directed the water into a leat which flowed parallel to Chapel Street, and after passing under a bridge in George Street the water was stored in a reservoir for Shepley Mill.

The curved stretch of the brook from the Market Ground to where it passes under High Street West is also artificial and was intended to provide a head of water in Shepley Mill reservoir. By redirecting the brook in a straight line past Wren Nest Mill and building a weir near the west end of the mill it was possible to provide a head of water, as can still be seen by comparing the level at this weir with the level as it flows under the bridge.

At Hurst Mill a different method was used to obtain a head of water. On the hillside to the south of the mill, two reservoirs were constructed and the water was conveyed to the wheel by an aqueduct. This arrangement gave a fall of 57 feet 6 inches, the greatest in the district.

In addition there were a large number of reservoirs built into the hillsides. Some were constructed by damming small streams, others by making an excavation and filling it from natural springs. Ten Foot Lodge was built to supply water to Wren Nest Mill. The water pressure in the valley bottom was sufficient to raise water from the mill to the lodge. At one

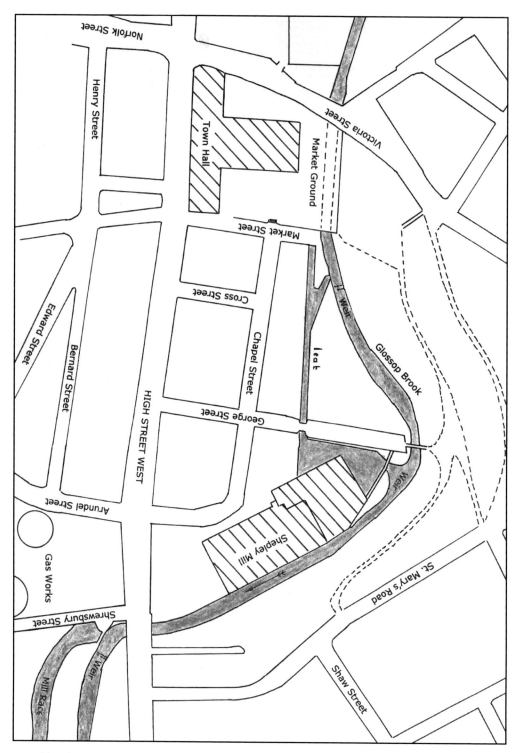

Map Six: Shepley Mill leat and other civil engineering works by Frederick Bateman.

Hurst Mill Aqueduct, 1940. (Supplied by Mr J.B. Shaw)

time it was the practice to fill this reservoir during the night using the mill sprinkler system and to draw off water during the day as required. The advantage of this skulduggery was that the water in the sprinkler system was not metered. Not quite the model behaviour we have been led to expect from our local mill owners.

Domestic Water Supply

When choosing a site for a farm, a reliable supply of drinking water would be vital. The six-inch Ordnance Survey map shows the symbol W – for well – amply distributed throughout Glossopdale and there are springs and water troughs shown. All the old farms would have a well and such are indicated at Lower Jumble, Cloud, and Higher Dinting Farms. The names Spring Street and Wellgate are reminders of the days before a piped water supply was laid on. Before industry invaded the valley the streams and wells would be free running and relatively pure.

Some of the old wells still exist, if not in pristine condition. Among the best preserved is the Town End Well built into the wall outside All Saints Roman Catholic Church. Within the grounds of All Saints, built into a wall outside the Rectory, is the stone inscribed with the motto of the Duke of Norfolk: "SOLA VIRTUS INVICTA: AD 1853". This stone once graced a well which stood some distance further east, close to the school.

Not far from this well was another in Manor Park. At one time it was capped with a column and headstone with the legend "WG 1660". Stories went the rounds concerning secret passages leading from this well to Glossop Hall and even to Shire Hill. Such yarns can safely be discounted, but not far away is a culvert which passes under the road to re-emerge near All Saints School. At one time it was the practice of more reckless students at the school

Well head in Wellgate.

The Town End Well, Church Street.

Well Head now in the grounds of All Saints Roman Catholic Church.

Horse Trough near the Quiet Shepherd, Tintwistle.

to enter the culvert at the entrance in the park, crawl through, and emerge near the school. These antics might be the origin of the stories about secret passages.

Wells in Charlesworth have been the subject of dispute. When Rev Goodwin Purcell became vicar at St John's he was soon in conflict with the Independent Top Chapel and its devotees. He launched an attack upon them by suggesting that the water in the wells was contaminated by flowing through their graveyard. The expression he used was, "They were drinking the broth of their ancestors' bones." The Chapel authorities had the water analysed and it was found to be fit for consumption. By a strange twist this was to rebound on the Vicar, because just below St John's graveyard was the Mousey Well, and as the graveyard started to fill it was the Mousey Well that became contaminated and went out of use.

Property owners renovating their houses have been surprised to discover that they have a well under the house. In older parts of the hamlets you will find small patches of cobblestones which were laid to prevent the ground around the well from turning into a mud bath. These medieval cobbles are different from the cobbles used when the streets of the town were paved. Instead of rectangular blocks of stone, they were laid by setting stones on edge. An example can be seen at Stocks Lane in Charlesworth.

Glossop Hall's water came by a pipe from two reservoirs on the Heath. Many of the mill owners lived in houses which had piped water from reservoirs on their land, Moorfield House for example.

The water supply position was worsening with population growth and effluents from the factories. Wells, pumps and streams could no longer cope and a piped water supply became imperative. A meeting of property owners was held at the house of George Hampson in Whitfield, on 10th March 1852, when it was agreed to "bring pure water in metal pipes from the old wells in Whitfield down the public road, and thence to the Turnpike-road". They agreed not to place the order for the pipes until "three-fourths of the money for the pipes shall be collected and deposited in the Liverpool and Manchester District Bank". They knew they were on doubtful ground for they bound themselves not to sell, nor divert the water from the wells, nor to use it for any but domestic purposes "on pain of immediate forfeiture of rights and privileges in the Society or Company".

The date establishes that the piped supply from Whitfield wells was the first in the Borough, but it was never legally founded. On one occasion, when a deputation from the Company met the Water Committee to enforce their rights, the Town Clerk suddenly produced the award and confounded them – an excellent example of municipal sleight of hand.

The principal partners in the Whitfield Water Company were Thomas Hampson, who owned property in Whitfield, and Joseph Robinson, a builder of Charlestown Road. It appears that it was not a simple matter to get their agreement to lay on a water supply to one's property. One gentleman found a way of outwitting this intransigence. He laid in a supply of iron pipe and surreptitiously excavated a trench from the rear of his house across Hampson's field at night, carefully replacing the turf, until he was able to draw water from a spring.

The Whitfield Water Company's supply was replaced by the Glossop Water Works, but during World War II several houses on Charlestown Road were still connected to the Whitfield wells and this proved very convenient when the town supply to other properties was cut off for several days.

With the building of turnpike roads and the increase in the number of horse drawn vehicles it became important for water troughs to be located along roadsides. Some of these are still in existence, but others are long gone, mainly due to frost damage.

Mrs Anne Kershaw Wood provided several fountains. In Howard Park is one with the statue of a cotton weaver. On either side are the heads of her husband Samuel and his brother Daniel in bas relief. The date is 1889. A second fountain stands near the traffic lights in the town centre, complete with drinking water for humans, horses and dogs. One cannot miss the carved inscription, commemorating Mrs Wood of Whitfield House, 1881, but note also in small letters on the base, Williams and Hope Dinting. David Williams was a Welsh mason who also worked on Dinting Church.

Other fountains erected by the Wood family were at the junction of Manor Park Road and High Street East, and where Victoria Street, St Mary's Road and James Street meet. These were demolished some years ago as an obstacle to traffic flow.

In 1852 the Duke altered an old mill reservoir at Swineshaw, laid pipes, and conveyed the water to the main streets of Glossop. This service became available in 1854 when property owners could apply for houses to be connected to the main for 2/6d per week in addition to paying for the labour and pipes required. No Act of Parliament was obtained, and this omission was soon to lead to trouble. Before this erupted, Lord Howard had constructed the Railway Reservoir (SK030966) in 1861 with water drawn from the Torside goit; this reservoir was to lead to the Hadfield Waterworks Company.

During the Cotton Famine, Lord Howard employed a number of unemployed men in constructing Padfield Reservoir number 1 in 1861–62, and in 1863–64 two more reservoirs at Swineshaw. This led to objections from mill owners that they were losing water power. In September 1864, Francis Sumner wrote a letter to the Lord of the Manor informing him that he had no legal right to the water or to charge for it, and that he must discontinue doing so, or legal action would be taken. Lord Howard immediately issued a notice stating his intention of discontinuing the supply after 30th September. This caused consternation, as many of the pumps were out of order and wells filled up. The threat of cutting off the water supply certainly speeded progress towards the town receiving its Charter of Incorporation. There was a public meeting on 22nd September 1864, where a deputation met with Lord Howard who explained the position. The problem was solved temporarily by Lord Howard agreeing not to charge for the water while an application was made for an Act of Parliament.

Padfield reservoirs number one and two.

Glossop Water Bill

On 23rd March 1865, Mr Edmund Potter, M.P., and Mr John France appeared before the Referees on Private Bills. Mr Potter opposed the Bill, and in his evidence he stated, "We require 3,600,000 gallons of water per day. It is essential that we have pure water." Mr Potter also pointed out that he had only established his factory in Dinting Vale because of the pure stream of water, since he could obtain coal elsewhere for £1,000 a year less. He had also constructed large reservoirs with a capacity of about 18,000,000 gallons at his own expense since there was no municipal corporation.

On 27th March, Mr John France, Mr G. Woofington and Mr F. Hawke appeared before the Referees. Mr France stated that he was one of those who agreed to call a public meeting, at which it was decided to take steps to put the place under the Local Government Act, to prevent the mill owners interfering with the supply.

At the next meeting in the Town Hall several manufacturers attended, and advocated making an application for a Charter of Incorporation. A petition had been signed by 923 persons in favour of the Glossop Waterworks Bill, and if it did not pass great distress would be caused by the end of June.

Mr Hawke stated that he was present at the meeting of 21st November in the Town Hall when the following resolutions were passed:

> "That in the opinion of this meeting the best way of settling the water question is by making the Waterworks the property of the ratepayers; that it is the wish of the ratepayers to petition for a Charter of Incorporation for the town of Glossop; that such petition be prepared during the present week, and the signatures of the ratepayers obtained thereto, and that a committee be appointed to effect the above object."

The Bill came before the Select Committee of the House of Lords on 22nd May 1865. Mr George Blackburne, the engineer, stated:

> "The effect of these works will be to give an annual supply to the inhabitants of 22,213,600 cubic feet, and to the mill owners of half that quantity. They would be able to give each person in Glossop 1,800 cubic feet per annum. The scheme was ample to supply a 50% increase in population, or 18,513 persons."

Mr Francis Hawke stated that when he arrived in Glossop 14 years previously there was a great deal of building in progress, and Lord Howard had increased the unregulated compensation supply to the mill owners at the same time as he increased the supply to the inhabitants. Lord Howard had expended around £16,000 on public works which included seven small reservoirs. If action was not taken there was real danger of some serious outbreak of disease as there was no other source of water and the streams were so fouled by the various mill owners as to be unfit for drinking. The Act was passed and received the Royal Assent on 19th June 1865.

Lord Howard was left in control of the new water company which made a start on the problems by converting the two small reservoirs at Swineshaw into a deeper one, constructing Upper Swineshaw Reservoir and the Cote Lodge, this work being completed by 1866. The mill owners insisted that Cote Lodge be used to supply compensation water at a constant rate for their use. In 1879 Lord Howard continued with his enterprises, building Padfield Reservoir number 2 to add to the reserves of the Hadfield Water Company.

The Glossop Corporation negotiated with Lord Howard for the purchase of the Waterworks. Lord Howard was paid £21,000, and the Corporation took possession on the 19th December

1879. In 1902 the question of additional water supplies was raised, and because it was felt that the cost was greater than Glossop could be expected to bear, a joint scheme with Hyde was mooted. The proposal was to build a reservoir on the Shelf Brook above Mossy Lea bridge, the estimated cost being £170,000. After due consideration of the cost, especially the laying of pipes to Hyde, the Hyde Council decided not to proceed.

When Lord Francis Edward Howard died in 1924 his heir sold off the estate, which led to the Borough obtaining the Glossop Water Order of 1928 to take over the Hadfield Water Company, so that they owned all the major local reservoirs.

In July 1928 the Waterworks Committee gave a report on the consumption of water in All Saints' and St James' wards. On 16th May 1928 the average consumption per head was 39.34 gallons; by 20th June 1928 the average consumption per head was 29.31 gallons. In the course of five weeks the consumption had been reduced by 24%, although in the meantime 1,406 pail closets had been converted to fresh water closets. Thanks to the discovery of leakages the amount of water lost at Glossop had been reduced.

The problems with the water supply at Hadfield are dealt with under Health in Chapter 12, and were solved when in April 1933, the Hadfield Filtration Works was officially opened. At this date, many of the water pipes to houses were still made of lead, and, because the local water was very soft, lead could be dissolved by the water with harmful effects, so after passing through the filters, lime was added to bring the water to the required degree of hardness. The supply to All Saints' and St James' wards benefited by having the water supply hardened by the injection of lime at Swineshaw Reservoir.

In 1938 a dispute broke out between the Medical Officer of Health, Dr E.H.M. Milligan, and the Borough Surveyor, Mr G. Faulds. There were some extraordinary exchanges at council meetings. Alderman J.D. Doyle stated:

> "It is time we had more co-ordination among our officials. We have been made to feel like perfect fools, for here we have our Water Engineer whose figures on water consumption are challenged by our Medical Officer of Health, and in such a fashion that we seem unable to get reliable figures."

A special meeting of the Council was held to consider the adoption or otherwise of a Water Commission authorising the borrowing of £20,700 for a water reserve at Hurst Reservoir for the domestic supply. Dr Milligan contended that the water consumption in Glossop was disproportionately high as compared with other towns. Further, with the decline in population a less ambitious scheme was needed. Might it not be more profitable to search for leaks? He pointed out that in the Swineshaw area there was an unduly large amount of water used for domestic purposes, quoting figures of around 40 gallons per head as compared with about 21 gallons per head in similar industrial areas.

Mr Faulds supplied reasons why in his view a further supply was necessary, and disputed Dr Milligan's figures. It was clear from the water flow at night that there was leakage in the system, but Mr Faulds stated:

> "The question has been raised as to testing for leakages, but in my opinion to go to the expense of testing during the period when the reservoirs are overflowing is a needless waste of public money. During droughts extra men have been engaged for night testing and the result has been that on no occasion has the night flow been reduced below 8,000 gallons per hour. The Council will understand it is impossible to get 100% efficiency, as in the borough there are 28 miles of mains and 50 to 60 miles of service pipes, and leakages are bound to occur."

Councillors spoke both for and against these views, but it may be significant that Councillor Leatherbarrow, who had a plumbing business, spoke in support of Dr Milligan. After a lengthy discussion it was decided to postpone the scheme, and that in the interim the engineer and his department were to make a thorough investigation into the water consumption in the Borough.

When Dr Milligan and Mr Faulds finally reached agreement, the Waterworks Committee decided against the Hurst Reservoir scheme and opted instead to enlarge Windy Harbour Reservoir. This plan was never proceeded with because World War II intervened. The Borough finally obtained possession of Hurst Reservoir under the Glossop Water Act of 1952.

The Borough may have got its hands on Hurst Reservoir, but that was not the end of the matter. The scheme involved alterations to Hurst Reservoir, the erection of a filter house and pumping station, and the construction of a concrete reservoir 800 feet above sea level at Brownhill.

The Brownhill Reservoir was intended to provide the pressure to supply higher parts of the Borough, but the building of this reservoir and pumping station to raise the Hurst Reservoir water involved considerable expense. Councillor Hurst caused a furore in the Council when he announced that he could save £100,000 by removing the Brownhill Reservoir and the pumping station from the scheme and instead connecting the Hurst Reservoir water directly into the mains after filtration. Councillor Hurst stated:

> "I am not prepared to pay for pumping a million gallons of water up to Brownhill Reservoir when we already possess two reservoirs at Padfield at the same level. The cost of the pumping station and the Brownhill Reservoir is calculated to cost £79,000. From bitter experience this is likely to be over £100,000 in practice."

Supporters of the scheme pointed out the additional costs of connecting Hurst Reservoir to the existing mains and the need for new mains. In 1959 the matter was taken out of the hands of Glossop Borough Council when Manchester Corporation Waterworks took control of various water undertakings as part of the regrouping of the water industry. All the work in progress, including the new Treatment Works to remove the impurities, was completed and Hurst Reservoir was officially opened on 18th July 1961.

In the *Glossop Chronicle* of 7th November 1958 appears the following comment:

> "When Glossop Council made its declaration in favour of regrouping with Manchester City Authority we may take it that the decision was made under duress. Whatever may be the views of the general public about the council, we could hardly believe that it would give away the service around which, in Glossop, the whole structure of local government has been built."

In April 1974 the water industry was nationalised and Glossop water came within the Eastern Division of the North West Water Authority. Since that date the water industry has been privatised and we have had the dubious pleasure of being able to buy back our own water supply.

Disposal of waste water is also part of water management and over recent years we have witnessed the sight of our public toilets disappearing at an alarming rate. There were once gentlemen's toilets inside the Market Arcade, in Manor Park Road, Primrose Lane, Shrewsbury Street, the High Street East entrance to Manor Park and Collier Street, to mention but a few that have gone.

As a postscript I should add that despite all the efforts to provide a satisfactory water supply, there are still folks who collect water from springs in a bottle, "Just to get a decent cup of tea."

Site of a lost gentlemen's toilet.

Glossop Gas Company

Today electricity is the main means of artificial lighting, but before the introduction of gas as an illuminant, the candle or rushlight was the principal light source. Later there were oil lamps which burned whale or seal oil fed into a wick. Still later the age of the paraffin lamp arrived. In every town there were chandlers' shops where tallow candles were made. Today we have little notion of what it was like to exist by candlelight, except perhaps when there is a power cut.

In 1792, the application of coal gas for artificial lighting was accomplished by William Murdoch who lit his offices and a street lamp at Redruth in Cornwall, and in 1798 he applied gas to lighting the factory of Bolton and Watt at Birmingham.

In 1804 the new illuminant arrived in Manchester when Murdoch was commissioned to light the house of a cotton spinning manufacturer. The work of displacing candles by gas commenced in 1805 with the lighting of two rooms of the mill and counting house, and the lighting of the whole factory was completed by 1807. Mill owners were used to innovation, and candles, whale oil and Russian tallow were costing more because the war made importation difficult. They also wanted a safer illuminant to cut their insurance premiums.

Murdoch's assistant, Samuel Clegg, was commissioned by the Borough Reeve of Manchester to light a lamp in King Street, in order to see if gas could be used for street lighting. Clegg constructed a gasometer, filled it from his own apparatus in Deansgate and then inserted it in a tank of water.

The Borough Reeve refused to accept Clegg's estimate of £140 to light the whole of King Street. Then the Commissioners of Police took a hand, and, having commenced to make gas in a small way, installed a light outside the door of the Chief Police Officer in King Street. The Police Commissioners had been considering lighting the principal streets of the town with gas instead of whale or seal oil lamps, and there followed the first serious attempt to manufacture gas on a commercial scale when the Police Commissioners proceeded to erect a

Gas Notice.

Former Offices of Glossop Gas Works.

gasworks in Water Street. From this point the use of gas in Manchester developed rapidly.

The simplest way of producing coal gas was to heat coal in a retort in the absence of air, partially converting coal to gas with a residue of coke. This is basically the method used by William Murdoch. At first there were noxious substances also produced, but ways of converting these into by-products such as oils, creosote, dyes and fertiliser were gradually discovered.

The Glossop Gas Company obtained Parliamentary powers giving it exclusive rights to manufacture and sell gas in a specified area on 21st July 1845. This was over fifty years after the invention of gas lighting by Murdoch, by which time financial risk had been virtually eliminated. There were already three small gas producing plants in the Glossop area, but none possessed Parliamentary powers. There were also three other industrial plants operated by Sidebottom's at Hadfield, Francis Sumner at Wren Nest and John Wood of Howardtown, for lighting their mills. The Duke of Norfolk owned a gas manufacturing plant which supplied a limited number of customers. This concern was the basis of the Glossop Gas Works. The Duke's original installation was located around the site of the Ambulance Station in Chapel Street.

In their prospectus of 1844, the promoters of the company stated:

> "The superiority of gas over every other mode of lighting public buildings, houses and shops, having already been demonstrated at Glossop, on a limited scale, it has been deemed advisable to extend the works now furnishing that article; and with a view to secure a provision of gas equal to the present and any future demand, to form a Joint Stock Company."

The first list of directors and shareholders of the Glossop Gas Company was dominated by the Howard estate management, local lawyers and tradesmen. We find Lord Edward Howard, John des Jardins, Michael Ellison, Richard Ellison, Michael Joseph Ellison and the Rev Theodore Fauvel among them. Clearly the new company was sponsored from Glossop Hall. The lawyer who promoted the Parliamentary Bill was the Sheffield solicitor to the Duke of Norfolk, Mr William Wake, who later became the first secretary of the Company. Among the names was an almost complete absence of the owners of the cotton mills.

The promoters decided to form a Gas Company and issued a prospectus inviting people to apply for shares in a company with a capital issue of £5,000 in £10 shares. The first meeting of the provisional committee took place on 22nd November 1844 at Glossop Hall, there being present Michael Ellison in the chair; John Dalton, calico printer; Matthew Ellison, Hadfield; John Kershaw of the Hurst; Thomas Collier and Joseph Robinson, both grocers in Howardtown. At this meeting the committee decided to increase the proposed capital of the new concern to £6,000, the applications being in excess of the amount originally proposed, and allotted the whole of the 600 £10 shares. Mr Kershaw was instructed to canvass the mills to ascertain whether they were likely to become customers, and the result being favourable, the committee requested the Sheffield United Gas Light Company to allow their manager to plan and estimate the cost of a new works and place a valuation on the Duke of Norfolk's works.

In presenting his estimate to the Provisional Committee, the Sheffield Gas Manager observed, "I would recommend that great attention be paid to the purity of gas so that it may not only be introduced into the mills, shops and public houses, but into the houses of the mill proprietors and other respectable houses."

With the passing of the Act of Parliament the Glossop Gas Company had the exclusive right to manufacture gas, to construct all necessary works, and to take up the streets. The extent of these rights was defined in a succeeding Act passed in 1855 as comprising the townships of Glossop, Whitfield, Chunal, Simmondley, Charlesworth, Dinting, Hadfield and Padfield.

The first meeting of the Board of Directors was held in Glossop Town Hall on 18th August 1845, and the Board set about supplying gas, and preparing to make good the promise contained in one of the clauses of the Act which permitted them to pay dividends of 10% on the invested capital. At the end of the year the first authorised gas fitters, John Shaw and Joseph Higginbottom, were appointed and the Company announced that "no other parties be allowed to do the work of this Company."

The superintendent and collector of rents was Mr George Tomlinson, at a salary of £30 per annum, while Mr James Gill, as works manager, received a salary of 21 shillings a week. By 12th March 1846, the new company had reached a position where they were able to sell gas and fixed the price at 7s. 6d. per thousand feet. Owing to their initial expenses the company decided not to pay a dividend on the first year's working. A year later they announced that the position of the company then was that the directors could have paid a dividend of 13%, but as they were contemplating an extension of the works to supply the Old Town of Glossop they placed some of their money in reserve, and paid a lesser dividend. In May 1847 the directors resolved "that gas be carried to the village of Glossop", and three months later applied to the Manchester, Sheffield and Lincolnshire Railway Company for permission to "lay pipes alongside the railway lines from Dinting in order to supply Hadfield".

At the ordinary meeting of shareholders held in the Town Hall on 28th February 1848 the directors announced the payment of a 10% dividend, the extension of the gas mains to Hadfield and a reduction in the price of gas. But at a later meeting the directors had to admit to their shareholders that increased consumption had not been realised, so they declared a dividend of 5%.

In 1849 the company was in difficulties. The consumption of gas had not increased and the clerical staff had made errors in the bookkeeping, and in consequence the directors were compelled to declare a dividend of 4%. In 1851 the mains were taken into Whitfield, but the financial promise of the 10% dividend had not been maintained, and in 1854, not only had the dividend fallen to 3.5 %, but the chairman announced that the company had exhausted its capital resources and would need to apply to Parliament for powers to raise fresh money. In this year also, trouble came from another direction; they were by now accustomed to depression in the cotton trade, but in 1854 they were confronted with the largely increased cost of coal, increased labour costs, and a reduction in the consumption of gas.

On 25th May 1855, the Bill received Royal Assent, and the company was authorised to raise a further £18,000 capital, but Parliament had restricted the dividend to 7.5% and the price of gas was limited to 6s. per thousand feet. The directors proceeded to issue two new shares to holders of each old £10 share and one new in respect of each old £5 share.

In 1859, the residents of Whitfield, Simmondley and Padfield asked for an extension of the mains. The mains were extended in all directions, the company stretching out all through their Parliamentary area except Charlesworth. The main under the railway at Hadfield was inadequate and an extension from Woolley Bridge to Waterside followed, and in 1860 the price of gas was reduced to 5s. per thousand feet, and the company were selling coke at 5d. per hundredweight.

In June 1860, the authorities applied to the company for the price of gas for lighting the streets of Glossop. Eventually, the lamps were lit at a charge of 3s. 3d. per thousand feet. On 25th February 1860, gas inspectors were appointed and on 12th May 1861, tenders were put out for the supply of lamp-posts and fittings required for street lighting. On 9th September 1861, the streets of the town were first lit by gas.

The American Civil War caused the consumption of gas and revenue to decline; dividends fell, and touched rock bottom at 3.5%. In 1864, the revenue and the actual sales of gas were but one third of those for the year 1861. After the Cotton Panic, the Company revived and expanded its sales. Ten years after the end of the American Civil War, the Gas Company was paying its maximum dividends; it was sometimes paying a little extra to repay the shareholders for their patience during the lean years; and it had reached the stage where, apart from temporary setbacks due to fluctuations in the prices of coal and the growing insistence of labour for better wages, it could look forward to being a sound investment which gave a good return.

In 1872 the Gas Company informed the Council that at the end of the current lighting season they would refuse to supply gas on the present terms. The Council's response was to apply for an Act of Parliament to make their own gas. The minutes of the Council for 5th February 1874 disclose that they were discussing the possibility of municipalising the Glossop Gas Company, and under the Mayoralty of Mr William Sidebottom passed this resolution:

> "That a sub-committee be appointed to consider the question of lighting and supplying the town with gas, and be authorised to ascertain the powers of the Glossop Gas Company, and to enter into preliminary negotiations to ascertain on what terms the Glossop Gas Company could become the property of the Corporation, and failing in the negotiations, to ascertain if there are any good and sufficient grounds that may warrant the Corporation in seeking Parliamentary powers to erect fresh gas works."

The directors of the Gas Company noted the newspaper report but said nothing. By September, the sub-committee had realised that they would find the Gas Company a hard nut to crack, and began to explore the possibility of getting a Bill through Parliament in order to run their own gasworks in the town.

The Council were in an awkward situation. Parliamentary Bills cost money in lawyers' fees; and who was to pay? The mill owners were not the only ratepayers; the directors and shareholders of the Gas Company paid rates and they would not willingly find money for mill owners to put into the pockets of lawyers, and also endanger the stability of their concern. So the sub-committee of the Council hit upon the idea of a local subscription to cover the cost of a Parliamentary Bill to establish another gasworks in Glossop. But there was a snag. If the Bill received Royal Assent, the cost of promotion would be a capital charge upon the new gasworks, but what if it failed? So the Mayor, Mr William Sidebottom, reported to the Council on 24th September 1874 that he had submitted the principle of the subscription to the principal ratepayers, and they would willingly subscribe but for the fact that if the Bill did not pass they would lose their money.

A meeting was called in the Town Hall on 10th February 1875 and the following resolution was passed: "That in the opinion of this meeting, the Glossop Gas Company do not afford to the inhabitants of the Borough a supply of gas of such illuminating power for domestic comfort, for working purposes, and for the proper illumination of the streets, and that such a supply as is afforded is inferior in quality, and sold at an excessive price." On 11th March 1875, they passed a resolution deciding to petition the Home Secretary to introduce a General Bill to enable all Local Authorities to erect gasworks and supply gas to their ratepayers without let or hindrance.

It is unlikely that the cotton masters contemplated the construction of another gasworks in Glossop, but if they gained control of the gasworks, their privately owned industrial gasworks could be closed down with capital savings.

In March 1875, the Council made an offer to purchase the whole of Glossop Gas Company and all its rights for the sum of £44,690. It was submitted to an extraordinary meeting of the shareholders on the same day as the receipt of the letter. The report of the directors states:

> "The quoted price has doubtless been influenced by the unjustifiable and unfair attacks, which for a considerable period past have been made against the Company and its Directors, the natural tendency of which must have been to depress the shares."

The Council gambled on the low market value of the shares stampeding the timid into selling out, but they were mistaken. After directly charging the Council and Corporation with unfair and unjustifiable attacks, they unanimously rejected the offer. This legal battle, which was won by the directors of the Gas Works, cost the ratepayers £1,080 18s. 6d. in 1880.

So far, the only means of lighting was by the fish-tail burner which burned with a yellow flame like a candle. A great improvement came with the invention of the Welsbach mantle around 1900. It was a vertical mantle and gave a far superior light to the fish-tail burner. The first works in Glossop to use the vertical incandescent mantle was the building contractor's shop of Cyrus Garside on Surrey Street, and the first shop to use the new mantle was the hairdressing establishment of Joe Bunting in Victoria Street. This invention caused a great extension of gas lighting for its adoption was universal and rapid. In order to let the public see for themselves the value of the new invention, the company offered to install incandescent lights round Norfolk Square, and the Town Council agreed on condition that the Company kept the lights in good order.

Five years later the inverted incandescent burner made its appearance. The popular notion was that it would be a failure because gas wouldn't go downhill. The inverted mantle gave such a good light that gas was able to compete against electricity for many years to come. About 1905 gas began to be used for cooking and heating, and the illuminant that was generally believed would disappear with the expansion of electricity took on an extended life.

In the year 1908 the Town Council suddenly revived its demand for municipalisation of the Gas Works, Councillor Eastham proposing that a sub-committee be set up to consider the advisability of purchasing the Glossop Gas Company. He secured a seconder, but the bulk of the Council refused to serve on the sub-committee. The sub-committee approached the Gas Company with a view to its municipalisation, but they got short shrift. The reply submitted to the Council intimated that "they had no desire to sell; the Gas Works was not on the market, but if the price were tempting enough they would recommend the shareholders consider it. They could not entertain a figure less than £100,000."

This campaign was also accompanied by offensive letters in the local press, with complaints that the gas stained brasswork in homes and was of poor quality, but unlike the previous effort it died a sudden death. The Glossop Gas Company was destined to remain independent until nationalisation by the post-war Labour government.

When electricity came on the scene the demand for gas still increased because gas was used for cooking and heating. At the time of the introduction of the incandescent mantle the Glossop Gas Company were producing annually some 58 million feet; ten years later, although the consumption of electricity was increasing, gas production was 84 million feet and in 1945 had reached 200 million feet.

In February 1957 the North Western Gas Board announced that the Glossop Gas Works was to close down and that gas supplies would come from either Hyde or the new works at Denton. All that would be retained were the gasholders and a maintenance team. Modern developments meant that gas could be produced more cheaply and distributed through the grid system and small gasworks like Glossop were obsolete. Now all that remains of Glossop gasworks is the original office building. A glance at this building shows the similarities in style to the Town Hall and the Railway Station, all having origins in the days when the Howards were Lords of the Manor.

There were other industries in addition to cotton adding to the town's prosperity. Some met with varying degrees of success; for example there was a Silk Mill in Silk Street and the Logwood Mill which stood on the opposite side of the Glossop Brook to the Junction Inn. The Logwood Mill was built around 1805 by the three Wagstaffe brothers, James, Joseph and Robert, and in 1831 it was worked by Messrs Samuel Oliver and Jones as a paper mill. Logwood was a dye made from logs imported from tropical America. The blood-red heartwood of the tree yields a black to purple dye used in the textile industry. The logs were fed against rotating blades which cut them into chips which were then ground into powder by millstones. The waste material must have been dumped in the Glossop Brook where apparently it had a detrimental effect on the products at the Dinting Printworks further

The Logwood Mill.

Civic leaders 1911.
Messrs Platt,
Edward Partington,
Reed, Ellison and
Herbert Partington.

downstream. Mr Potter, proprietor of the printworks, sued Oliver for damages and the case practically ruined Mr Oliver.

Turn Lee Mills had been worked by the Bennetts and Kershaws for the production of textiles and paper. Later, Thomas Hamer Ibbotson worked the mill but he was unfortunate after starting in business as a paper manufacturer. On 16th May 1860 he had a fire in which £1,500 of cotton waste was destroyed.

In 1873, Messrs Olive and Partington became tenants and made dramatic changes. Leading these changes was Edward Partington, who was prepared to invest time and money in inventions and experiments; not all were successful but others benefited the firm financially and the publishing trade also by reducing the cost of paper so that newspapers came within the reach of all.

With the introduction of Edward Partington's ideas the raw material for paper manufacture changed and whole trainloads of timber from Canada and Norway were transported to Glossop and carried to Turn Lee Mills on trailers drawn by the once familiar "Tiger" tractors. The mills were so successful that extra land was leased in 1876 and again in 1882, together with the old woollen mill further down the road in order to secure the water rights. By the end of the 19th century, Olive and Partington's Turn Lee Mills had grown into a huge complex.

Edward Partington's efforts were not confined to Turn Lee Mills; he had an interest in the Ramsbottom Paper Mill Company, Broughton Bridge Mills, Barrow-in-Furness Mills, Borregaard Mills in Norway and Hallein Mills in Austria. He was also a director of Glossop Ironworks and specialised machinery designed in the drawing office at Turn Lee was made there.

Glossop folks were of the opinion that Turn Lee Paper Mills were the largest in the world. This might have been true once but it was certainly to be surpassed in size later. Whatever its size it assuredly found employment for thousands during its life. There can be few local families without some connection with Olive and Partington's. It seems only the other day that men walked along Charlestown Road in cloth cap and bib and brace overalls carrying wicker lunch baskets or a basin wrapped in a red handkerchief.

The Gnathole Brook below Turn Lee Mills was known as the "Chemic Brook", because the processes at the mill caused the colour of the water to change frequently and some peculiar odours were emitted. Among the waste flowing downstream was a substance which left a grey residue, which when it dried out resembled the material used for egg boxes. A new industrial chemist started at the firm and was aghast at this waste and immediately introduced changes to the process which cleaned up the brook and increased the profits simultaneously.

Turn Lee Mills have known disasters in the past. Production has been halted by serious flooding; employees have been killed and injured in industrial accidents. The worst disaster occurred on Friday, 25th June 1943 when there was a tremendous explosion just before

Tiger Tractor. (Photo supplied by *Glossop Chronicle*)

eight o'clock in the morning. The first impression was that a bomb had struck the mill, but it was a spherical boiling pan which had burst, completely wrecking the solidly constructed mill building. Four men were killed and five seriously injured.

Turn Lee Mills became part of the Inveresk Group and it was believed that Turn Lee would never close as long as Tom Smith was a director of the Group. Whatever substance there was in this suggestion may never be known, but Turn Lee closed five years after his death in 1958. A reason given for the closing of Turn Lee Paper Mills was that the machinery turned on phosphor bronze bearings and so could not run at the higher speeds that were by then standard practice in the paper trade.

Most of the buildings were demolished and the last major part to go was the Jubilee Mill which was destroyed in a catastrophic fire in September 1994.

Isaac Jackson came to Glossop from Hyde and set up in business as a saddler. His business developed steadily and he took larger premises in Victoria Street and went on to own a fine block of shops. It was while he was working in Victoria Street that he invented and patented a belt fastener which eventually came into worldwide use. At a time when virtually every piece of machinery was belt driven, the market for an efficient belt fastener was enormous.

By 1901 he was employing 50 people and had added tool making and the manufacture of nuts and bolts to his product line. In 1905 he moved his works to Hawkshead Mill, a former cotton mill. At Hawkshead he installed gas engines running on gas made on the premises, and the mill was equipped with the latest machinery imported from America. Isaac Jackson went on to produce other inventions and products and by 1911 his workforce had grown to 150. During the Great War parts were made for high explosive shells and he also developed a reliable shell detonator. In 1919 Isaac Jackson and his wife bought the Town Hall and Market rights from Lord Howard and presented them to the Borough as a memorial to the men who were killed in the Great War.

Disintegrator. One of the machines designed in the drawing office at Turn Lee Mills and built at Glossop Ironworks. (From a paper read before the Manchester Association of Engineers in 1911 by T.W. Sharpe, M.I. Mech.E)

Isaac Jackson was made a Freeman of the Borough in 1920. By 1980 the firm was in difficulties, redundancies were declared and in 1982 Isaac Jackson's ceased trading.

Another local industry was rope making, carried on at Lee Vale Ropeworks in Charlesworth and at Levi Jackson's Hobroyd ropeworks. At one time rope piecers from Charlesworth travelled all over industrial Lancashire and Cheshire fitting new cotton driving ropes to mill engines. On occasion, when extra long ropes were made at the Hobroyd Mill, the rope walk was extended right down the lane past High Lawn and across Turn Lee Road onto the forecourt of Stanley Shaw's garage. Levi Jackson's Rope Works was destroyed by fire in 1985.

The fire which destroyed the Jubilee Mill, September 1994.

Hawkshead Mill.

8

THE DEMISE OF COTTON AND THE ARRIVAL OF NEW INDUSTRIES

Henry Ford is often quoted as saying "History is bunk". I beg to differ, because if we take a look at Glossopdale much can be learned. It would seem there is a right time to get involved in an industry. None of the early cotton masters were as successful as later entrants like John Wood or Francis Sumner. The introduction of steam engines provided a death blow to many of the smaller cotton masters who had commenced business with borrowed capital which had been used in the purchase of machinery and mill building. Consequently they were unable to purchase steam engines or erect engine houses. Matters were made worse because steam engines were required to drive larger and more efficient machinery. Slowly they were driven into bankruptcy or forced to let out their mills to others.

After John Wood's death, Howardtown Mills continued to expand under his three sons, but they did not continue to live in the modest style of their father. John Hill Wood built Whitfield House; Daniel and Samuel moved from Howardtown House to more splendid accommodation at Moorfield. John Wood and Brothers became a limited company in 1875 with Daniel Wood as Managing Director and the firm continued to grow until there were nearly 4,000 looms and 221,000 spindles. John Wood senior had made sure his sons were brought up knowing every aspect of the trade, but inevitably it seems that all the members of the Cottonocracy gave later generations a "good" (?) education and they moved into politics, the law and other fields, leaving the mills in the hands of managers.

The cotton industry provided a livelihood for the bulk of the population throughout the 19th century. With most of the family working, folks had a fairly comfortable existence, but prolonged unemployment soon exhausted their savings and debts with local shopkeepers and landlords would soon be run up. In the 1897 slump, the Hadfield Distress Fund was set up to alleviate the suffering. The situation was again serious in 1909 and 1910. An appeal was issued in December 1909 for families in Charlesworth and Chisworth who were without food or fire. In April 1910 there were insufficient monies in the Mayor's Fund to pay out further relief. By September of the same year the headline in the *Glossop Chronicle* was "Glossop's Starving Children". The article stated that there were around 1,000 starving school children in Glossop and Hadfield. The Glossop and Hadfield Independent Labour Party was distributing 60 free breakfasts consisting of bread, butter and jam, with tea and coffee, a full meal every morning, with a dinner on Saturdays, to children attending day schools in St James' Ward.

These downturns in trade tended to be cyclic, but it was becoming obvious that cotton would never return to its former dominance. Some of the problems could be put down to overproduction, and others to foreign competition. There was a popular misconception that workers in Japan and elsewhere were subsisting on a bowl of rice. The truth was that the foreign industrialists were setting up in business with the advantages of learning from the

British and only buying the best machinery from U.K. manufacturers or from mills that were closing.

There was an improvement for a time after the Great War, but by 1921 the local newspaper held reports of large numbers of unemployed who had exhausted their Labour Exchange benefit marching to the Guardian's Office in ranks of four. The local paper dated 21st January 1921 carried the headline: "THE SHORT TIME IN THE GLOSSOP DISTRICT. About 7.500 receiving Out of Work Pay."

By the late 1920s the position was becoming serious. Wood's Mill failed in 1924 but was kept open by its creditors. In 1931 Glossop had an unemployment rate of 57% and Hadfield 67%, compared with a national figure of 19%. This desperate state of affairs led to many folks leaving the area to seek work. There was a fall in population and in the number of marriages and the birth rate.

The 2nd Baron, Francis Edward Fitzalan-Howard, died in 1924 and his heir sold off the entire Glossop Estates the following year. Payment of death duties was probably the main reason for the sale, but it must have been obvious that the estate income from quarries and ground rents on various properties was falling and that the Howards might do better to transfer their assets elsewhere. Whatever the reasons for the sale, it was another blow to the town since the Howards had often acted as benevolent landlords in addition to providing employment in times of distress.

To their credit the Glossop Council took action, forming the Glossop Industrial and Residential Development Committee. Their efforts were all the more praiseworthy as the leading families who had built up the cotton industry had departed and the Council no longer contained many with experience of running large concerns.

Wood's Mill 1960. (Supplied by Mr J.B. Shaw)

The objects and aims of the Glossop Industrial and Residential Development Committee were as follows:

(a) To undertake the immediate preparation of information for insertion in the "Come to Derbyshire" guide, and the preparation of an up-to-date local guide, and to collect and collate information in regard to the amenities and advantages of the Borough whether commercial, historical, scenic or recreational.

(b) To foster the introduction into the town of new industries.

(c) To do everything to improve the welfare of the existing industries.

(d) To collect the fullest information respecting: (i) Building sites, both industrial and residential; (ii) Vacant industrial premises; (iii) Industrial properties available for purchase.

(e) To act as a central authority to receive representations and to answer enquiries on the foregoing matters.

The Committee consisted of councillors and representatives of industry and commerce. The task facing them was made difficult because similar conditions existed throughout the industrial north-west of England.

By February 1936 the Committee was able to report some success. They had used their influence to obtain cheaper railway fares and electricity. One mill had been restarted and three new industries had been introduced. Ferro-Alloys had commenced work in the Glossop Ironworks; part of Rhodes Mill, Hollingworth, had been acquired by Hadfield Silks; and a new brickworks was being constructed at Mouselow by Messrs J. Greenwood. Although the new companies employed small numbers, between them they made an impact on the number of unemployed.

The position was further improved by events in Europe where Hitler's persecution of the Jews caused many of them to emigrate, bringing their skills and, in the case of the more fortunate, their capital with them. Germany's loss was certainly Britain's gain with the influx of numbers of talented and industrious people. One is reminded of earlier persecutions such as that of the Huguenots.

There is usually a tendency to resent folks from outside regardless of their origins, but the prospect of renewed employment certainly muted complaints. One question which needs asking is why were there not more Glossopians with the initiative to start some venture?

There follows a survey of some of these industries.

Volcrepe

First registered as a company on 3rd July 1931. It was formed in Northamptonshire to acquire the business of a small firm of shoe manufacturers whose chemist had developed a shoe-soling material. It incorporated wool with crêpe rubber and had certain advantages over the crêpe rubber in general use. This was called *Vo-la-Crepe*, from which the name of the company was derived.

To provide accommodation for the expanding business, a weaving shed at Wood's Mill was acquired in 1931 and the manufacture of shoes and Vo-la-Crepe started in 1932 at Milltown. During World War II shoe making at Glossop was stopped under the Government's scheme for the concentration of industry, and was undertaken for Volcrepe by G.H. Palmer near Leicester. After the war this collaboration continued with the formation of High Peak Shoes, based in the Albion Mill at Hollingworth.

During the war a wide range of products was made for the war effort. These included gas masks and earphone pads for service radio equipment; Volafelt shock pads for steel helmets; inflatable lifebelts for airborne troops; balers for air-sea rescue dinghies; parts for aircraft; and soling for aircrew boots. At one stage during the war, the Axis powers controlled 98% of the world's supply of raw rubber, and the scientific and technical staff had to overcome all the difficulties appertaining to the use of synthetic rubber and substitute materials.

In the post-war period a wide variety of products was made, including miners' kneepads and shoe soles. In the early 1950s latex foam product manufacture was started and in the mid-1950s the Polyurethane division was formed, Volcrepe being one of the first companies in Britain to enter this field. This division was sold in 1960 and became Coolag Ltd. Lack of space at Milltown became a problem and in 1956 a new Bridge Banbury rubber mixer was installed at Wren Nest Mill.

More recently, due to increased competition in the footwear industry, the company decided to specialise in the manufacture of cellular rubber which is used in a wide variety of industries from automotive and aerospace to judo mats and packaging. In 2001 two companies within the Evans and Reid Group, Volcrepe and St Albans Rubber, merged to form E & R Polymers.

Testing in the laboratory at E & R Polymers.

Ferro-Alloys & Metals Ltd

This company commenced work in April 1934 manufacturing Ferro-Tungsten, Ferro-Molybdenum, Ferro-Vanadium, Chromium and other metals used in the production of high speed steels. The company came into prominence with the erection of the 300 foot chimney in 1977 despite widespread public opposition. This has been the subject of ongoing agitation ever since.

In view of the recent troubles with regard to emissions it is of interest to note that as early as 1937 there were complaints from 66 residents of Shrewsbury Street, Wren Nest Terrace, Surrey Street and Edward Street regarding alleged nuisance and damage by fumes and dirt emitted from Ferro-Alloys' chimney.

Flexy Brushes

Dr Bob Cohen and Ken Rosenfield came to Britain from Germany after Hitler came to power, and having technical knowledge of brush making set up in business in Manchester. One of their early products was a flexible scrubbing brush which did not have water passing through; they also made artists' brushes. The company came to Glossop around 1945 and started work in Brook Street. After a few years they had made sufficient profit to buy Old Dover Mill outright. On the death of Dr Cohen the business was sold by the family and Flexy brushes continued to be made at the Old Dover Mill in Chunal. The business changed hands several times, and, as the new owners were not interested in the artists' brush products part of the business, Mr Peter Mellor set up High Peak Brushes for the manufacture of a wide variety of brushes from artists' to make-up. Mr. Mellor sold his successful business in 2002, but after a few years High Peak Brushes closed.

Workers at High Peak Brushes 2002.

Lancashire Chemical Works

Founded as a private company limited on 5th February 1937, the works being installed in the old electricity generating station at Dinting, which was gradually converted into a chemical factory. The company produces mineral tanning compounds, mordants and adsorbents. These products are used chiefly by the tanning, textile and various sections of the chemical industries, with some being exported. The directors of the company were Dr Walter Hene and R Heckscher.

The Glossop Electric Company, now occupied by Lancashire Chemicals.

Ferrostatics Limited (1937)

Two Hungarian brothers, after escaping from the continent before the Second World War, set up an engineering firm in Hollingworth employing five men. The company expanded, moving into Robert Wilson's Old Bakery in High Street West. The workforce consisted almost entirely of highly skilled toolmakers. At first they made precision jigs and fixtures, but after the war, with the growth of the plastics industry, they moved into the mould-making field. Among their moulds were battery moulds for Chloride, and eventually Chloride built up their shareholding in Ferrostatics until they were able to take over the firm.

Maconochie Bros.

The Second World War was to bring further benefits to Glossop so far as employment was concerned. The London factory of Maconochie Bros at Millwall was badly damaged in the Blitz and was rebuilt in 1940 at the site in Hadfield next to the branch railway line. The trade names Pan Yan Pickle and Kep Sauce were well known, and there were even old employees of the company who came up from London who were known as Pan Yan Mary and Minnie Kep respectively. Another famous product was Maconochie's meat and vegetable stew. If old soldiers who served in World War II are to believed, they existed for the duration on a diet of Maconochie's M and V.

In 1959 the firm was taken over by H.S. Whiteside, who introduced the Sun-Pat range of products. In 1967 Rowntree and Company bought the factory. More recently the company has closed with consequent job losses.

The Admiralty

Also in 1940, an Admiralty depot in Portsmouth was bombed and moved into part of Wood's Mill which was derelict and had been empty for over 12 years. The workforce grew from 280 to 772 and the space occupied from 90,000 square feet to 240,000 square feet. Essential workers were billeted in the town, and this is an aspect of wartime which has been largely forgotten. If a householder had spare accommodation then essential workers could be billeted in his house compulsorily. The Admiralty depot was closed in 1945.

After the Second World War, the cotton industry enjoyed a brief revival. Francis Sumner's turned a building behind the mill into a hostel and also took over Redcourt House for accommodation. Girls were recruited from Eire, and later from Italy and from amongst displaced Europeans. Despite their diverse backgrounds and language difficulties quite a

Above: Wilman's Station Mill.

Right: Demolition of Wilman's Mill. (Supplied by Mr E. Lord)

number of these people became permanent members of Glossop's population. Some efforts at modernisation of plant were made with machines being fitted with individual electric motors. At Wood's Mill, the Engineer, Bert Clough, developed and patented a device known as a centre weft fork and his assistant Arthur Tomlinson travelled to various mills fitting the device.

Having seen the equipment in the maintenance workshop at Wren Nest Mill when Volcrepe took over part of the mill in 1955, I can only say it would have made a fine museum with its collection of 19th century tackle. Wren Nest closed completely in 1956 and Wood's closed their weaving sheds in August of the same year. Wood's Mill spinning rooms shut down in April 1959. Waterside was the last of the big concerns to close in 1976.

The textile finishing companies survived longer than most. Dinting Printworks, once the world's largest, closed in 1966. John Walton's, Bleachers and Dyers, moved from Charlestown to Woolley Bridge in 1950 and closed in 1985 with the loss of 260 jobs. The last textile mill to close was Wilman's Station Mill in 1989.

Most of the mills have been demolished to make way for various developments and their disappearance has been speeded by several fires, the most dramatic of which was the conflagration of 1996 when the eastern end of Wren Nest Mill was consumed utterly.

The days when a child's name was put down to work at Wood's Mill or Turn Lee while he was still in his pram have long gone, as has the notion of working for the one company

A Spinning Room.

throughout one's working life. Today folks are glad to have a job that lasts six months. Sadly the concepts of loyalty to the company, or of a paternalistic attitude on the part of companies, who would continue to employ workers for as long as possible during times of recession, have been lost.

Since 1945 a whole range of firms have come and occupied parts of empty cotton mills. When the Admiralty vacated part of Wood's Mill, the Ritz Manufacturing Company moved in, starting with six sewing machines. In 1956 they employed 250 girls and had to bus in workers from outside the town, but by 1981 they were laying off workers in large numbers.

Pickerings, part of the Fison's Group, took over the weaving shed at Wren Nest and used it as a food canning factory. In 1969 the Fison's Food Factory was taken over by Heinz Ltd, who promptly closed the works with the loss of 170 jobs.

W.M. Allan occupied the smaller weaving shed at Wren Nest for the manufacture of refrigerated shop display units. They were taken over by the CWS and later closed. Mentor shirts used the Old Liberal Club on the corner of Railway and Edward Streets.

Keith Blackburn is an example of a local entrepreneur who had his ups and downs in the textile trade, manufacturing and printing stretch covers, cushion covers and car seat covers. Others who have come for a while and then departed include Beaufort Air-Sea Equipment, Rowpak, and North's, who occupied the old Littlemoor School.

One industry which has enjoyed success is the manufacture of plastic foams. In 1965 Coolag moved into part of Olive and Partington's Turn Lee Mill in Charlestown. Drakafoam set up in part of the Dinting Printworks and in 1991 the American firm Carpenter's took them over.

L. and A. Middleton's built a few houses post-war and had some success manufacturing the Eskimo and Igloo draught excluders. Other builders have found plenty of work with the erection of new estates. G.A. Lomas and Egerton's spring to mind.

What does the future hold? It would seem that Glossop is destined to be a commuter town for the foreseeable future, but perhaps there is another entrepreneur of the calibre of John Wood already planning to set up in business.

9

Travel Through The Ages

Ridgeway from Mam Tor heading towards Lose Hill.

The earliest trackways were along ridgeways or the sides of hills because the valley bottoms were marshy and liable to flooding. Within the Peak are two old ridgeways. One is on the limestone plateau running roughly north and south passing close to the stone circle at Arbor Low. The Roman road from Derby to Buxton followed the same general line, as does the modern road. The second runs along Rushup Edge, Lord's Seat, the Iron Age fort on Mam Tor, past the site of Hollins Cross and on to Lose Hill.

Two ancient routes over the Pennines are via Longdendale or by Doctor's Gate and the Ashop Valley. In both, the tracks follow the north side of the valley where possible to make the most of the winter sun, and after crossing the inevitable mountain stream head for high ground to make the shortest exposed crossing. Ancient travellers took the best route possible. In Longdendale the track between Pikenaze and Saltersbrook only crosses one stream at Audernshaw Clough, but a route along the south side of the valley would have crossed dozens.

Along Doctor's Gate the exposed section over the summit is the only part where paving remains. Dr John Talbot, an illegitimate son of the Earl of Shrewsbury, was Vicar of Glossop from 1494 until 1535 and he would have had to travel between Glossop and his father's castle in Sheffield. There was mention of a Doctor Talbot's Gate in a document of 1627 and it is possible that he was responsible for improvements to the ancient track.

Some materials would be unobtainable in a given locality and have to be brought from afar. Salt is an example, which would have been essential to preserve the meat of animals slaughtered at the start of winter through to warmer times in the following year. The trade was centuries old, and is recorded in the Domesday Book where, prior to 1066, the Cheshire wiches belonged jointly to King Edward and Earl Edwin. Later, Basingwerke Abbey was a monastic owner of salt wiches.

Longdendale formed a natural route for packhorses to travel from Cheshire into south Yorkshire, and this is why, until the county boundaries were altered in 1974, a long tongue of Cheshire intruded between Derbyshire and Yorkshire so that the Earls of Chester could avoid tolls. There are reminders of this trade in place names along the way, Saltersbrook being the best known. The bottom of Wellgate in Old Glossop was formerly known as Salford, which may be an indication of another salt route via Doctor's Gate.

With the departure of the Romans, roads fell into neglect. Bridges and culverts collapsed, drains silted up and metalling sank into the subsoil until travellers had to make their way round the obstacle as best they could, widening the road in the process. For most, travel was on foot with only the wealthy travelling on horseback. The frequent passage of livestock converted roads into lengthy dung heaps. Oxen were preferred for the pulling of carts because their cloven hooves splayed out, giving them a better purchase in the mud where a horse would quickly become bogged.

Elizabeth I was the first monarch to have a coach, and from the early middle ages until the 17th century packhorses and mules were almost the sole means of transport for goods. In the Peak, packhorses were common into the mid-19th century because they could travel over routes impassable to heavy wagons.

The Statute of Winchester of 1285 made it the responsibility of manors to keep the king's highways in order and gave manor constables the task of supervising the work. This legislation was ineffective and in 1555 an Act was passed ordering Surveyors of Highways to be elected in every parish. Each parishioner owning a ploughland in tillage, or keeping a draught animal or plough, was liable to supply a cart for four days a year for use in road repair. Each able-bodied householder or tenant was required to give four days' "statute" labour a year. The post of Surveyor of the Highway lasted in parishes until the setting up of councils in the 19th century.

In addition to the carriage of salt, packhorses were used to transport coal from the pits, broken stone for making and repairing roads, and finished cloth to markets. Dr Aiken, writing of the agriculture of the district, says; "The manure for the land is lime, brought from Chapel-en-le-Frith on the back of small Welsh horses, which run up and down the hills with as sure a foot as goats and have little other food than what they pick up by the road side on their return."

A narrow causeway was cheaper to make and maintain than a road of a width suitable for carts. Bridges also could be narrower, but in many cases the horses could plod straight through streams. Most of the packhorse bridges were built of wood and so no trace remains. Such

Above: Holloway on Coombes made by passage of packhorses.

Left: A roadside reminder of the days of the packhorse.

Bottom: Slatelands Bridge, built in medieval days and repaired several times since after flash floods.

bridges were narrow with low parapets to leave clearance for the panniers. In places where a paved causeway was not provided, the constant passage of horses' hooves cut into the soil and over the years formed a deep depression, or holloway.

Quite apart from the evidence on the ground, many place names on modern maps give clear indications of the packhorse trade, Jagger's Lane, Packhorse Inns and Hollowgate being typical. Slatelands Road was once known as "Stoney Causey", which fits in with the old bridge and being on a packhorse trail.

The population of England was growing and, as farmland was encroached upon, local farmers could no longer supply all the food required by large cities. This led to a growth in droving and large flocks and herds were driven along drove roads, some still known as "Green Roads". To ensure that animals arrived at market in good condition they were moved at a steady pace, allowing them to graze at the roadsides. Farmers could add to their income by providing pasture for the beasts at the end of each day's drive. An example can be seen just after crossing the Saltersbrook Bridge into Yorkshire, where the remains of the field walls stand to the left of the road behind the site of the Miller's Arms.

When trade started to recover after the English Civil Wars an Act was passed in 1697 intended to improve the condition of roads, and among its provisions was one for the erection of guide posts, or stoops. The best locality to see examples is in Bradfield Parish where there are still eleven standing.

The only possible trace of a guide stoop in Glossop is a stone built into a wall in Carr House Lane at SK038935. On one face of the stone are the words "To Glossop", and on a second "To Dinting". The faces hidden in the wall cannot be read, but the stone would have stood on a pillar.

Left: A Bradfield Guide Stoop.

Below: "To Glossop" stone.

To make a guess at what is written on the hidden faces it is necessary to understand that the convention was that the traveller should turn right at the face indicating his destination. If this stone previously stood close to the top of Whitfield Cross then the hidden words could be Sheffield and Chapel.

While packhorses might have been adequate for the clothiers distributing yarn and collecting the woven cloth for delivery to Manchester and Stockport, the new textile mills needed better methods of transport. The solution was found by improving existing roads and tracks. A broad-wheeled wagon with 9 inch rims drawn by six horses could move the same load as thirty packhorses, so good roads made economic sense. Often, the new turnpikes were just the old tracks which were improved by placing a bar across the road and charging tolls to certain classes of users. The tolls thus raised were to be spent on improving the surface. Before the construction of turnpike roads there were few bridges. When a lane came to a stream there would be stepping stones.

Map Five suggests that on the Derbyshire side of the Etherow/Goyt boundary there were mere tracks while in Cheshire the Manchester Saltersbrook turnpike has milestones indicated. One traveller described the situation in the following words: "Glossop till recently, was a place difficult to approach, and under some circumstances almost impassable, they seem to have no roads, but what the Romans had left."

Carr House Lane, a packhorse route heading for Doctor's Gate.

Manchester to Saltersbrook Turnpikes

The first local turnpike road was made by turnpiking the old track from Manchester to Saltersbrook after an Act of Parliament in 1732. This was followed in 1741 by a complementary Act providing for this road to be continued from Saltersbrook to Doncaster through Penistone and Barnsley with a branch to Rotherham. This turnpike did not follow the modern road along all sections. One stretch passed along Longside Edge, and after crossing the stream at Saltersbrook continued along the packhorse route past the Saltersbrook Inn and the Lady Cross on the summit. The so-called packhorse bridge at Saltersbrook was a bridge on this turnpike, and when it was rebuilt in 1985 by James Chatterton, Robert Sheldon and Jack Haynes it was found that although the remnants of the arch were only about half a metre wide, the foundations were for a bridge of 5 metres' width. There were toll bars on the Manchester to Saltersbrook turnpike road at the Gun Inn, the George and Dragon, and near the summit where the road to Dunford turns off.

Chapel-en-le-Frith to Entreclough Turnpike

The next turnpike was the Chapel-en-le-Frith to Entreclough Bridge. This road followed the same route as the A624 and B6105 except where it passed through the town centre of Glossop. Before the building of Victoria Bridge in 1837 the road passed in front of the Trap Inn and after crossing the Glossop Brook by a humpback bridge emerged at Smithy Fold, and after passing the Howard Arms went along Ellison Street. Entreclough Bridge spanned the River Etherow in line with the site of the George and Dragon Inn, but, with the building of Woodhead Dam, the road was diverted over the dam and the bridge submerged. There was a branch which passed along Cemetery Road and Hadfield Road to Woolley Bridge and then up Woolley Lane to a toll at the Gun Inn where it joined the Manchester to Saltersbrook Turnpike. Traffic from Old Glossop would travel along Church Street to meet the turnpike road at Smithy Bar.

Known toll bar sites were at the Drover's Arms; Glossop (near the Howard Arms); Smithy Bar; Torside bar and finally at the George and Dragon where the road met the Manchester to Saltersbrook turnpike. On the branch road there were bars at Hadfield Cross and Woolley Bridge.

George and Dragon at Woodhead. A very old hostelry demolished in 1961 by Manchester Corporation.

Bridge on the first turnpike road at Saltersbrook. Usually called the packhorse bridge.

Plaque on the Saltersbrook Bridge with the initials of the men who rebuilt it.

Howard Arms 1960. (Supplied by Mr J.B. Shaw)

Smithy Bar Toll House.

Glossop to Marple Bridge Turnpike

In 1803–4 a third turnpike road was made from Glossop to Marple Bridge with a branch from Charlestown Bar to Dinting (Turn Lee Road and Primrose Lane), and a branch from the Plough Inn to the Spread Eagle Inn. In 1803, Shepley Mill Bridge and Corn Mill Bridge were built, and in 1804 Dinting Mill and Primrose Bridges. In 1840 there were four toll bars and six side gates. There were other toll bars near the Junction Inn; opposite the Plough Inn; at Woodseats Lane; at Holehouse where New Mills Road meets Glossop Road; and at Rose Brow near the Windsor Castle Inn at Marple Bridge.

The tolls were adjusted on sliding scales, taking account of weight, number of horses and width of wheels. This last point caused argument and even litigation. The trustees were concerned with damage done to the road by heavy wagons with narrow wheels, while wagon owners were convinced that narrow wheeled wagons were easier to draw. Animals on the hoof and even flocks of geese and turkeys paid tolls, though foot passengers were exempt.

Manchester to Sheffield Turnpikes

In 1758 a turnpike was authorised which led on from Sparrowpit through the Winnats Pass, Castleton, Hathersage, and so to Sheffield, crossing the Derwent at Mytham Bridge, thus linking Manchester with Sheffield. The steep gradient of 1 in 5 up the Winnats might have sufficed for packhorses but was a serious obstacle to coaches and wagons, so in 1811 a new road was cut along the flank of Mam Tor, and then below Rushup Edge to Chapel-en-le-Frith. The section which wound up the unstable face of Mam Tor has been a constant problem due to the shale slipping and it was abandoned in 1976.

The old pack way from Sheffield passed through Stannington and by Moscar Cross. It crossed the Derwent at Cockbridge and then ascended to Rowlee Farm and threaded its way by Upper House on Oyster Clough to Doctor's Gate and Old Glossop. This was once the main road to Manchester used by drovers and packmen who refused to pay tolls on the roads over Woodhead and Midhopestones, or through Sparrowpit and Castleton.

Sheffield to Glossop Turnpike

In 1821 Thomas Telford's new turnpike was opened, running along the Rivelin Valley to Ashopton and then via the Hope Woodlands and the Snake Pass to Glossop. The object was to make a road from Sheffield to Glossop and join the Marple Bridge Turnpike Road and so to Manchester. There was already a bridle road along the Woodlands valley but Telford built a new road between Glossop and Doctor's Gate Culvert.

The chief promoters were the Dukes of Norfolk and Devonshire, and there were other trustees, largely Sheffield men who saw the road benefiting their businesses. The growing traffic on turnpike roads led to the building of inns to cater for travellers and to provide stabling for horses, the Snake Inn, the Norfolk Arms and The Royal Oak being examples.

There were exemptions for users of turnpikes. Horses, cattle or carriages crossing and not going more than 100 yards along the road were exempt, and mail carriers, yeomanry riding in uniform and drivers of poor law and election vehicles could travel free. A fine not exceeding £2 could be imposed for making bonfires or playing football in the road. There were also general Acts relating to all turnpikes. One Act gave magistrates the power to sentence anyone found guilty of pulling down or damaging a toll gate to "Transportation to one of His Majesty's Plantations Abroad for Seven Years".

There were toll gates at Ashopton; a bar near Hey Ridge Farm to catch riders coming over the Roman road from Hope Cross; at the Snake Inn; and at a place called Cross Poll which may have been where the Doctor's Gate track met the new road since there is no other point where tracks join the road between the Snake Inn and the toll house at SK056943.

Telford's Road was well engineered but built too late to prosper and when the Woodhead Tunnel opened in 1845 all hope of running at a profit disappeared. Eventually the turnpikes became the responsibility of the County Councils.

With the completion of this road, Glossop had the basis of all the major roads in the area. These roads caused the local authorities to make connections with other roads, and build footbridges. In 1821 the Old Town Hall, Old Cross and Turn Lee Bridges were built.

During the 1820s stagecoaches were coming onto the road to cater for increasing numbers of travellers. The first regular coach to run from Manchester to Glossop commenced in May 1821, on Tuesdays and Saturdays. In 1825 there were two coaches, *The Merry Tradesman* and *The Norfolk*, fares 5s. each. Letters were sent by mail coach and mail gig until 1852, when on 19th January a great snowstorm made the roads impassable. The mail coach was snowed up at Woolley Bridge and could get no further, and ever afterwards letters were sent by rail.

There were five mail coaches from Glossop to Manchester in 1840. The *Norfolk*, every morning at eight, and afternoons at half past five, went through Ashton, Stalybridge and Mottram. To Sheffield, there was a coach from the Commercial Inn, every morning except Sunday at a quarter past ten, and from the Royal Hotel every morning at half past ten; both went through Ashton, Mottram and Glossop. The *Park Ranger* left the Swan, Market Street, every morning at a quarter past nine, travelling via Ashton and Glossop. The *Umpire* left the Swan and Eagle Hotels at twelve noon, also via Ashton and Glossop. A coach left Glossop every Friday for Stockport at 8.30 a.m., returning at 8.00 p.m.

The life of a toll keeper was hardly one of leisure when not collecting tolls. His income was regular but rarely sufficient for him to make a decent living, so he had to be prepared to tackle other work. Some worked at tailoring or shoemaking, while others repaired the roads. The only perk of the job was that he usually had a rent-free house and garden.

An interesting case involving toll dodging appeared before the magistrates in Glossop in October 1874. A gentleman with a corn dealer's business opposite the toll house at the top of Milltown had found an ingenious way of avoiding paying the toll when corn was being taken to the corn mill in Corn Street. He used a detour which involved his carts going up Manor Street, round the back of his property, and then back onto the turnpike road beyond the toll bar. This stratagem had the Turnpike Trust nonplussed until they were able to show that the last part of this unofficial route was over private property belonging to the Duke of Norfolk, who was a trustee of the turnpike road.

Imagine a trip over the Snake Pass in winter, clinging desperately to the outside of the coach with snow driving past horizontally. The driver the worse for drink before the coach even started on its journey and many of the passengers little better, cursing dreadfully as they tried to avoid being flung from the top and dashed to pieces. On reaching the bottom of a steep hill, all the able-bodied passengers had to alight and walk to the top regardless of the weather and, as if this was not bad enough, unscrupulous coach proprietors would overload their coaches beyond the legal limit of six inside and six outside passengers.

Travelling downhill could be a hazardous affair as the braking system consisted of a block of wood pressed against the rim of the wheel. If this primitive device failed, or the coachman, emboldened by drink, decided to dash downhill without applying the brake, coach, horses and passengers would go hurtling down the hill with a good chance of a serious accident.

Accidents were caused by axles and poles breaking, wheels coming off, and coaches overturning. Coaches weighed around 18 cwt. unloaded, and as much as two and a half tons fully loaded. Much of the weight was carried on the top of the coach, making it unstable.

Despite these problems, the advent of the turnpike roads and coaches meant that travel was infinitely more comfortable than previously. The times of journeys were reduced due to improvements in road surfaces, better designed and lighter coaches, with steel springs to

Left: Bar at end of Woodseats Lane, now demolished.

Above: Milestone on the Snake Road: Manchester 23 miles, Sheffield 15 miles.

Above: Glossop to Sheffield Turnpike in the Woodlands Valley.

give a more comfortable ride, quicker changes of horses at the end of each stage and horses pulling for shorter stages. Coaches also enabled letters and news to travel more speedily.

At the start of the Turnpike Era there were no road engineers and the trustees and their surveyors had to proceed by trial and error, but by 1840 there were 22,000 miles of good roads in Britain. In 1837 the London to Edinburgh mail coach regularly completed its 373 mile run in 45 hours, compared with 10 days in summer and 12 days in winter a century earlier.

Older folks often think that things were done better in the past. On some topics they are correct. One example that immediately springs to mind is that roads, drains, roadsides and hedges were kept in a far better state when the lengthmen were at work, patrolling their regular stretch.

After a blizzard near the Quiet Shepherd. Such winters seem to be a thing of the past.

The Arrival of the Railway

Horse-drawn wagons running on cast iron trackways had been employed long before the first successful locomotive appeared. The Stockton and Darlington Railway was designed as an outflow for colliery production to replace an inadequate coal road. Such a railway had been proposed as early as 1810, but the Act of Parliament granting permission was not obtained until 1822.

George Stephenson was appointed engineer of the line. Stephenson suggested that the company seek permission to use steam locomotives. At first, the freight wagons on the Stockton and Darlington line were generally hauled by horses, although it quickly became apparent that locomotives were 30% cheaper to run. As a precaution against locomotives breaking down a horse would be carried on a wagon. The railway caused the price of coal in Stockton to fall and within eighteen months the cost was halved and the railway was already making a profit.

Stephenson's fame spread rapidly, and before the Stockton and Darlington had opened he was approached by the directors of the Liverpool and Manchester Railway. Stephenson became the engineer who designed the first railway which incorporated all the elements of an intercity railway for freight and passengers. The significance of the Liverpool and Manchester scheme was that it connected two centres of industry and commerce, both of which were growing rapidly, and could only contribute to the economic strength of the region. It was the first public railway to operate entirely with locomotives, to have a double track throughout, to operate passenger trains to a timetable, and also the first to operate all the traffic with its own rolling stock and locomotives.

The opening day of the Liverpool and Manchester Railway was on 15th September 1830 and the line attracted passengers and freight because of its all-steam image. More than half the stagecoaches between Liverpool and Manchester were off the road within three months. By the end of 1830, the Liverpool and Manchester Railway had made a net profit of £14,432 on just three and a half months' operation. The age of steam transport had arrived.

These developments were not lost on local manufacturers, whose businesses were handicapped when competing with rivals who had access to a railway. They banded together to construct a railway from Manchester to Sheffield. Their first attempt, in June 1833, failed because they were unable to raise sufficient capital. This failure did not deter them and soon another committee was formed and the railway engineer Charles Blacker Vignoles was authorised to draw up a scheme. Local mill owners were eager to see a line opened, not only to bring raw cotton into the town and finished goods out to Manchester, but also to bring in cheap good quality coal from the Yorkshire coalfield. The Sheffield steel trade would also benefit from the line, and at a meeting in Sheffield on 4th January 1836 it was agreed to form a company with a capital of £800,000. It was also determined that the country should be resurveyed separately by Vignoles and Joseph Locke, each to furnish estimates.

Among the directors or shareholders in the Sheffield, Ashton-under-Lyne and Manchester Railway Company were local men: Thomas Ellison, Michael Ellison, George Sidebottom, Joseph Sidebottom, William Sidebottom, John and James Sidebottom, of Waterside; James Rhodes, Mr Dalton, John Wood, and Francis Sumner.

By 3rd May 1837 the railway bill had passed the committee of the House of Commons and been read for the third time in the Lords. On 1st October 1838, at Woodhead, Lord Wharncliffe took his spade, cut and threw out a sod and declared the ground duly broken for the Sheffield and Manchester Railway.

The main obstacles to building the line were the need for large bridges to span the Etherow at Broadbottom and the Glossop Brook at Dinting, and the boring of a major tunnel from Woodhead to Dunford Bridge. Other difficulties were encountered when trying to raise capital to keep the project going. Vignoles resigned in February 1840 and Joseph Locke took over responsibility.

It was essential to get part of the line into operation to provide the revenue to keep the engineering works ongoing. The line was opened from Manchester to Godley Bar in November 1841, and omnibuses were laid on between Glossop and Godley Bar to connect with the trains. The line reached Broadbottom on 10th December 1842, and Broadbottom Viaduct was completed a fortnight later, enabling trains to run as far as Gamesley, then known as Old Dinting Station.

With the completion of Dinting Viaduct the line was opened to Woodhead on 8th August 1844, where coaches were provided to take passengers to the Yorkshire towns. *White's Directory* of 1857 describes Dinting Viaduct in the following terms: "On entering this vale, the viaduct of 16 arches, constructed of wood and stone, which crosses the valley and turnpike road, strikes the beholder with astonishment at the daring of the present generation."

The first tunnel was opened for traffic on 14th July 1845, and the second on 22nd February 1852. At the time it was the longest tunnel in Britain at three miles and thirteen yards.

Travel for first class passengers was luxurious, in covered coaches with some degree of furnishing and candle or oil lights. Second and third class passengers travelled in open wagons little better than cattle trucks. Second class passengers had the luxury of plain wooden seats; third class had none and were known as "stand ups". To add to the joys of lower class travel they had to contend with extremes of climate plus smoke and cinders flying from the locomotive.

The new line was of immediate benefit to manufacturers in Broadbottom and Hadfield, and with the subsequent building of the branch line, Dinting Vale Printworks, Mersey Mills, Waterside and Bridge Mills also gained access. Major cotton manufacturers like John Wood and Francis Sumner, and mills in Old Glossop, were not so well served. The Duke of Norfolk came to the rescue by constructing the branch line from Dinting to Glossop. On 8th November 1842 the Duke's woodmen started clearing the route. By building the line on his own land the Duke was able to avoid the expense involved in obtaining an Act of Parliament, and on its completion sold it to the Railway Company, and made a profit on the project. The branch railway was opened on 18th July 1845. After selling the line, the Duke retained one privilege, his own private waiting room.

When the first locomotives were built, the only concern was to get them to pull a load and no thought was given to methods of stopping them. Much greater efforts were put into building faster and more powerful locomotives than into braking and signalling methods, hence there were numerous serious accidents.

There have been accidents at Glossop Station due to trains failing to stop. In 1869, Jack Mort, better known as Hell Fire Jack, drove through the buffers and another driver repeated the feat in 1889; on this occasion the train travelled almost across Norfolk Street. At 3.30 p.m. on Wednesday, 14th May 1941 the train again failed to stop, demolishing a section of the wall and a bus standing outside.

In September 1855, there was an inquest at the Plough Inn on three people killed at Dinting Viaduct. The deceased were John Healey, 23 years of age, back tenter; Thomas Priestnall, 30, a weaver; and Jane Hadfield, 35, a winder. Healey was the first to jump out of the carriage, saying as he stepped upon the parapet, "This is the way out." He then held out his hand for Jane Hadfield, who took it, and as he stepped back they instantly disappeared. The train had stopped on the viaduct because there was already a train standing in the station.

On Monday, 11th December 1882 there was a serious collision on the Manchester, Sheffield and Lincolnshire Railway at Dinting. The 4.15 slow passenger train from Manchester, bound for New Holland, was standing at Dinting Station. The guard had just got into the brake van and the train was about to proceed when he heard two sharp whistles indicating danger. Looking around he saw the Liverpool express coming over the viaduct. The express was travelling at about 40 mph and came so suddenly round the curve that it was impossible to avert a collision or even to decrease the speed.

Left: Built-up doorway of Lord Howard's Waiting Room at Glossop Station.

Atlas, a goods locomotive built for the Manchester to Sheffield Railway.

Broadbottom Viaduct pre-1919.

The guard had barely time to jump from his van and run up the embankment before the express dashed into his brake van, completely telescoping it and rearing it on end. The force of the collision was such that the next carriage, a third class, was also telescoped, and the engine at the other end was dislodged from its shackles and sent spinning down the line. The driver jumped off and escaped unhurt, but the stoker, who remained on the engine, had his arm injured. Two compartments of the third class carriage were completely smashed and three passengers were injured; one had both legs broken and his head cut. The impact of the express was so great that every one of the carriages of the standing train was destroyed and both lines were blocked.

Bad as this accident was, it could have been far worse if the stationmaster had not realised that the five o'clock express from Manchester was due and sent a man to wave a red danger lamp in front of the advancing train. As the man was going over the viaduct, his lamp went out and he had only one match left. He managed to relight his lamp before the express came into sight and was able to stop it on the other side of Dinting Arches. But for this prompt action the Manchester express could well have plunged off the top of the arches with all its carriages and passengers. The blame for the collision was put on a block of signals being out of order due to a recent snowstorm. One can only wonder at the railway company allowing express trains to run at speed over a section of line where signals were out of order.

The opening of the line had an impact on Glossopdale. Cheaper and better coal from the Yorkshire coalfield meant the end for the local pits and cheaper gas for lighting; Welsh slate could be brought in enabling lighter roof construction; perishable foodstuffs, meant that local farmers had to concentrate on milk production and rearing sheep and cattle; mail services were speeded up.

The drive for greater speed and more powerful locomotives, heavier rolling stock and longer trains necessitated improvements to the viaducts at Broadbottom and Dinting. In February 1862 the timber arches were replaced with wrought iron sections by William Fairbairn's company without interruption to the flow of traffic. The extra brick piers to support both viaducts were a later addition, work commencing in October 1918 with completion in the following year.

There were once 250 railway companies in Britain but they were consolidated into four by the Railways Act of 1921. The railways were regarded as a national asset as in the event of war they could run on coal.

The Sheffield, Ashton-under-Lyne and Manchester Railway has changed its name several times. In 1849 it became part of the Manchester, Sheffield and Lincolnshire Railway and later the Great Central Railway until the formation of the London and North Eastern Railway in 1923. With the nationalisation of the railways in 1948 the big four companies became British Railways.

On 5th November 1936, a scheme to electrify the line between Manchester and Sheffield, at a cost of £2,000,000, was announced, and in March 1939 new coaches and motor coaches were ordered for the electrified line. The great advantage of electrification was that it would allow more trains to pass through Woodhead Tunnel. The number of steam locomotives that could pass through in a given time was limited because the fumes on occasion were so thick that drivers were incapacitated. Work was started on electrifying the line, including Woodhead Tunnel, but the scheme halted on Tuesday, 9th January 1940, because of the war.

In August 1947 it was announced that the L.N.E.R. was to resume work electrifying its Sheffield to Manchester main line, together with other lines, a total of 75 route miles. It was estimated that the work would cost £6,000,000, take four years to complete and save 100,000 tons of coal a year. The L.N.E.R. also obtained parliamentary powers to build a new double line tunnel parallel with the existing Woodhead Tunnel. The route carried heavy traffic, about 60% of trains carrying coal. Nearly 100 trains a day passed each way through the tunnel, and electrification was estimated to increase its capacity by 25%.

Electrified line on Dinting Viaduct, 1960. (Supplied by Mr J.B. Shaw)

Railway accident at Hadfield Station.

Express train travelling up Longdendale.

On 11th December 1954, the *Times* carried a report that the electrification of the Manchester to Sheffield line had increased the number of passengers using the service. Further, by Monday, 25th April 1955, both freight and passenger traffic had increased since electric traction came into use and on the Manchester to Glossop section trains were already carrying 237 passengers for every 100 who travelled on the steam trains.

It seemed that the Manchester to Sheffield line was to be given a new lease of life when it became the first all-electric line in Britain with the opening of the new Woodhead Tunnel in September 1954. The original tunnels were closed in 1956. Rail travel through Woodhead Tunnel had the advantage that the line could usually be kept open through the worst of winter weather, when the Woodhead and Snake Passes were closed.

The Beeching Plan of 1963 put a stop to this progress, and among its proposals was one to close all passenger services to Glossop. At a public meeting in the town Mr C.A. Howell, Labour M.P. for Perry Barr, said the railways had actually made a profit up to 1955 and had lost money only since the Government interfered with them and road hauliers had taken much of the freight. On Saturday, 26th April 1966, Mrs Barbara Castle reprieved the Manchester to Glossop line.

Despite the ever growing heavy goods traffic on the inadequate road through Longdendale, passenger services were withdrawn on 5th January 1970, and freight services on 18th July 1981. In *Railroaded: The Battle For Woodhead Pass*, by Simon Fain, appears the following:

"In closing Woodhead, Britain abandoned an electric railway at a time when every other major railway nation was constructing new ones; abandoned a route carrying 5 million tonnes of heavy freight a year between its major conurbations and across a national park; scrapped 45 locomotives, which were the most efficient and advanced on the network, while building no replacements; sealed up the best tunnel on British Rail; and deceived the public by juggling public accounts while ignoring public costs."

If the Liverpool and Manchester Railway could make a handsome profit within a few months of the line opening, it might be pertinent to ask why, with the advantage of modern technology, it appears to be impossible to run a paying concern today?

A crack in Dinting Arches in 2004.

Glossop Station in 2002.

Glossop Tramways

The Glossop Tramways Provisional Order Bill was published in November 1900, the application to run the scheme being made by the Urban Electricity Supply Company. The tram depot and power station were built at Dinting.

The Glossop Electric Tramway was the smallest in Derbyshire and at one stage had nine tramcars running along the four mile route. The lines ran from the Queen's Arms in Old Glossop to the Palatine in Hadfield with a half mile branch up Victoria Street to John Wood's gates. The first tram left the Queen's Arms on 21st August 1903. When the first trams ran, the Electricity Company was already supplying 50 customers with electric lighting and it was hoped to increase that number and later to light the streets of Glossop. The population of Glossop was too small for the company to be viable and the intention was to link up with the Stalybridge, Hyde, Mossley and Dukinfield system which had a branch as far as the Dog and Partridge in Mottram Road, Stalybridge, only a couple of miles from Woolley Bridge.

There was a mania for tramways with new lines being opened regularly. In 1901 a scheme financed by the Manchester Suburban Electric Tramways was proposed to build tramways from Stretford through Cheadle, Hazel Grove, Marple, Charlesworth and Mottram. This would have enabled passengers in outlying districts to make a connection with the tram lines already in existence spreading out radially from Manchester.

There seemed a real possibility of the link with the S.H.M.D. being achieved in 1915, but the Great War killed off the scheme. The tramway was offered to Glossop Council in 1920, but the proposal was turned down. Eventually the tramway was forced to close, the last trams running on 24th December 1927.

Tram Terminus at the Dog and Partridge.

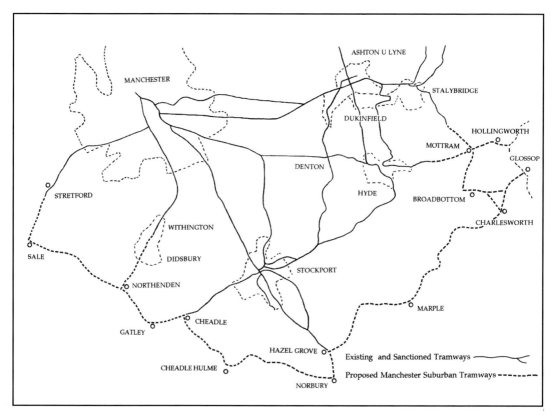

Map Seven: Proposed Manchester Tramways.

The North Western Bus Company started a service on the Boxing Day immediately afterwards. Most Glossopians found work within the town and those who worked in Manchester could travel by train, so at first there was not a great demand for bus services. Nevertheless, these grew steadily until there were regular services to Manchester via both Hyde and Ashton with S.H.M.D., North Western and Manchester Corporation buses running at regular intervals. From Hyde it was a simple matter to travel to Stockport and from Stalybridge and Ashton one could reach Oldham and Mossley. The North Western also ran services to Marple and Buxton. With the decline of the cotton industry more and more people sought work outside the town and bus services enjoyed their heyday. Few people owned cars before World War II and it wasn't until the mid-1950s that the situation changed. Possession of one's own transport conferred a certain status, but also opened up other employment possibilities. At the same time the quality of bus services plummeted, with strikes, rudeness on the part of bus conductors, and increases in fares all providing further encouragement to buy cars.

From that point on there was a steady decline in the number of bus services, and a corresponding increase in the number of privately owned vehicles until the present situation was reached where the roads in the area are totally inadequate to handle the traffic during busy periods, streets are blocked with parked cars, and car parks are half empty due to the charges. To add to the problems, additional housing has been erected, doubling the population and increasing the number of vehicles, but insufficient has been done to improve the roads to cope.

Tram in Station Road, Hadfield.

Before the Great War, the wealthy had their own coaches and coachmen. A hundred years ago virtually all transport on roads was horse-drawn; coal, milk, and groceries were nearly all delivered in this way until after World War II. At one time Hampson's of Whitfield were reputed to have a hundred carts on the road. Goods brought into the town by rail would be distributed by carters to your front door if necessary. Really big items such as steam engines and boilers were towed on trailers drawn by steam traction engines.

One of the first contracts obtained by the local haulage company of A.B. Taylor was for hauling the stone to build Stockport Town Hall. This company later used steam tractors to haul a train of three trailers, which was legal at the time, and in the 1930s used Foden steam lorries to move coal from the coal hoppers on Surrey Street to feed the rows of Lancashire boilers at local mills. During World War II these Foden lorries were stored in a garage at the Victoria Street end of the Top Sandhole as a precaution against petrol being unobtainable. Olive and Partington's used Tiger Tractors built by John Fowler of Leeds to haul logs from Surrey Street to Turn Lee Mill. The last drivers to work them were Owen Williams and George Wilmot.

The worst bends on the Snake Road and Chunal have been straightened out and the roads widened, but the B6105 is little better than it was in the days of the stagecoach. The A628(T) has been widened in places but is still inadequate to cope with the flow of juggernauts over the Woodhead Pass. On occasion I have counted as many as 36 crawling along with a stream of cars behind them. There has been pressure for a bypass to relieve the villages of Mottram, Hollingworth and Tintwistle for years and at last it appears to be imminent. One wonders why the motorway from Hyde was built as far as the island at Hattersley if it was not intended to extend it further.

What remarkable changes have taken place over such a short period. Walking the route of the packhorse way which runs along Coombes Rocks, one can watch aircraft circling, waiting their turn to land at Ringway Airport. One can only speculate what form of transport will be in use in the next hundred years.

10
LAW AND ORDER

In Anglo-Saxon times the land was divided into tithings. These were groups of ten or twelve households held collectively responsible for the behaviour of each member. The tithing was also responsible for ensuring that any member accused of an offence was available to answer to the charge. This system was known as "Frankpledge", and at the Manorial Court Leet a View of Frankpledge regulated the working of the tithings. In the event of a crime the whole community was expected to join in the hue and cry after the culprit.

In 1266, at the "Assize of Bread and Ale", a law was passed to fix the price of these articles, and to punish the baker and brewer if their wares were not of good quality. A local official known as the Ale Conner tested the quality and measurement of ale and bread. He was the forerunner of our present day Inspector of Weights and Measures.

At the Court Leet, disputes between tenants of the Manor were settled; the Court had power to deal with false measures, selling bad meat, smoky chimneys, privies in offensive condition, defects in bridges and highways, destroyers of ancient boundaries, neglecters of hue and cry, scolds, and many others. Punishments were rough and ready; dishonest tradesmen could be nailed by the ear to the door post of their shop, or have their rotten produce burned under their noses.

Formerly the Lord of the Manor held Court Leets twice a year, at which the Constable or Headborough, the keeper of the stocks and pillory, and the pound keeper were elected. Courts Leet were held in Glossop, but with the passing of the County Courts Act of 1846 they were superseded and became just a social occasion.

The office of constable first appears in the Statute of Winchester (1285). The constable was appointed by the manor or parish and was responsible for a range of duties which varied over the centuries, but could include the upkeep of the stocks or lock-up; the inspection of alehouses; the supervision and where necessary the removal of itinerant strangers and beggars; the suppression of riots and unlawful assemblies; the collection of child maintenance from fathers of illegitimate children; and the building, repairing and surveying of bridges.

The Statute of Winchester in towns introduced the system known as "Watch and Ward". Watch was the term for the night guard of constables, and Ward referred to their duties in the daytime. Here we have the origin of the Watch Committee which supervised the work of local police forces.

The stocks were originally intended for the constable to secure prisoners until he had time to place them in safe custody, but later, prisoners were held by the legs and pelted by the mob. There were formerly stocks near to the Old Cross, and at Stocks Lane in Charlesworth.

The following are some who served in the office of Constable for Glossop.

1689	William Newsome
1702	Henry Booth, of Charlesworth
1703	Thomas Hadfield, of Hadfield
1704	Samuel Wagstaffe, of Dinting
1705	Wm. Higginbottom, Ludworth
1706	William Chatterton
1707	John Morton, Lees Hall
1708	Samuel Robinson, Milltown
1709	Samuel Bray, Mouselow
1710	John Bennett, Chunal
1711	John Ratclyffe, Arnecroft
1712	Booth Waterhouse, Simmondley
1713	Thomas Rowley for Smithy Land
1714	Samuel Hybbert, of Millbrow
1715	Wm. Harrison, Simmondley Hall
1716	Daniel Nield, Mouselow
1717	John Hollingworth in Ludworth
1718	Jonathan Henshaw, Ludworth
1719	Robert France, Glossop
1720	John Creswick, Padfield
1721	James Shaw, Stirrup
1722	John Dewsnap, Glossop
1723	William Shepley, of Cold Harbour
1724	John Bancroft in Ludworth
1725	Armfield, Charlesworth
1726	Beeley, tenement in Charlesworth
1727	John Shepley
1823	John Wood
1827	Thomas Wilkins

The Liberty of High Peak was under the supervision of a High Constable, and because of the religious troubles of the day it was sometimes necessary for the Privy Council of Elizabeth to interfere in such appointments. On 24th January 1592, the Council received a letter from Robert Bainbridge, of Derby, concerning John Tunstead, who had been appointed Bailiff of the High Peak, "an office of much credit by reason of the few justices inhabiting the place through its wildness"; he reports that the whole hundred is fraught with recusancy to the number of 300, and states that the bailiff's eldest brother is a fugitive and traitor of Anthony Babington's conspiracy.

After Henry VIII's break with Rome and during subsequent reigns, professing a particular religious belief could be an expensive and even life-threatening activity. Recusants were those who would not, or did not, attend divine service on Sundays or holidays in the Established Church; they included both Roman Catholics and members of nonconformist sects. For dissenting recusants the fine was 12d. for every offence. In 1641, Robert Bagshaw, of Glossop, was fined 21s. for being absent 21 Sundays. Against popish recusants the fines were heavier. The penalty for attending Mass was £66 13s. 4d.; for saying it, double that amount, plus 12 months imprisonment.

From the Recusant Rolls in the Record Office, in Queen Elizabeth's reign, AD 1558–1603, we find that Elizabeth Beard and Dorothy Ridge were recusants in Glossop. Again, in King James I's reign, 1603–1625, Roger Hide and Helena Whitall were listed. It was not until

1829, when the Catholic Emancipation Act was passed, that Roman Catholics recovered their civil rights, the then Duke of Norfolk being the first to take advantage by taking his seat in the House of Lords.

Glossop, 4th October 1841: Head Boroughs (Constables). The following were nominated and submitted to the magistrates for approval: Samuel Shepley, leather cutter, Head Borough for Glossop. His assistant constables were: James Sheppard, Howard Town; Edward Ford, Rose Green; James Cooper, Rough Town. The Head Borough for Padfield was Joseph Bramhall, Waterside; assistant, John Barber, Padfield. Head Borough for Hadfield was Joseph Woodcock, Brookfield; assistants, William Bradbury, Waterside and Thomas Nield, Hadfield. Benjamin Platt was assistant constable for Dinting. The Head Borough for Whitfield, Chunal and Simmondley was Joseph Oates; assistants, Thomas Fielding and James Jackson. Head Borough for Charlesworth, Joseph Board, assistants, John Booth, cotton band maker, Holehouse; John Wilde; and Samuel Shaw, Long Lane. At the same meeting the following were appointed pound keepers: James Dewsnap for Glossop; Reuben Warhurst for Padfield; George Rothwell for Hadfield; Jonathan Heys for Whitfield, Chunal and Simmondley; and Abraham Goodwin for Charlesworth.

Every able-bodied householder was liable to be sworn in as a Special Constable. At one time Special Constables' staffs were purchased by friends of the appointee and were kept afterwards as a souvenir. Ordinary staffs were provided out of the poor rates.

Glossopdale was run by the Vestry which met in the vestry at the Parish Church. Later, with the building of the Union Workhouse, they used the boardroom. With a larger population it was no longer an efficient way of conducting the town's affairs if every householder attended meetings. The minutes of the Vestry for 1st June 1801 indicate how the problem was dealt with:

"Formation Of The Select Vestry: Whereas numerous men attend at the monthly vestry meetings who are not particularly interested in the concerns of the Parish, and many of whom do not pay Poor Rates and whose interference in the Vestry retards the business of the township. For the better regulation of the business of the township it is agreed at a meeting held this day that a select committee be appointed to assist the Overseers of the Poor in the business of the Parish for one whole year from the day of the date hereof – conjointly with the Churchwardens.

It is further agreed that 16 persons should be chosen to assist the overseer in the discharge of his office. It is further agreed that the Rev Howe be appointed clerk to the meeting. Committee: Mr Matthew Ellison, Mr James Robinson, for Glossop; Mr Thomas Frost, Mr John Hadfield, for Padfield; Mr John Thornley, for Hadfield; Mr Joseph Cooper, Mr James Platt, junior, for Dinting; Mr Roberts, Mr John Kershaw, Mr John Bennett, for Whitfield; Mr Joseph Hadfield, Mr Thomas Bennett, for Simmondley; Mr John Lawton, Mr Joseph Jackson, for Charlesworth; Mr James Nield, Mr John Nield, for Chunal. Witness our hands: Christopher Howe, Vicar of Glossop; Thomas Winterbottom, George Siddal, churchwardens; Joseph Jackson, James Robinson, John Thornley, John Winterbottom, John Wood, James Nield, John Bennett, John Kershaw, Joseph Shepley, John Knott, Robert Lees, Roger Goodeson, Henry Kelsall, Joseph Cooper."

Extracts from the minutes show the problems they had to deal with:

15th April 1824: Ordered that £10 be allowed to Mr Thomas Ellison for the improvements to the bridge near the parish offices, and the erection of a foot bridge near Mr Wilkinson's house, and also that the further sum of £15 be allowed to Mr Ellison for the widening of the bridge at the foot of Little Moor.

9th April 1829: A reward of £2 2s. was offered for the apprehension of William Mather and Joseph Peters for deserting their families.

17th October 1833: Ordered that John Rhodes be allowed the sum of 2s. 6d. as temporary relief, and if he does not obtain employment between now and the next meeting that he be sent to the treadmill.

16th December 1842: Ordered that the Master of the Workhouse provide a number of stone hammers for the use of the paupers, and that the able bodied be set to work breaking stone. A widow, in receipt of a weekly allowance, was refused any further relief in consequence of having had an illegitimate child and refusing to name the father.

The system of policing by local constables worked when populations were small and everybody knew his neighbour and strangers were watched carefully. However, the growth of villages into thriving industrial towns meant that the old methods were no longer applicable. With the building of railways, gangs of navvies could descend on some quiet country area and cause a drunken riot at short notice. Before the establishment of local police forces it was necessary to send for the military to suppress large scale public disorders.

The enclosure of land meant that folks who had formerly been able to roam freely over common land found themselves before the magistrates on a charge of trespass. At the October Sessions of 1832 we find Joseph Wyatt of Glossop trespassing on the Duke of Devonshire's land in pursuit of game, and George Heathcote of Chunal doing likewise on the Duke of Norfolk's land in the plantation in Chunal.

At the Quarter Sessions of July 1833, Joseph Cooper of Chisworth, publican, was convicted for permitting drunkenness in his house at Chisworth during the hours of Divine Service on 15th July contrary to the licence granted to him whereby he had forfeited the sum of one pound and six shillings, being his first offence. The costs were assessed by the Justices at 14 shillings.

At the same Sessions Samuel Hadfield was convicted for riding upon a cart on the turnpike in Chunal without having any person on foot to guide the same, the said cart not being such a light cart as is usually driven with reins. The Justice fined Samuel Hadfield the sum of two pounds together with 14 shillings for costs.

In 1833 there was a county-wide check into the use of false weights and measures and at the October Sessions the following were all found guilty of offences: John Beard, James Ashton, John Hall, Joseph Bennett, John Thorneley, all of Charlesworth; Samuel Shepley of Woolley Bridge; Henry Smithies of Simmondley; Robert Buckley of Charlestown; Isiah Lee and Thomas Wilkinson, of Glossop; James Waterhouse of Ludworth; Joseph Moss of Waterside. These gentlemen were shopkeepers, but four Glossop retailers of ale were also convicted: Jerry Sykes, Thomas Linney, John Woolley and Aaron Howard.

On 31st October 1838, Thomas Manning was walking on the road from Sheffield to Glossop when he was murdered just below the bridge over Ramsley Clough. A man was arrested but there was insufficient evidence against him to secure a conviction. No one was ever found guilty of the crime. Afterwards a stone was set in the wall near the spot where the body was found with the letters MMH cut in it, signifying "man murdered here". The stretch of wall with this stone collapsed long ago and the stone has disappeared.

On 27th August 1839, the County Police Act was passed which enabled the Justices of the Peace to set up paid county police forces. Opposition on the grounds of cost was strongest in country districts where there was little crime. Naturally, the criminals who found their activities restricted in areas where police forces had been set up moved their operations to those areas without a police force. Five of the Derbyshire justices sent a requisition to the Clerk of the

Peace for an adjourned General Quarter Sessions to be held on 1st November 1839, at the County Hall, Derby, to consider carrying this Act into execution within the shire. It was resolved to adopt the Act, and a committee appointed to report to the next sessions.

The committee drew up a report, which recommended that the Act should be adopted throughout the county, and that the extent of the force should be as follows:

1 chief constable, at a salary of £300 per annum	300
6 superintendents, £75 each and clothing	486
60 constables, 18s. per week	2808
Clothing for 60 constables, £6 per man	360
Total annual expense	3954

The force recommended was one man for every 3,000 inhabitants, only one-third the size of force sanctioned by the Act.

In Glossop the system of voluntary police started to break down, and a public meeting was held on 9th March 1853, when it was decided to have paid constables. Derbyshire was slow to set up a county force, but the County and Borough Police Act, 1856, required the Justices of the Peace to establish a force for any parts of the county not covered. Thus Derbyshire County Police Force came into existence in March 1857.

On 3rd January 1860, William Sidebottom and George Andrew, J.P.s, attended Derby Quarter Sessions and obtained sanction to erect a new police station in the Royal Fields (Ellison Street).

The new county force were too few to deal with the situation in Glossop. Robert Hamnett has left a description of the state of affairs when the first meeting of the Glossop Borough Council took place on 26th December 1866:

> "They faced a daunting task; the Borough was not in a financial position to put affairs in a proper condition. The Cotton Panic had caused hundreds of ratepayers to emigrate or remove to other places; the shopkeepers were almost bankrupt; the middle classes impoverished; and the cotton masters had suffered losses through their mills being stopped and paying heavy rates. The main roads that run through the Borough were turnpike trusts, which trusts had only a few years to run before they expired so little money was spent on the repair of the roads. The streets were badly lit and were neither sewered, paved, flagged nor channelled, and the sanitary system was shocking. People swealed their chimneys when they thought fit, the factory chimneys belched forth volumes of black smoke, the water supply was insufficient and the pipes worn out.
>
> The police were insufficient in numbers and subject to assaults. The morality of the Burgesses was low, drunkenness and theft rife. The public houses were open until 12 o'clock; sectarian and racial hatred was bitter; and when the public houses closed, especially on Saturday night, a free fight would ensue and when the police interfered, often as not, the contending parties would join forces and rout the police. The cotton operatives were paid fortnightly on Saturdays, and when paid their first move was to their favourite pub. It was a common sight to see wives or children waiting to get what they could out of their husbands or fathers before they drank too much. At twelve o'clock men could be seen staggering home with their cans and dinner basins, their wages considerably reduced."

In February 1867, the Borough Council decided to have their own Police Force. The first Watch Committee of the Borough Council consisted of eight mill owners, one mill manager, a shopkeeper, and the landlord of the Norfolk Arms.

On 18th March 1867, Inspector Kershaw of Stalybridge was appointed Chief Constable at a salary of £100 per annum. James Bohan, of the Cheshire Constabulary, was appointed Sergeant at a weekly wage of 25s. Six policemen were appointed at a wage of 21s. per week. The police had to be paid, and on 9th May 1867 a Borough Rate of sixpence in the pound was levied. A Sanitary Inspector was also required, so on 21st March 1867 Chief Constable Kershaw was appointed at a salary of £15 per annum.

The police entered upon their duties on 2nd April. The lock-ups at the Town Hall had been condemned as insanitary, more fit for the middle ages. Application was therefore made in April, at the Derby Quarter sessions, to use the County Lock-ups in Ellison Street.

Borough Magistrates were necessary, and the following were recommended: Francis J. Sumner, John Hill-Wood, William Shepley, Frederic Buckley, Thomas Rhodes, Samuel Wood and John Hadfield, cotton masters, every last one of them.

The police being numerically few to deal with the rough element, the Council on 26th October 1867 obtained 12 cutlasses. Whatever became of these cutlasses? Are they in some police museum?

In the second annual report of the Chief Constable, for the year ending 29th September 1871, it was stated that 241 persons had been apprehended and summonsed, 60 males and 6 females for drunkenness; there had been 56 robberies, £127 11s. 4½d. value stolen, of which £93 15s. 11½d. worth had been recovered; 108 places had been found insecure; 90 persons had been fined 1s. each for swealing their chimneys; 63 persons had pedlars' licences granted to them; and 223 pedlars had their licences endorsed. In 1876 the County Lock-ups were bought by the Town Council for £1,886 8s. 6d.

The Fire Brigade, also the responsibility of the Borough Police, made their first public appearance on 6th February 1886. When news of a fire was received, the first task was to collect the horses from the Carriage Company. In the old Fire Station in Ellison Street there is a beam, mounted in the roof, used to suspend the harnesses for the horses so that they could be backed into position ready for a rapid exit with the appliance.

Fires were common in the days before the introduction of electric lighting. The destruction of the Bridge Mill in 1899 was such a catastrophic event that witnesses were still talking about it fifty years later. Another incident which could have had serious results occurred in January 1902 when fire broke out in the Market Hall. There were concerns that the fire would reach the Drill Hall where arms were stored, or even the old police cells containing the Volunteers' ammunition. Fortunately the fire was spotted by PC Samuel Chatterton who ran to the Police Station and rang the fire bell, which brought firemen and members of the Police Force to the scene. The hose cart and fire extinguishing apparatus was despatched, followed by the manual fire engine, and soon water was being poured onto the conflagration. Hosepipes were attached to the mains in Victoria Street at the rear of the Market Buildings and also at the front of the Town Hall. The presence of water mains close by undoubtedly saved the day. The damage to the buildings which belonged to Lord Howard was estimated at £600 and the place was insured. The wreckage was cleared away so that the market could open on Saturday 25th.

In 1900 a new fire engine was purchased for £531 8s. 1d. This purchase was the result of the Chief Constable's report on the inadequacy of the old manual engine on the occasion of the Bridge Mill fire. The Glossop Police remained responsible for the town's fire and ambulance services until the early years of World War II.

On 8th June 1886, the Borough Police Force was inspected by the Hon. C.J. Legge, Inspector of Constabulary, who recommended that the Force be increased in numbers. The Police Force in 1913 consisted of 1 Chief Constable, 1 Inspector, 4 Sergeants and 24 men. In 1943 the Police Force had 1 Chief Constable, 2 Inspectors, 6 Sergeants and 13 Constables.

At one time the buildings in Ellison Street housed the police station, the fire brigade, the ambulance, the mortuary and the weights and measures office. The new ambulance station

Glossop Police Station, Ellison Street.

Ruins of the Bridge Mill after the fire.

National Fire Service and Police during World War II. (Supplied by Mr J.B. Shaw)

was built in 1968 and the Fire Brigade moved to the new station in the grounds of Whitfield House in May 1972. In 1948 the Fire Brigade became part of Derbyshire Fire Service.

As a result of the Police Act of 1946, 45 non-county police forces were abolished and the watch committees in those boroughs lost their police powers. Glossop was once more amalgamated with the county force in April 1947.

Chief Constables at Glossop

Samuel Kershaw, appointed 8th March 1867, resigned on 30th April 1870, on becoming Chief Constable of Southport.

William Beard, appointed on 10th May 1870, discharged on 19th June 1873.

Henry Hilton, appointed 11th August 1873, resigned 17th January 1875 on being appointed Chief Constable of Huddersfield.

William Henry Hodgson, appointed 18th January 1875, who died 20th January 1899. Mr Hodgson served in several police forces including Manchester, Liverpool and Rochdale. When police forces have to deal with tough customers, the usual procedure is to appoint a suitable constable to that beat. Mr Hodgson was the ideal appointee for such posts, being a very powerfully built man, who handed out good thrashings as required. Mr Hodgson's career took him to the Dinting Printworks at one stage and eventually he rejoined the police at Glossop as Chief Constable.

John Gregory Hodgson, his son, was appointed on 6th February 1899. Mr Hodgson has been described as the biggest man you ever saw, so big that when he mounted his horse, the animal's stomach almost touched the ground. Mr Hodgson junior sprang to local fame at the great Bridge Mill fire on 5th June 1899, when he led his men in a futile battle against the flames with the old manual fire engine. This puny device was humbled by Hyde's splendid new steam fire engine, the famous "Maggie".

The *Glossop Chronicle* of 3rd July 1903 carried a report of an invention of Mr Hodgson's. The device enabled a branch pipe to be fixed so as to deliver a jet of water in any direction or angle so that it could be left without an attendant, and the jet adjusted to any position at a safe distance from falling debris and well away from heat and smoke. This device would work in combination with the new steam fire engine. Mr J.G. Hodgson died on 10th December 1921.

On the death of Mr Hodgson, Mr W.R. Wilkie came to Glossop from Macclesfield, where he held the position of Inspector. He started on 10th February 1922, and appears to have shaken up the system by lecturing members of the force on Police Law and Administration. Those who did not come up to his expectations would find themselves in his office on the receiving end of a good roasting.

During Mr Wilkie's stay the horrific Simmondley Pit Murders came to light. Inspector J. Chadwick led the investigation and Constables Roe, Ruck and Bradbury all played a part. By this date the horse-drawn steam fire engine of 1900 had been replaced with one powered by a petrol engine. The steam pump from the old appliance was employed to pump water from the air shaft. Mr Wilkie left at the beginning of 1929 to take up a post with the force at South Shields.

The next to hold office, starting in March 1929, was Robert Collier Greensmith, a local man. He also worked at Dinting Printworks, which he left to join the Hyde Police Force where he rose to the rank of Inspector. The new Chief and the Watch Committee were often at loggerheads and they made several attempts to get rid of him. The reasons for this ongoing battle have never been made public, but he did book two aldermen for drinking in the Bridge Inn outside licenced hours, a piece of police work not calculated to endear him to the gentlemen concerned. The Council minutes for 1937 noted that Mr Greensmith's application to be placed on maximum salary was refused.

The efforts of the Watch Committee to rid themselves of Mr Greensmith were thwarted again and again. Just when they thought they had the skids under him, he always managed to redeem himself by a piece of police work which received popular acclaim from the public and press and thus the machinations of the Watch Committee were foiled.

PC Ruck at scene of accident opposite the Plough Inn (1928).

Group at the top of the air shaft during investigations into the Simmondley Pit Murders. On the left are PCs. Ruck and Roe. Inspector Chadwick is holding the shovel near the human remains, and on his right is the Chief Constable, Mr Wilkie.

Mr Greensmith may have upset the Watch Committee previously, but the events that resulted from the purchase of the new refuse cart came in a different category. In 1935, the Borough Council purchased a new petrol-driven refuse cart to replace the horse and cart used previously. This was seen as an ideal opportunity to save money and the Council gave instructions that the vehicle was to be operated by one man who would both drive the lorry and empty the dustbins into it. Lorries of the day had to be started by swinging on the starting handle, an exhausting and even risky business. Not surprisingly the driver opted to leave the engine running when he alighted to empty bins.

To leave the engine running with no one at the controls was clearly a breach of the law and the Chief Constable instructed one of his sergeants to watch the driver and book him if he left the engine running when out of the vehicle. The unfortunate driver was between a rock and a hard place. The Council insisted that the vehicle was to be operated by one man, and the Chief Constable was equally insistent that if he left the engine running then he would be booked. Clearly the driver could not be expected to start and restart the lorry engine hundreds of times a day, and he soon found himself in the magistrates' court. The magistrates had no option but to find him guilty of a motoring offence.

The Chief Constable, with the law on his side, was in a strong position, but that did not prevent the Council appealing to higher and higher courts, losing on each occasion as was to be expected. The true victims of these capers were the ratepayers when the litigation eventually put a penny on the rates. Mr Greensmith retired from the Glossop force on 7th March 1941 and took up the position of Weights and Measures Inspector in Dorset.

Chief Constable R. Greensmith with the Fire Brigade and the new Fire Engine, *Beatrice.*

Glossop's last Chief Constable, Percy Hawkins, came from Sheffield on 25th May 1941, and held the post until March 1947 when the merger with the County Force occurred. Mr Hawkins had an interesting career. In the army, he served with the K.O.Y.L.I. on the North-West frontier, and in Mesopotamia and Iraq. In the police he held the ranks of Constable, Sergeant, Inspector and Chief Inspector in the Sheffield City Police Force, Chief Constable at Glossop, Commandant at the Police Training College and Superintendent in the Derbyshire Constabulary.

Whilst at Glossop he gave distinguished service during the Turn Lee Mills explosion of 1943, the floods of 1944 and the three outbreaks of foot and mouth disease of 1945. At the time of the floods he earned admiration for his handling of the situation and his ability to overcome difficulties.

He was secretary of the "Stay at Home Holidays" during the war years. During those weeks he organised events in Glossop, which included visits from Derbyshire County Cricket team; there was something happening every day and every night in Glossop or Hadfield to attract holidaymakers. It was doubtless due to his organising ability that Glossop made a profit from the stay at home holiday schemes. Each year between £30 and £50 was handed over to local hospitals. He was awarded the King's Police Medal in 1948.

In the pre-Great War years there were only two cars in Glossop, owned respectively by Lord Howard and Sir Edward Partington. This situation gradually changed and speed limits and driving tests were introduced. Belisha beacons were installed in the town centre in February 1935 and three years later they were replaced with traffic lights.

The Chief Constable was already provided with a car, but with the introduction of speed limits the police thought they should have another car to enforce the law. The Council were not convinced of the need for some time. Councillor "Honest" John Hague could see no reason why they could not use the Chief Constable's car for chasing speeders, and suspected they would waste their time joyriding around the Borough.

In 1938, during the Sudetenland Crisis, the President of the British Legion, with the consent of Prime Minister Neville Chamberlain, flew to Berlin to place proposals before Herr Hitler, to the effect that if agreement could be reached between Germany and Czechoslovakia, the British Legion offered its services as an impartial body in the areas concerned. As a result, after the Munich agreement, a body of volunteer police went to Czechoslovakia to oversee the Czech referendum. One of these volunteers was Glossop PC Stonewall Jackson.

A feature prior to World War II were charity football and cricket matches between the police and such opposition as local butchers, or the North Western Bus Company, the money raised going towards local hospitals or the Clog Fund. These activities helped to ensure good relations between the police and public.

There were plenty of criminal activities to keep the police busy from the formation of the Glossop force: local volunteers firing rifles at random, bookies' runners, gambling in public houses, drinking outside licensed hours, unemployed men playing pitch and toss, farmers watering the milk, and domestic disturbances, to mention just a few.

21st October 1871. Simmondley Highway Robbery. Sarah Anne Firth of Charlesworth, a cardroom hand working at Wood's Glossop, alleges that she was stopped on Friday evening not 200 yards from Simmondley by a man who seized her by the throat and threatened her life if she did not give up her money, and she gave him her fortnight's earnings.

1872. Removing night soil. John Thornley was charged with an offence under the Local Government Act, by laying a quantity of offensive matter on the street, to the annoyance of the residents. He pleaded guilty. PC Hague proved the case. On 14th March he felt an offensive smell in Victoria Street and he found the breadth of the street half covered with night soil. Thornley was fined 1 shilling and costs.

In September 1902 the police were instructed to deal with an outbreak of card playing on the Pygrove. The miscreants were boys from the Glossop Technical School.

In 1921 there was a coal shortage due to strikes and folks were desperate for fuel. Two youths were summonsed for chopping down trees in Castle Wood, and a man was caught stealing coal from Sumner's Mill yard.

Wednesday, 5th April 1922. A warrant was issued for the arrest of James Cockcroft, who had been postmaster of Glossop for the last two years, on a charge of stealing £1,300 from the Postmaster General.

On Thursday, 19th June 1929, Lloyds Bank was robbed in a very amateurish fashion. PC Cresswell entered the bank on hearing the alarm bell where he found the cashier, Arnold Baldwin Whiteley, behind the counter with his hands tied with string behind his back and over his mouth was a cotton wad. When the manager, Mr Ashton, returned from lunch he found the till and the cash safe open. After checking the books he found £2,718 was missing.

Chief Constable Greensmith went to Brighouse on the Sunday evening where he arrested Henry Farrar, managing director of Henry Farrar and Sons Ltd, in connection with the alleged disappearance of £2,718 from Lloyds Bank. Whiteley was arrested on reporting to the Police Station on Monday morning. Both men were brought up at the Glossop Police Court on Monday and remanded on a charge of stealing £2,718 from Lloyds Bank.

The Chief Constable read Farrar's statement, in which he said that he and Whiteley had been trading together in cotton futures. Whiteley became indebted to him for large sums and he was obliged to ask Whiteley to trade in his own name. The Chief Constable went on to say that when he met Whiteley outside the police station, Whiteley had an attaché case containing £1,857 and a bunch of keys belonging to the bank.

The court committed the pair for trial at the Derby Quarter Sessions in July, where Arnold

Above: PC Ralph Shaw giving a
Road Safety Demonstration at
St Andrew's School.

Left: PC Stonewall Jackson,
from a postcard sent from
Czechoslovakia.

Baldwin Whiteley, 33, cashier, pleaded guilty to stealing £2,718 from his employers, Lloyds Bank Ltd, and Henry Farrar, 35, secretary, of Brighouse, Yorkshire, pleaded guilty to counselling, procuring or commanding the offence. Whiteley was sentenced to eight months' imprisonment in the second division, and Farrar to two months' imprisonment in the second division.

The Great Train Robbery of 8th August 1963 took place far from Glossop; nevertheless, one of the perpetrators hid in a local farm for some months. The *Guardian* of 19th April 1966 reported that the Scotland Yard Flying Squad had been conducting searches in London for James White, and two days later that the search had been narrowed to the Cockfosters area. White was believed to be short of cash and wearing horn-rimmed spectacles to hide his conspicuous staring eyes.

On Friday 22nd James White, aged 46, was arrested at a resort home at Littlestone-on-Sea and taken to Lechlade, where he appeared before the local magistrates. The sum of £30,440 was later found in a caravan at Tadworth, Surrey, concealed in panelling. James White appeared in court at Aylesbury on 6th May 1966 and was remanded to the Leicester Assizes where on 20th June he was sentenced to 18 years. Of the original £2,595,997 stolen, only £343,448 had been recovered by this date.

Mrs Clarkson, a farmer's widow who lived at Cown Edge Farm, had put the farm on the market, but was surprised when a buyer turned up with a suitcase full of notes. She sold the farm, but insisted that the sale be carried out through the proper channels. On 3rd November 1966 a market trader called Alfred Place, aged 42, of Maltby Road, Mansfield, appeared in the Mansfield Magistrates' Court accused jointly with his wife Jean, Henry Isaacs, aged 52, and Joanna Isaacs, both of Mount Road, Canterbury, of conspiring together to harbour James Edward White while the police search was in progress. Money from the robbery was used as part of the purchase price – £4,250 – of Cown Edge Farm, where White was hidden from April 1964 until September of that year.

Alfred Place had a brother-in-law who was a police officer in Nottinghamshire and learned from him that enquiries concerning White's whereabouts were being made in the Glossop area. As a result he decided to sell the farm, and White was seen there no more. Isaac's son Michael, a farm worker, said he went to work at Cown Edge Farm to get experience. "Mr and Mrs Lane" also lived there. White was brought into court and identified by Isaacs as "Mr Lane".

This chapter cannot finish without a mention of Samuel Roe. He was invalided out of the Lovat Scouts during the Great War, but came to public notice during the investigations into the Pit Murders. In 1924, PC Roe received the King's Police Medal. The report in the Glossop Chronicle read as follows: "It will be remembered that during the inquest and court proceedings in connection with the Glossop Pit Murders, he was warmly commended for his courage. PC Roe played an heroic part in bringing to the surface the human remains recovered from the Simmondley Pit, the task being one of great danger and difficulty, extending over several weeks."

Later he became the Fire Chief and several stories are related about him. During the Second World War he was reputed to keep ducks in the bottom of the Fire Station tower. On one occasion the Fire Brigade were called out, and as the men struggled into their gear a fireman was dismayed to find that one of his boots was missing. When they returned from the blaze he had to report his loss to Fire Chief Roe who was in the Conservative Club testing the whisky. "I know your boot's gone missing," roared Sam. "I have it here. Some bloody fool threw it through the Conservative Club Window."

One of his tasks was to go round schools during the war and give talks on the static water tanks in the area. Sam was definitely a character with no "edge" to him and a strong local accent. I can still recall him saying, "If these 'ere tanks are 'arf full of rubbich, then it stands to sense that they'll only old 'arf as much waiter."

Glossop Police Cricket team at North Road. Includes officers Shaw, Henshaw and Morrison.

Fire Chief Sam Roe's medals.

11
LOCAL MILITARY HISTORY

In Anglo-Saxon times all able-bodied men were expected to fight, since defeat meant slavery for men and women worth taking. The *fyrd* was the local militia in which free men were expected to serve, normally within the shire they inhabited. At the time the typical warrior was the *thegn*, a hereditary noble who held land in return for military service.

Shortly after 1016, King Cnute introduced a body of fighting men into England known as the *housecarles*. They were a standing force until 1051, acting as the king's bodyguard. After 1051 most of them were granted lands on which they settled, while remaining available for military service. William I introduced in 1070 a system called Knight's Service, whereby his tenants-in-chief had to provide a number of knights equipped and ready for duty.

For years after the Norman Conquest Englishmen were involved in a series of wars in France under the leadership of an alien aristocracy as the Norman kings attempted to add to or defend their lands on the continent. One vital component of these armies was the English longbowmen who were highly trained and able to have an effect on the outcome of battles out of proportion to their numbers.

In medieval times each township had its complement of archers who would practise at the butts. The Whitfield butts were on the Little Moor at Em Butts, now Todd Street, near the Roebuck. Hadfield butts were on a level piece of ground between Woolley Bridge Road and where the track of the Waterside branch railway ran.

In 1433 the Abbot of Basingwerke leased his lands in Glossopdale to John Talbot, first Earl of Shrewsbury, who was engaged in the Hundred Years' War in France for much of his career. He was killed at the battle of Castillon in July 1453 when, at around seventy years of age, he led an Anglo-Gascon army in an attack on a superior French force, thus bringing to an end the Hundred Years' War. Some 4,000 were slain in the battle and we may surmise that there were Derbyshire men among them.

With the claims of English kings to be also kings of France effectively ended, it was time for the aristocracy to get on with managing their estates and think of themselves first as Englishmen. The final defeat in the Hundred Years' War was one of the best things that could have happened for England. The treasure wasted and taxes levied in pursuit of a war against a country which at that time had a greater population and resources constituted a tremendous drain on England.

In Tudor times the forces consisted of the county militia, with the Lord Lieutenant of the county nominally in charge. All able-bodied men between 16 and 60 were liable for service, and it was the duty of the parish constables to ensure that the local levy was raised. General musters of county forces to inspect equipment were held at least every three years and more frequently in disturbed times.

By an Act known as an Assize of Arms, kings would set down a list of weapons to be supplied by various classes of citizen. No sooner had Elizabeth succeeded to the throne than she tested the legislature of her predecessor by calling out the county forces in several shires. Extracts from the Peak also give an indication of the importance of villages in the mid-16th century:

Eyam: Thomas Barlow, gentleman hath one coat of plate furnished, one black bill, one long bow, one sheaf of arrows and one steel cap. Christopher Eyre, gentleman hath one coat of plate furnished, one black bill, one long bow, one sheaf of arrows and one steel cap. The said township of Eyam hath harness and weapons in readiness for one archer: able men without harness in the same town, 7 bill men.

Glossop: hath harness and weapons for one archer and one bill man; able men without harness in the same constabulary; archers 22; bill men 22.

Bowden: Henry Bagshaw, gentleman hath one coat of plate, two long bows, two sheaves of arrows, two steel caps and black bill; the township of Bowden hath harness and weapons for two archers and one bill man; able men without harness in the same constabulary; archers 7; bill men 24.

Not an impressive array, especially when one considers that regular practice at the butts was becoming a thing of the past. Just as well that England's sailors, thanks to spending their time robbing Spanish treasure fleets, were better prepared for battle.

On 26th May 1559, Elizabeth appointed George, Earl Talbot, Lord Lieutenant. "We have thought fit to commit to your charge the lieutenancy of the Counties of York, Notts., and Derby, for which purpose we have addressed you our commissioner under the Great Seal."

He received a further nomination in July 1565: "The Queen further tells her lieutenant not to trouble his counties with summoning the general musters unless the Scots are coming," but it gave him "power to command our subjects in your shires on any sudden events".

To call out the militia in a national emergency, beacons were placed at prominent points so that the whole country could be alerted within hours. The Glossop beacon was sited on Whiteley Nab at SK026926.

On 17th March, 1580–81, the Queen issued her warrant to the sheriff and justices to levy 150 able men in the county of Derby for service in Ireland "against the rebels and other undutiful subjects". They were not to be taken from the musters of the county; 60 were to be supplied with calivers; 30 with corselets; 30 with bows and arrows; and 30 with black bills: they were to be sent to Ireland, by Chester, before 15th April, where the Mayor of Chester was to be responsible for their conduct money.

The poorness of weapons and insufficiency of clothing were two of the causes of English defeats in Ireland. Much of the trouble was due to funds provided being siphoned off by those in command, and there were instances of men refusing to board ships until they had received the pay and equipment promised.

Up to 1660 the defence of England relied upon the County Militias because of opposition from Parliament to the King having an army at his disposal. The limitations of the militia system were revealed during the English Civil Wars when militia companies refused to cross the county boundaries and the contending sides were forced to rely on volunteer companies.

As far as Derbyshire was concerned the main actions took place in the south of the county, the chief personality involved being Sir John Gell of Hopton Hall near Wirksworth, who raised a regiment of foot for Parliament and established a garrison at Derby.

The sympathies of many Glossopians would lie with Parliament since they relied upon Stockport and Manchester as markets for their woollen cloths and these places were Parliamentary strongholds. The only local men known to be involved were Captain William

Garlick of Laneside, Captain Thomas Hadfield of Hadfield, and Colonel Randle Ashenhurst of Beard Hall.

Ashenhurst became a Captain of John Gell's own Troop of Horse around 1643, but there is a record that "He ran away with about 40 horse... but he is since become Major." When Bolsover Castle fell in August 1644 to Major General Crawford, Ashenhurst was made its governor. It was probably shortly afterwards that he was promoted to the rank of Colonel by Fairfax. Garlick was Captain under Randle Ashenhurst at Bolsover Castle, and was probably in his company previously in Gell's regiment at Derby.

Captain Hadfield served in the Derby regiment, probably as Lieutenant to Captain Randle Ashenhurst in Colonel Gell's own troop. He may have been with those who ran away with Ashenhurst. He became a Captain in Ashenhurst's regiment at Bolsover Castle, where he was involved in a covenant concluded between the servants of the Earl of Devonshire and himself in June 1648. This was confirmed by the committee in London and, under its terms, Chatsworth House would be rendered untenable, the gates being taken to pieces and breaches made in the wall. No forces would be put in the house, which would not be spoiled.

Whatever their sympathies, the demands for cash by the combatants were unpopular with folks who had little enough to start with. Nothing was safe from the depredations of the soldiers whose pay was usually in arrears. Both sides supported themselves by plunder. Lead from the font or church roof was melted and cast into bullets. The husbandman's fowls and pigs would be slaughtered, cooked and eaten without hesitation.

The Second Civil War ensued with Royalist uprisings, but was ended with Cromwell's defeat of the Scots under the Duke of Hamilton at Preston on 18th August 1648. The Scots infantry were scattered and many tried to conceal themselves in the valleys of the Peak. Chapel-en-le-Frith Church was used to imprison 1,500 Scotsmen and it is recorded that 44 died and were buried in the churchyard. There are stories that not all were captured, but stayed on as farm workers in Derbyshire. After the Restoration, fears of the king having a standing army remained, and ultimately led to the Stuart Kings being replaced by the Hanoverians. The Derbyshire connection with these events was the first Duke of Devonshire, a prime mover in the "Glorious Revolution" of 1688.

The 1715 and 1745 Rebellions had no impact on Glossop, although during the latter Prince Charlie's Army must have passed within striking distance of the town as it marched from Manchester through Ashbourne and on to Derby.

In response to the French Revolution, in November 1796 an Act was passed for the raising of Supplementary Militia for the defence of Great Britain. On 24th June 1797 payments were made to 34 local men in the Militia, and their wives were supported by the Parish during their husbands' absence on duty.

In 1803 a Militia Act was passed which caused many Glossopians to enlist in the Regular Army, and they served during the Peninsular Wars. Sergeant Thorpe enlisted in 1803 and served 21 years. Others were Joseph Harrop, nicknamed Blucher, who was in the artillery and William Booth of Wellgate was one of Napoleon's guards at St Helena.

Those who were not balloted for the Militia, and did not enlist, formed on 31st October 1803 two companies of volunteers, named The Glossop and The Padfield and Hadfield Volunteers. The officers were Captain Commanding, George Hadfield; Captain, John Thornley; Lieutenants, John Wood, of Hadfield, and Joseph Hadfield, of Lees Hall; Ensigns, Moses Hadfield and John Kershaw. The Glossop Volunteers drilled in a field opposite Meadow Mills and their uniform consisted of a scarlet coat with yellow collar and cuffs, white trousers and the officers had gold lace.

The Local Militia Act of 1807 raised battalions in the counties. Most of the old Infantry Volunteers transferred into the new force. Any shortfall in the required quota was made up by ballot. Unlike the County Militia, the Local Militia was not liable to serve outside their own or adjacent counties, and whereas the County Militia continued in service after the end of the Napoleonic Wars, the Local Militia was disbanded in 1816. The Local Militia may be likened to the Home Guard, a purely local defence force. The County Militia, on the other hand, was more akin to the Territorial Army.

Patriotism was not the sole motive for men enlisting in the Army. Often it was a matter of economic necessity, with the offer of a uniform and three square meals a day being the alternative to starving. With the large numbers of unemployed weavers in the area it is not surprising that many ended up fighting in the Peninsular War.

In 1859 a meeting was held in an attempt to form a Volunteer Corps in response to a request from the Lord Lieutenant of the County. The principal supporters were George Andrew, William Sidebottom, John Hill-Wood and T.H. Sidebottom. Mr Edmund Potter, Mr Thomas Ellison and the Rev Thomas Atkin were against the formation of a rifle corps and there was an amendment that "The present system of the formation of Rifle Corps would be destructive of the morals of young men, and if the vast commercial establishments in Manchester were carried on by some who led semi-military lives they would wither and decay as fast as they had grown up." Twenty-six voted for the amendment and only sixteen for the resolution so the idea was shelved.

The Franco-Prussian War of 1870 brought about a renewal in interest and in June 1875 over 150 persons agreed to enrol. The Mayor, Samuel Wood, called a meeting in the Town Hall for Monday, 14th June at which the Mayor called upon Alderman J. Stafford to propose the following resolution: "It is desirable to form a rifle corps." Mr T. Rhodes seconded it. Mr Charles Chambers of Hadfield moved an amendment that there should be no rifle corps; this time the resolution was carried.

Application was made to the War Office for permission to form a corps and steps were taken to raise funds to defray the cost of uniform and equipment. Over £600 was received, the principal subscribers being the cotton masters and Edward Partington. Lord Howard promised the use of land for a shooting range and part of the Market Hall for a drill hall and armoury. In October, Captain Egerton visited the sites of the proposed shooting range and drill ground and gave his approval.

The first rifle range was situated to the north of the Grouse Inn and involved firing across the Turnpike Road from Chunal Plantation at targets on the opposite side of the road. An odd choice of site since it meant breaks to allow traffic to pass when the longer ranges were being used. It was replaced by a new range at Mossy Lea, opened in 1877.

The 23rd Derbyshire Rifle Volunteers paraded for the first time on Saturday, 26th February and were inspected by Captain W. Sidebottom. On 7th March the members of the corps were measured for uniform and on Saturday 11th they had their first open air drill.

When the Regular Army suffered reverses during the Boer War, additional forces were called for. The War Office could not accept all volunteers, but formed an "Active Service Company", composed of men selected from the volunteer battalions in Cheshire. The Glossop detachment was allowed to send eight men, who went to Chester on 19th January 1900 and embarked for South Africa on 17th February. On Monday, 4th February, 18 more volunteers left for Chester to join the Second Service Company, and on the 25th embarked at Southampton for Cape Town.

During their absence the local committee of the War Fund looked after their wives and families. On 14th February 1903 there was the presentation of Coronation medals to the South African service men and long service medals to Privates F. Stokes and W. Howard. The Mayor, Councillor E. Partington, made the presentations.

The Volunteer movement expired on 31st March 1908 when the Territorials came into being. The Glossop Detachment of the 4th Volunteer Battalion, Cheshire Regiment, became H Company, 6th Battalion, Cheshire Regiment.

The Great War was a disaster for all nations involved with the shocking waste of young lives. The *Times History of the War* serves to show how out of touch with reality people of

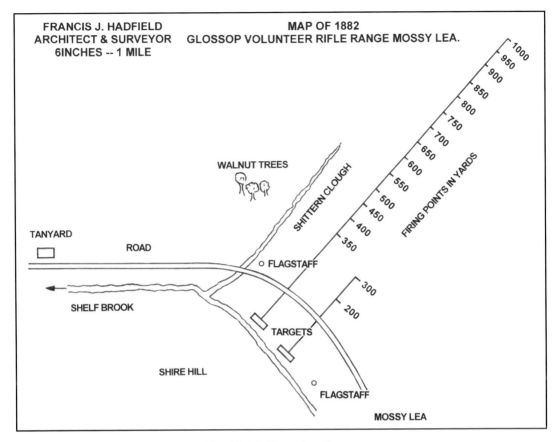

Map Eight: Mossy Lea Range.

all classes were at the outset. The earliest copies are full of photographs of Grand Dukes and similar grandees. Members of the aristocracy were making their homes available as hospitals and convalescent homes. Cartoons showing Germans with their hands in the air were also popular until it dawned that if they were all surrendering, why wasn't the war already over?

Kitchener had the foresight to see that a long war was in the offing and he set out to create a mass army capable of taking on the continental armies. At first he called for 100,000 volunteers, and by the end of the year he had over a million. By September 1915 this had risen to two and a quarter million. Kitchener built the New Army around the old Regular Army by forming Service Battalions of the existing County Regiments and grouping them into divisions. Thus there were 14 New Army divisions by October 1914, but with insufficient weapons, uniforms or instructors to train them.

However, this is part of a wider field. Let us take a look at what occurred in Glossop and district. A host of voluntary organisations sprang up to provide support for the men at the front and other victims of the conflict. These included the Local Committee for the Prevention and Relief of Distress, the Belgian Relief Fund, the Mayor's Fund for Wounded Soldiers' Comforts, Glossop Prisoners of War Fund, Littlemoor Wounded Soldiers' Rest Room, and the provision of Christmas parcels for soldiers and sailors. The Partington Home served for the reception and occupation of wounded Belgian soldiers.

Lena Matthews, as a girl during the Great War, knew the young men who set off with eager faces, proud to fight for their country. She could also describe the efforts of ordinary folks to make a contribution:

Tom Slater of Hollingworth with Lee-Metford Rifle. Tom was one of the Glossop Volunteers who went to South Africa in January 1900 as a member of the 1st Service Section. (Supplied by Mr J. Chatterton)

"What about those who waited? That wasn't easy, but we tried to keep our end up by helping where we could, knitting socks for soldiers and sea boot stockings for sailors. We made light of our troubles; always someone worse off than ourselves. Mrs Kief, a Gamesley lady, baked currant cakes, wrapped them up with a message in and threw them to t'lads in t'troop trains as they came through Gamesley. We used go and sit on t'banking at Gamesley. 'This cake was made by Mrs Kief – good luck, lad.' Not much, but it brought a smile to some mother's lad's face, didn't it?"

Young men were under pressure to enlist. Walter Kinder had a slating and plastering business which he ran from a yard at the rear of his house in Sumner Street. In 1914 he had the contract to work on houses being erected in Tredcroft Street. Men leaving his yard had to pass number 12 Sumner Street on their way to the job. At number 12 lived James Edwin Hamnett, a recruiting officer, who would buttonhole them and say, "I think you should be in the Army, my lad." He was so successful as a recruiting officer that Walter Kinder lost his entire workforce and had to finish the work himself.

Generally the men who had survived the Great War said little about their experiences, but if you could get them to talk it would sometimes come flooding out:

"One day I was a lad in Charlesworth, bird's nesting along the hedgerows, the next I was in the trenches in Flanders."

Newspapers from home were welcome. At one stage it was the practice to have meatless days. We were quite taken with the reply of one grand dame when asked how she managed on meatless days. 'Oh, we usually have a chicken,' she said."

One soldier on leave from France missed his train at London Road station when returning to his unit. He was promptly arrested and placed in the Glasshouse and shipped off with the next draft. When asked what he thought of Military Prison he replied, "It was great; there was a roof over your head, three meals a day, and nobody was shooting at you."

As the war progressed grim reality started to sink in. Newspapers carried pictures of men awarded decorations for gallantry, but also those killed or wounded. There were letters of thanks from troops in the field who had received Christmas parcels, and letters from men in distant parts telling of their experiences. There were also articles concerning men who failed to return from leave. These few were outnumbered by those who stuck it out to the end. There was also a portent of the future when Zeppelins flew over the Glossop moors on 25th September 1916.

Physically many of the troops were very small, for the obvious reason that they had not had sufficient to eat in their formative years. A recruiting poster for the Cheshire Regiment in 1915 stated that men must be 5 feet 4 inches and upwards. They were, however, a tough bunch; I suspect much hardier than we are today. They must have been to survive the shocking conditions in the trenches.

George Bocking was typical of the thousands of men who played their part in the war. Volunteering for the Sherwood Foresters in August 1914, he survived despite being wounded four times and finished with the rank of Sergeant and the Military Medal. He spent the rest of his days as a farmer.

Glossop Territorials in Howard Park during the celebrations of the Coronation of George V, June 1911.

Above left: George Bocking in the Sherwood Foresters 1914. (Supplied by Mr J. Bocking) and above right: George Bocking on his tractor at Intakes farm, Ludworth. (Supplied by Mr J. Bocking)

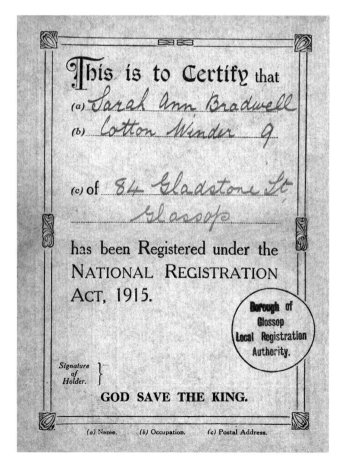

This is to Certify that
(a) *Sarah Ann Bradwell*
(b) *Cotton Winder   9*

(c) of *84 Gladstone St Glossop*

has been Registered under the NATIONAL REGISTRATION ACT, 1915.

Borough of
Glossop
Local Registration
Authority.

Signature
of
Holder.

GOD SAVE THE KING.

(a) Name.   (b) Occupation.   (c) Postal Address.

Left: First World War Registration Card. The number 9 designates some group because Sarah was around 15 at the time. (Supplied by Mr T. Gledhill)

Above: Grave from World War I in New Burial Ground, St James'. There are several of these graves, some of men who died at Moorfield, which are cared for by the British Legion.

The War Memorial in Norfolk Square was unveiled on the last Sunday in March 1922. It is difficult over 80 years later to realise just what this meant to the people of the town, but if you read the names of the fallen there is a good chance you will recognise a family member that you never had the privilege of knowing. Try for a moment to understand what it meant to bereaved parents, widows, fiancées, brothers and sisters. Remember also that these were the men who had played together in local football and cricket teams, attended the same schools and churches. Glossop was once a place where everyone seemed to know everybody else.

When the unveiling ceremony was over, the steps of the Memorial were covered with wreaths. Perhaps the most poignant was that laid by Mr C. Haughton on behalf of the ex-servicemen of the town; he had lost three sons. For years afterwards it was a common practice for men to raise their hats when passing the War Memorial.

It was obvious that Britain was again heading for war in the 1930s and steps were taken to prepare for the inevitable. In September 1935 the National Government issued the first circular on Air Raid Precautions to local authorities. In 1936 construction of "Shadow Factories" commenced, to produce aircraft and other armaments. Car and aircraft manufacturers experienced a boom, and shipbuilding in depressed areas received a boost. The cotton trade also benefited from the need for uniforms. The ARP services were mobilised on 25th September 1938, and on the 29th the government published its plans for the evacuation of two million people from London. Gas masks were issued to men, women and children.

May 1939 saw the introduction of the Military Training Act which introduced conscription. It only applied to young men aged 20 and 21, who were required to undertake six months' military training. The size of the Territorial Army was doubled and in Glossop two companies of the Royal Corps of Signals were formed with each volunteer signing on for a four year engagement. In July and August of that year the Glossop men were in camp at Skegness, and with the outbreak of war one section was sent to France.

With the declaration of war, Parliament passed the National Service (Armed Forces) Act, which made all men between 18 and 41 liable for conscription. Military reservists were called up on 24th August 1939 and the ARP services warned to stand ready.

As part of air raid precautions, citizens had to buy blinds, curtains and paint to eliminate the possibility of lights being spotted by enemy aircraft. The blackout was enforced by air raid wardens and police. To prevent flying glass, strips of tape were stuck on windows.

Once war had been declared, gas masks were to be carried at all times. Air raid shelters were built in various parts of the town, the largest being where the Telephone Exchange stands today. Others were built in Turn Lee Road, King Street and Bank Street. Some Glossopians built their own private shelters, but there were no Morrison or Anderson shelters in Glossop. Static water tanks were set up to guard against water mains being cut during an air raid. Everyone had a ration book and an identity card. One bureaucratic stroke of genius introduced in 1939, shortly before the declaration of war, was to lop a fortnight off the school summer holiday. This decisive action failed to deter Herr Hitler from attacking Poland.

Children from large towns were evacuated into the comparative safety of the countryside. Glossop received a contingent of evacuees from Manchester and the ones I knew all came from the same school, Varna Street in Gorton. The Manchester evacuees, each carrying a gas mask, were met at Glossop Station by Charles Casey, acting as reception officer. The school population had a sudden increase and we had a whole new crowd of playmates. Many of these children had never been outside of Manchester before and to be able to climb trees and carve your initials in the bark was a whole new experience. Not surprisingly, they found the sight of a cow with those dangerous horns somewhat frightening and they never discovered where the condensed milk trees were, but on the whole we got on together.

A picture has been painted of the generous way in which these children were treated. Both evacuees and their hosts had mixed experiences. There were instances of well-to-do folks

Remembrance Day at Hadfield War Memorial.

Glossop Peace Medal.

Memorial Plaque in Hadfield Primitive
Methodist Chapel.

whisking away the better-dressed children, leaving the poorest to the last. One family took in three boys and within hours it was found that they were verminous, and all their clothes had to be destroyed and fresh outfits found. On the other hand, one Glossop woman found herself in court because she was not feeding one of her charges properly. There were plenty of folks in Glossop struggling to keep their heads above water after years of unemployment, but some of the evacuees looked positively destitute with only plimsolls on their feet. One positive long-term effect was that it opened the eyes of many to the conditions under which other people lived.

Most of the evacuees soon drifted back to their homes when air raids did not occur, only for some to move out of Manchester once more with the arrival of the Blitz. For these unfortunate folks it was a very trying time, because the winter of 1941 was one of the worst on record, with huge snowdrifts and houses literally buried under the snow.

After the fall of France, when the east coast towns were at risk, 600 evacuees came to Glossop from Lowestoft. This time things ran efficiently; many of their teachers came as well and Littlemoor School was reopened to house the new arrivals. They were met by Mr Cecil Lord, Headmaster at the Grammar School, who was acting as Chief Billeting Officer. Mr Lord lived in a large house in Sheffield Road, but did not take in any evacuees. Other Glossopians, despite living in much more humble accommodation, had evacuees or essential workers at the Admiralty billeted with them. Presumably this was one of the perks of being the Billeting Officer.

Rationing was intended to ensure that everyone received the basic necessities so far as food and clothing was concerned. A ration book was not all that useful if you hadn't the cash to buy the goods. Before rationing could be introduced there were instances of wealthy women buying all the sugar and tea they could get their hands on. There was an incident outside Bradley's fish shop in High Street East when one affluent lady marched to the front of the queue under the impression that she was entitled to special treatment. She was rapidly disabused of the notion by ladies from rougher parts of the town who held more egalitarian views.

Rationing was in the hands of the Ministry of Food, and ration books and identity cards were obtained from Food Offices. Feeding the population was a priority and the lend-lease shipments of dried eggs, evaporated milk and canned meat, including the famous "Spam", were vital if people were to have a reasonable diet. The basic weekly ration was fixed at 4 oz of bacon, 2 oz of tea, 8 oz of sugar, 1 lb of meat, 8 oz of fats, 3 oz of cheese and two pints of milk. Folks were exhorted to grow vegetables and every possible way of cooking potatoes and carrots was advertised. The wealthy were at an advantage at first because it was still possible for them to purchase meals in restaurants, but as the war progressed British Restaurants were opened for industrial workers. Subsidised school meals were introduced and by 1945 a third of schoolchildren were fed at school.

The mass call-up of volunteers of 1914 was not repeated as it was pointless to recruit men if there were not the uniforms and weapons to equip them. It was important that workers in essential industries remain where they were. Other men were sent to work in the coal mines and were known as Bevin Boys after Ernie Bevin, who was Minister of Labour and National Service in the War Cabinet. For some reason the notion gained credibility that the Bevin Boys were conscientious objectors. Some Bevin Boys were, but most were not; they had no choice in the matter, but were drafted into the pits.

In May 1940, when the German attack through Holland and Belgium got under way, rumour was rife and there was concern about the possibility of paratroops landing in various disguises. On the evening of 24th May 1940, Anthony Eden made the following speech:

"Since the war began, the government has received countless enquiries from all over the kingdom, from men of all ages who are for one reason or another not at present engaged in military service and who wish to do something for the defence of the country. Now is your opportunity. We want large numbers of such men in Great Britain who are British subjects, between the ages of 15 and 65, to come forward now and offer their services in order to make assurance doubly sure. The name of the new force which is now to be raised will be the Local Defence Volunteers."

Within 24 hours over a quarter of a million men had volunteered. There was no medical examination and the upper age limit of 65 was not strictly enforced. The intention was to have a force who would know the locality and be capable of tackling paratroops until regular forces could arrive.

The recruitment was in the hands of the British Legion and the officers drawn from those who held commissions in the Great War. Captain Lanceley, president of the local branch of the British Legion and in civilian life Managing Director of Charlestown Bleachworks, became the Commanding Officer of the local Home Guard Company with the rank of Major. His second in command was Captain Len Capper, a manager at Turn Lee Mills; the company HQ was located in the Municipal Buildings.

Captain Lanceley made an appeal for members of the public to hand over rifles and revolvers for use by the Home Guard. This was not the time to make enquiries as to whether the weapons were licensed or not. Volunteers consisted of old soldiers from World War I and young men either too young to enlist in the forces, or in essential trades, or awaiting call up. Equipment tended to consist of what the Army had no longer any use for. The uniform could be described as a khaki boiler suit and leather anklets, plus a Glengarry cap with a Sherwood Foresters badge. At the end of July 1940 the LDV were renamed the Home Guard.

By late June 1940 the following were commissioned officers in the local Home Guard:

Lieutenants: J. Seville; C.C. Smith; S. Beever; F. McDonnell; W.H. Brindley, MC. Second Lieutenants: J. Wood; C.J. Casey; J.W. Haigh; J. Gerrard, DCM, MM; B.P. Sewell; J. Wildgoose; A. Beever; G.F. Furniss; G. Busby (Vicar of Charlesworth).

The unit was organised into three platoons. Number 2 platoon trained in the old Liberal Club in Railway Street, with Charles Smith as Platoon Commander and Charles Casey as his second in command. The NCOs included Sergeant Frank Mitchell, who had a hardware shop in the High Street, Corporal Owen Williams, who drove a Tiger tractor, and Lance Corporal George Wain, who was employed by a firm of printers.

Rifle practice was on the Crowden range, whilst the Lewis gunners used an old quarry near Lees Hall. House to house fighting was practised at Lower Blackshaw Farm. Equipment gradually improved, but some of the improvised weapons were capable of executing a lot of damage. The faces of Blackshaw Quarry were covered with the burnt out remains of Molotov cocktails.

The Home Guard posted a guard outside the Town Hall and at outposts where a lookout could be kept over moorlands thought of as possible paratroop landing sites such as the Snake and Chunal. There was also a sentry box under Dinting Arches beside the path which leads up from Dinting Vale to the station. Railway workers needing to cross the arches carried a loudhailer to let the guard know as there was a distinct possibility that the guard might let off a few rounds.

A machine gun post was set up in the south-west corner tower of the Roman fort and the loopholes cut in the wall overlooking Moodsbottom Bridge are still to be seen. The Home Guard proved useful, especially early in the war, by guarding local installations, thereby releasing regular soldiers to man the threatened areas of the south-east.

Loopholes overlooking Moodsbottom Bridge. Made by the Home Guard during World War II.

From August 1940, the Home Guard became increasingly regularised when units were affiliated to the county regiments. There was a steady improvement in weapons with the issue of Sten guns and the Northover Projector which consisted of a long steel pipe mounted on a tripod that fired bottles of phosphorus to ignite enemy tanks. The projector was a forerunner of the Piat anti-tank weapon.

The Home Guard was stood down at the beginning of December 1944, by which date the officers were as follows:

Major Lanceley
Captain Len Capper.
Capt. Mc Shannon   Medical Officer
Lt. W. Brindley MC.   Admin
Lt. G. Furniss   Intelligence Officer
Lt. A. Beever   Q.M.
Lt. G.C. Potter   Liaison
Platoon Officers   J. Seville, J. Wood, C.C. Smith, E.F. Muller, J. Haigh, L.C.
     Neild, C.J. Casey, J. Gerrard, DCM, MM, S.A. Bamford.

Charlesworth Section   Lt. G. Busby
C.P.A.   Lt. B.P. Sewell
Railway section   Lt. J. Wildgoose.
J Mcrone was the C.S.M.

One group who did a wonderful job with little publicity was the Royal Observer Corps. Their job was to watch for enemy planes after they had passed through the radar chain and pass on this information so that fighters could intercept them. Most of the approximately 30,000 observers were part-timers who exposed themselves to bad weather and danger in crudely protected posts, without uniforms and often without even a steel helmet. The Glossop Corps were stationed at SK043947 in Old Glossop.

One task which called for a special type of courage was bomb disposal. The most famous unexploded bomb was one that entered the ground close to St Paul's on 12th September 1940. It was extracted on the 15th, driven in a lorry through the East End of London and exploded on Hackney Marshes. One member of the disposal team was a Glossop man, Bill Arrowsmith, who you may remember better as a bus conductor. A genuine Christian gentleman, he was not in the habit of talking about the exploit.

Virtually the whole population was involved in some capacity: Special Policemen to replace officers who had joined the armed forces; the Auxiliary Fire Service; Civil Defence, which included wardens, rescue and stretcher parties, staffs of control centres and messenger boys; Red Cross and St John; and the Women's Voluntary Services; are just some that spring to mind. All these duties were carried out in addition to normal occupations. Workers in essential industries worked a seven day week throughout the war and faced fines and even imprisonment if they took time off without sufficient excuse.

The Air Ministry launched the Air Training Corps in January 1941 for boys between 16 and 18 and shortly afterwards Sea Cadets and Army Cadets were started. Volunteers were issued with uniforms and received instruction which must have shortened their training when they were called up.

No bombs dropped within the Borough boundary although some fell on the surrounding moorland. During the blitz on Manchester, the fire brigades in surrounding towns such as Hyde and Ashton would come to their assistance and the Glossop appliances would move out in support. Air Raid Wardens were on nightly lookout for incendiary bombs, which were tackled with stirrup pumps and sandbags. At first stirrup pumps were effective, but the Germans started to drop incendiaries which contained a small explosive charge. These were dealt with by dropping a sandbag on them until the charge had gone off and then the fire was extinguished.

Much could not be reported in the press, but one part of the war effort where Glossop could make a contribution was in providing storage, thanks to the number of empty mills. Any spare space in Glossop was requisitioned by the Ministry of Supply or Ministry of Food. These included the Logwood Mill, Meadow Mills, and the rear of Woolworth's Stores. There were secret food stores at Padfield Top Mill and part of Volcrepe. Workmen entering Shepley Mill in the early days of the war got a surprise when they found coffins piled up ready for the deaths expected as a result of bombing raids; later it was used by the RAF for the storage of ammunition.

The contribution of Volcrepe, Maconochie's and the Admiralty in Wood's Mill has been mentioned, but silk charge bags for naval guns were woven at Wilman's Station Mill, and Bancroft's made gun sights for aircraft.

It was vital that nothing went to waste. Dustbins were placed at various points so that food scraps could be put in them for pig food. Waste paper was collected at a site behind the Fire Station. Folks were asked to hand over any scrap aluminium to build aircraft. Probably the best remembered of the salvage campaigns was the compulsory collection of wrought iron railings from parks and gardens. In September 1940 Alderman 'Dick' Sellers went round with a barrel organ raising money for the Spitfire Fund.

One effect of the war was that unemployment was cured and gradually a shortage of manpower became the problem. Women were conscripted for the first time. With production concentrated on war essentials there were shortages of many goods. It became almost

Glossop WVS. (Supplied by Mr J.B. Shaw)

Remains of a Liberator Bomber which crashed on Mill Hill.

impossible to purchase an alarm clock. Folks who had struggled on the dole suddenly found themselves with a few bob in their pockets and nothing to spend it on.

Special drives to encourage saving and put spare cash to work were arranged. As part of the publicity for these events parades were held. In Glossop there was a War Weapons Week in May 1941, and a Wings for Victory Week in May 1943. There were also Warship and Salute the Soldier Weeks.

Many incidents which occurred during the Second World War could not be reported for reasons of security, but are worth recording before they are forgotten altogether. In 1943 it was learned that a unit of Commandos was training at the bottom of Small Clough. Teenage boys flocked to the site to see them firing Bren guns, mortars, and Piat anti-tank weapons. Ammunition was used liberally and at the end of the day boys would rummage through the piles of cartridges to find those which had not been detonated.

The Commandos were a wild bunch of young men and taught their teenage audience a few skills they might have been better off not knowing. Amongst these tricks was how to extract cordite from a .303 round and what could be done with this raw material afterwards. One afternoon the Commandos made a rocket by filling a large cardboard tube with cordite and strapping it to a long stick. This projectile soared over Shire Hill, to the boys' delight. Werner von Braun would have been impressed, but the officer in charge was definitely not. For some time afterwards the town resounded with loud unexplained explosions.

One surprising piece of deployment occurred when Frank Wood, a farmer who was with the army in the Anzio bridgehead, was transferred home to Glossop to help get the harvest in. With that task completed he was off back to Anzio.

During the early years of the war, when night raids on Sheffield and Manchester took place, piles of old car tyres were stacked in isolated spots with the intention of lighting them to deceive the Germans into dropping bombs on the decoy instead of the cities. One of these decoys was on top of Whiteley Nab, not far from Sitch Farm, and another was situated on Chunal Moor. In July 1943 there was a tremendous thunderstorm and the lightning struck the decoy on Chunal Moor and ignited it.

12
Progress in the Field of Health

Medical provision in medieval times must have been a hit-and-miss affair in a place like the Glossop valley, far from any monastery where care might have been provided.

Toilet arrangements were basic; probably a midden outside, close to the back door. Flies had little distance to travel from refuse to the food that people ate. The manner in which disease could be spread by bacteria was unknown and parasitic worms were common.

Middens in close proximity to dwellings could also pollute wells and thus be the cause of infectious disease. Baths would be unknown for most and it would take hardy characters to bathe in streams in winter. Farmhouses could have common entrances for humans and animals; indeed in some cases the animals were a source of heat in winter. Early inventories sometimes include a pile of manure, but make no mention of beds because ordinary folks slept on a pile of straw laid on an earth floor, and rheumatic complaints were widespread. Houses were built from timber and thatched with turf and heather which would provide an ideal haven for rats and mice. Woollen clothing would encourage fleas and other vermin.

Medicines consisted of herbal remedies, and until recent times folks swore by the efficacy of Goose Grease for chest ailments and Dog Fat for rheumatic pains. The smoke inhaled from open fires was a further health hazard. At least when most people could not read eyes were not strained and spectacles unnecessary.

It was believed that scrofula could be cured by the king's touch, or by treating it with his bathwater. Hence the disease was known as The King's Evil. The Stuarts continued the practice both in and out of exile. This alleged power of kings was used as an argument in favour of Charles I during the Civil Wars. The last British monarch to use the touch was Queen Anne. In the registers at Mottram Church there is a record of the curate, Hamnett Hyde, going to Greenwich to be touched by King James I on 27th May 1610.

The Glossop Parish Church Registers for 1623 and 1636 show a considerable increase in the death rates. The average for the time was 27 deaths a year but in those years it rose to 67 and 66 respectively. Clearly the valley had suffered the visitation of some epidemic disease, possibly the plague.

There was a cholera epidemic over much of England in 1849. Three people named Bennett died at the Heath and workers on the Woodhead Tunnel, crowded together in insalubrious conditions, were badly smitten and 28 people died. Many of the victims are buried at St James' Chapel, Woodhead and at Christ Church, Tintwistle. Dr J.G. Harrison of Manchester prescribed port wine as a remedy, but the men kept dying and the doctor then prescribed hot coffee and brandy. This was in line with medical opinion of the day which held that regular meals, a little port wine, and above all strength of character could ward off cholera.

On Tuesday 1st January 1884, there was an inquest on the bodies of four persons who were found suffocated at Milltown on the previous Saturday. Richard Townsend, an army pensioner; Dorothy Stafford, a married woman with whom he cohabited; and Ruth and Sarah Stafford, her daughters. Dr Mackenzie and Dr Rhodes, who made the post mortem examination, stated that there was a very strong smell of gas in the house, but nothing to indicate where it came from. Gas was not laid on in the premises. The house where the victims lived was stated to be destitute of sanitary arrangements and the bedroom where the deceased slept had no ventilation whatever. The source of the gas was never established, and the Gas Company were not found to blame.

In January 1890 there was an influenza outbreak with 100 cases reported. Without proper sewerage systems the ideal conditions were created for the spread of disease. The refuse from the backyard privies was emptied during the hours of darkness by the night soil men who carted it away and spread it out to dry, later to be used by farmers. There was a scandal towards the end of the 19th century when there was an outbreak of cholera caused by a gang of night soil men who were spreading the refuse in a backyard within a stone's throw of the town centre.

Progress in medical matters was slow; the circulation of the blood was only discovered by William Harvey in 1628. In 1798 Edward Jenner published the results of his experiments which showed that inoculation of human patients with cowpox gave them immunity to smallpox. In 1865, Lister proved that by insisting on the utmost cleanliness in the operating room and using carbolic acid as an antiseptic after surgical operations the incidence of infection fell sharply. These and other advances improved the life expectancy and quality of life, but until the discovery of modern drugs such as penicillin and streptomycin the major reasons for the improvements in health and life expectancy were better housing, improved sanitation, plus pure milk and water supplies.

Demolition of early 19th-century houses in Milltown. (Supplied by Mr J.B. Shaw)

Wood's Hospital.

The Napoleonic Wars gave a boost to the practice of surgery. The French surgeons were more proficient than their British counterparts, partly because they were integrated into the French Army, whereas in the British Army surgeons were usually men known to the Colonel of the Regiment who were called upon when needed, but also because they had better opportunities to practise on dead bodies. British surgeons were restricted to the use of the bodies of executed criminals within the county and even in those times the numbers of people who ended up swinging from a gallows was insufficient for their needs. The result was a rapid growth in the nefarious trade of bodysnatching, by which degraded scoundrels could make themselves a useful income resurrecting the bodies of the recently buried and delivering them to the surgeons.

There is no record of any bodies being snatched from the graveyard at Glossop Parish Church, but that is no reason for assuming that it did not happen. On the contrary it is extremely likely that a graveyard within easy striking distance of Manchester should be visited at dead of night by such fellows. Bradfield, Hope and Eyam were certainly targeted by resurrectionists based in Sheffield, and the bodysnatcher's grave in Mottram Churchyard can be seen there to this day.

Medical provision improved when Wood's Hospital was opened in January 1889. The Hospital cost £6,986 11s. 10d., and the furnishing £699 19s. 9d. Towards this Daniel Wood subscribed £6,000; John Wood, £1,000; Mrs Anne Kershaw Wood, £599 17s. 1d. After 1892 John Wood contributed £100 annually and Mrs Anne Kershaw Wood £50. Daniel Wood endowed the Hospital with £19,000 invested in Railway Bonds. Other Glossopians left sums and each year Hospital Saturday and Sunday collections raised money, and charity football and cricket matches made further contributions. In 1948, Wood's, Partington and Shire Hill Hospitals passed to the Manchester Hospital Board.

Glossopians held Wood's Hospital and its staff in high regard and there were stormy public meetings held when, in 1988, Wood's Hospital was threatened with closure. Nevertheless, in 1990 Wood's Hospital became a care home for elderly patients needing extra nursing care.

At Glossop Council on 15th February 1900, the question of extensions to the Gamesley Isolation Hospital arose. Alderman Rowbottom thought that nothing should be done for the moment. The hospital site had been chosen as a halfway house between Glossop and Marple Bridge and both contributed their share to its upkeep. He had been examining the accounts and some items seemed extraordinarily heavy. In cabs it cost close upon £30 for this year, and according to the report there had been but 63 cases. That being so, they ought to have the hospital nearer, and if they could they should let Marple Bridge have the present one.

Another matter he wished the Council to consider was the spirits, ale and porter account. Whilst the doctor was present he wished to ask how it was so much was used, the bill for February last being £4 8s. That included £1 19s. worth of bottled beer and porter and wines and spirits amounted to £2 8s. There were no cases of amputation in which a lot of brandy was required, and yet it was nearly three times as much as the Wood's Hospital account.

The Chairman said the late medical officer used to order the patients what he considered they required but he believed there were two patients who helped themselves. He felt rather surprised at the Inspector allowing it to accumulate as it had done, for it must be laxity on the part of the Inspector or the Medical Officer in allowing it.

Inspector Samuel Dane said he held the authority of the Medical Officer for the supplies of brandy, and of a pint of stout for the nurses. But he might state that some of the patients had been kept alive by stimulants, and by them alone. If the stimulants had been given except by the authority of the medical officer then he knew nothing of it.

Councillor Furniss said that the comparison by Alderman Rowbottom was hardly fair, because the Gamesley Hospital was an infectious hospital. They could not get anyone to go there and do the work unless they had what was requisite. It was not everybody who would nurse typhoid and scarlatina, and they should not be niggardly.

Dr Mackenzie said he was not responsible for the housekeeping arrangements. In his official capacity he had given orders for beer and spirits for certain patients, but the matron dealt with housekeeping arrangements. Typhus and typhoid reduced the system very much, and at a certain point patients had to be maintained by stimulants. He was not an advocate of beer, and he would as soon the nurses did without it, but he had been obliged to give an order for beer for the nurses, or they would not have stopped at the hospital and put them in a worse fix than before.

The complaints about the cost of cabs led to the purchase of a horse ambulance in 1902. The cost was £132; the result of the Publicans versus Butchers charity football match. It could be drawn by one horse or a pair, and was equipped with splints and the latest medical equipment. The splendid new ambulance was drawn by horses supplied by the Glossop Carriage Company. It was offered for sale in December 1940 after 38 years in use.

From personal experience I can tell something of the "Fever" Hospital. At the age of five I was diagnosed with scarlet fever and was taken to the hospital in the horse-drawn ambulance. Meals were the high spot of the day and rice pudding the best of the lot. In the next bed was a little tot of about three years of age who drew a lot of attention from the nursing staff because of the manner in which he ate his rice pudding. I couldn't see what he was doing wrong as he appeared to be shovelling it down like the rest of us. The nurses took a very different view. "Do what Neville does, chew your rice pudding." The poor little mite didn't know the ropes; the correct thing to do was to go through the motions of chewing; that way you got a second helping.

Visitors were not allowed. The nearest parents could get was to peep through the windows at the end of the ward. Even after release from hospital, matters were not at an end. The house had to be fumigated; quite an interesting business. All the doors and windows were sealed up with tape and brown paper and the Sanitary Inspector lit a device which looked like a large firework, and we all had to leave the house while the fumes filled the place.

The Isolation Hospital was originally built as a smallpox hospital to cope with a sudden outbreak and it later became the infectious disease hospital for the Borough. It was not an imposing building, being a collection of huts. However, it claimed never to have lost a patient. After its closure by the Ministry of Health around 1950, it was sold back to the Council who offered it the Youth Hostels Association.

Council troubles were not limited to the Isolation Hospital:

The Times, Saturday, 20th November 1897

> At Manchester on Thursday before Mr Justice Ridley, the case of "Warrener v Barnes" was an action brought for damages for slander. The plaintiff Ellen Warrener was Matron of Wood's Hospital, and the defendant was the Mayor at the time he was said to have uttered the slander. The hospital was under the control of the Town Council, and the plaintiff was appointed matron in 1888. In November 1895, Mr Barnes was elected to serve upon the visiting committee, and during 1896 and 1897 he visited the hospital frequently. On July 28th this year, at a meeting of the committee, a resolution was proposed, and was seconded by the defendant, that three months notice should be given to the plaintiff, and the motion was carried. Upon the resolution coming before the Town Council for confirmation on August 11th, the defendant uttered the following words, which constituted the subject of the present action:
>
> "The reason I seconded the resolution was from personal observation at Wood's Hospital. From what I have seen of the nurses and persons there I regard them as neither more nor less than white slaves. I would never submit to Miss Warrener or any other woman in England that had such tyrannising control over human life. From what I have seen personally the girls at the hospital have been in terror, and it would be a disgrace to me to flinch one inch."
>
> The defendant pleaded that the words were spoken on a privileged occasion, and that they were true. The plaintiff, in her evidence, said that although she had been matron for nearly ten years no complaints had ever been made against her by the committee, nor was the notice to leave given to her upon the grounds that she was guilty of cruelty to nurses or patients. At the conclusion of the plaintiff's evidence a consultation took place between counsel and their clients which resulted in an apology being given to the plaintiff with £10 10s. damages and costs.

The Partington Nurses' and Convalescent Home was opened on Saturday, 27th June 1908. In 1906, Mr Edward Partington gave a sum of £30,000 to provide a Nurses' Home and Convalescent Home combined, and the building was erected so that Queen Victoria Nurses could minister to the poor in their own homes. The home had also accommodation for eight convalescent patients. The donor invited the Mayor and corporation, magistrates, and officials to tea and inspection of the new buildings, which had been handed over to the Corporation handsomely endowed. Edward Partington was made the first Freeman of Glossop in 1906 and knighted in June 1912. This was in part due to his philanthropic work in providing the hospital and also contributing to the Public Library.

Some of the workforce at Olive and Partington's were less impressed with his generosity, being of the opinion that he needed to build a convalescent home to accommodate folks injured in his mill. In 1920 Mrs Partington, daughter-in-law of Lord Doverdale, changed the use of the Partington Convalescent Home to the Partington Maternity Home. The Partington Home was closed in 1983 and reopened in 1990 as a private nursing home.

The following reports give a picture of the health problems besetting the area at the start of the 20th century.

Report of Samuel Dane, Sanitary Inspector, 9th May 1916.

Owing to war conditions and shortage of men it has been necessary to reorganise the collection and disposal of dustbin rubbish. It has also brought the work under the Housing and Town Planning to a temporary stoppage, the owners being unable to get tradesmen to do the work.

The excrement and urine, tripe dressers' and butchers' offal, and fish dealers' refuse are all regularly collected and removed in covered vehicles to the Sewage Outfall Works.

The ash-bin system is still advancing, and the ash-pits are being gradually cleared away. This bin refuse is now collected weekly by the department. The number of bins in use is 1,484, as against 1,343 last year. Usually there are two cottages using one bin.

There were 95 cases of Scarlet Fever treated at the Gamesley Isolation Hospital. The total number of houses disinfected after the removal or recovery of the cases was 101 and the number of rooms disinfected were 302. Several beds have been destroyed by fire at the request of the owners, principally after cases of tuberculosis, or owing to being verminous.

With regard to milk there are still some who persist in ignoring "new fangled methods" of keeping the cow houses and cattle clean. Five persons were prosecuted for abstracting milk fat or for adding water to the milk. During the year 301 inspections of cow sheds and dairies and 14 inspections of milk shops in the Borough have been made.

The Meat Inspector has made 513 inspections of the slaughter houses in the Borough during the year. The method of slaughtering might be improved, especially in the slaughtering of pigs and calves which are often bled to death without being stunned into unconsciousness before bleeding. 473 visits have been made to places where other foods are in preparation, such as tripe dressers, cow heel establishments, pork butchers, sausage and brawn makers.

There are 55 bakehouses on the register and 71 visits have been made. All defects found have been remedied.

I am able to inform you that 45 houses have been re-drained or re-sewered during the year. 18 new houses have been drained and the drains connected with the main sewerage system.

Progress in public health got a boost with the arrival of Dr E.H.M. Milligan, M.D., D.P.H., on 27th August 1920 as the town's first full-time Medical Officer of Health. It is no exaggeration to say that he started a health revolution in Glossop.

Before introducing reforms, Dr Milligan set about gaining the public's confidence by educating them. In his early years in Glossop, he would put on health exhibitions, at which some of the foremost experts in public health were invited to speak, the earliest of which, in October 1920, was one of the first mounted in England.

The following is the report for Glossop presented in October 1922 by Dr Barwise, County Medical Officer, and Dr Milligan. It serves to illustrate the progress already made and as a base to compare with later.

	1891–1900	1901–1910	1911–1920	1921
Birth rate	27.05	22.04	17.03	17.87
Death rate	20.44	16.44	14.39	13.08
Deaths from Typhoid	0.31	0.14	0.65	-
Deaths from Phthisis	2.01	1.29	0.95	0.76
Infant mortality per 1000 births	173	141	111	78

In his annual reports to the Health Committee of the Borough Council, Dr Milligan was working to a plan. In his first report he listed several deficiencies and suggestions for their removal and these items stayed on his agenda year after year until the problem had been dealt with to his satisfaction. Further to this strategy, as shortcomings were dealt with, he would add yet others to his list.

Dr Milligan did not pull any punches and his comments must have upset many with entrenched ideas. It is not difficult to imagine the response of landlords whose property was deemed unfit for human habitation and who found themselves faced with bills for improvement. Most of these substandard houses have been demolished or completely overhauled. At one time there were houses in Bernard Street and parts of Edward Street which came into this category, and also courts hidden away off Cross Street and Chapel Street which have all disappeared. Back Kershaw Street, Shivering Row and Dearnley Row were hardly salubrious properties. In defence of the folks who lived in these houses, many managed to keep them clean and tidy.

In 1926 there were still approximately 300 back-to-back houses. Francis Sumner is reputed to have built a row of through houses for his workforce and, when they were completed said, "These are too good; convert them into back-to-back."

In his report as School Medical Officer in March 1922, Dr. Milligan stated:

Left: Dr Milligan, Glossop's Medical Officer of Health. (Supplied by Mr R. Turner)

"Dozens of homes have been found in which ventilation is provided by a small pane of glass about 8 inches by 6 inches, opening like a casement. The unpaved yard is the rule, WCs are rare in working-class homes, and baths almost unknown. It will be under-stood that the inculcation of hygiene among school children is a mockery unless better living conditions can be obtained.

In last year's report I mentioned the desirability of separate pens and pencils in the school to prevent the spread of infection. In one instance owing to an outbreak of scarlet fever, this course was adopted, and the outbreak ceased."

The Doctor suffered from malaria, which he caught while on holiday in Suffolk. Mosquitoes are present in the south of England and during wartime there were thousands of troops who had served abroad where the disease was prevalent, so to catch malaria in Britain was not unknown.

As a result of this affliction he always wore a topcoat and thick muffler on the warmest days. He was, however, fanatical on the subject of fresh air. On entering the bedroom of a patient his first move was to make a dash for the window and fling it wide open. The moment he was off the premises the patient went through a brief wonder cure which caused him to leap from his bed of sickness and slam the window shut before staggering back to bed.

The Glossop health revolution can be followed from the official facts and figures of Dr Milligan's own annual reports. For instance, in the matter of ash-bins and water closets, in 1920, 2,578 houses were served with ash-bins, and 2,864 served with ash-pits. By 1940, there were only 30 houses in the Borough who had to use ash-pits, and they were covered. In 1920 there were only 799 water closets in the borough and 2,512 pail closets. By 1940, there were 3,878 water closets and no pails. There were still 4 privies on farms in outlying districts. This improvement in sanitation caused a considerable saving on the rates, by removing the need to employ night soil men, as well as improving the health of the people. The conversion was rate-aided with the Council providing the labour and the property owners providing the materials.

Dr Milligan had difficulty in his early days trying to understand the Glossop dialect. Most of the old dialect words have gone out of use, but 60 years and more ago it was a different matter. He was not alone with this problem as Glossopians had equal difficulty in understanding Dr Milligan's Irish accent, which was made even more indecipherable by being filtered through a thick muffler. When examining the children at school he was handing out advice and firing questions, the vast bulk of which were not understood. One of his favourite pieces of advice was, "Eat more milk and cheese." Either free or very cheap milk was provided at schools but how children were expected to obtain extra cheese during wartime rationing was not explained.

In 1920 there was only one child welfare clinic. Soon a series of clinics were opened and staffed. They included a dental clinic started in November 1921; minor ailments clinic; orthopaedic clinic; ultraviolet ray clinic; tonsils and adenoids clinic; and the maternity clinic with facilities for expectant mothers.

On 22nd May 1925, Dr Milligan was able to report as follows:

> During the last year 500 pail closets were converted to WCs under a scheme to give work to the unemployed.

> The year 1924 brought widespread unemployment. The hardship resulted in a higher death rate and the birth rate is the lowest ever recorded in the Borough.

> I call the attention of the Council to various matters.
> 1. The Housing Question and overcrowding.
> 2. The air pollution caused by dusty roads and the firing of chimneys.
> 3. The tipping of refuse in various parts of the Borough.
> 4. The high death rate from respiratory diseases and the high maternal mortality during childbirth.
> 5. Improvement of the Hadfield water supply.

To emphasise problems with the Hadfield water supply Dr Milligan would produce a bottle of coloured water. This water came from Torside and Ogden Cloughs and was discoloured due to peat, but the main concern was that it dissolved the lead in the pipes with harmful effects on those who drank it. Hadfield people were in the habit of running their taps first thing in the morning to clear out the water which had been in contact with lead pipes between the main and the tap. This meant excessive use of water which was another reason for remedying the fault.

It was impossible to improve the water quality until the Corporation had bought the

Hadfield supply from Lord Howard. It is unlikely that, during the 19th century when the supply was laid on, anything was known about the dangers of soft water dissolving lead. With the erection of the Hadfield Treatment Plant in Padfield Main Road these problems were overcome. The result was that the number of cases of inflammation of the kidney was halved.

Smoke from domestic chimneys was a further source of pollution, made worse by the practice of "Swealing", or cleaning flues by setting fire to them. This practice was almost universal throughout the Borough and no legal action was taken against those who carried it out between 4.30 a.m. and 6 a.m. Dr Milligan pointed out that it was illegal and injurious to public health. Furthermore, soot was not harmless as continued application to the skin causes cancer; and continuous application of it to the interior of the lungs is harmful, no less from 4.30 a.m. to 6 a.m. than at any other time.

Another Glossop health problem was tuberculosis, and, on coming to the town, Dr Milligan was asked by the County Medical Officer of Health, Dr Sydney Barwise, to undertake a campaign against this disease, as Glossop was a blackspot in the county as regards death from consumption. In his report of April 1928 Dr Milligan was able to report that the death rate from pulmonary tuberculosis was the lowest recorded and the lowest of any of the larger towns in Derbyshire.

Another health field in which Glossop was a pioneer was in immunisation against diphtheria, being one of the first districts to adopt the method. Although diphtheria still occurs, deaths that result from it are very much fewer than formerly. Figures for the year 1940 showed that the death rate had fallen to nearly one-sixth of that in 1920.

There were no school meals in Glossop when Dr Milligan was appointed. Children who lived at a distance from school would bring sandwiches. During the 1930s, with thousands out of work, many children were starving. Dr Milligan arranged for special sandwiches to be delivered to schools for the children of the unemployed. These sandwiches were especially nutritious; brown bread and butter with cheese, eggs and watercress. As a matter of fact they were so good that some of the children whose parents were still in work and thus not entitled to the sandwiches thought they were being badly done by.

Children whose health was thought defective at examination were sent to an appropriate clinic; several, including the Sun Ray, Dental and Eye Clinics were situated in the Municipal Building.

A visit to the dentist was not something to be looked forward to. Before you set off there were the cheering words of your schoolmates: "They aren't proper dentists down there, they are only practising on you." On the other hand the teachers loved to tell us how lucky we were to have such services provided free.

Having screwed up enough courage to go to these allegedly untrained dentists you began to wonder if there wasn't something in these comments. Fillings were generally agreed to be the worst experience of the lot. The gums were not deadened so you just had to sit there with a drill which felt like a road drill removing the rotten part of the tooth and every few seconds a stabbing pain shooting through your mouth.

Unsatisfactory housing was another area where Dr Milligan set to work. In his report of 1924 he pointed out the number of houses with only two bedrooms; 3,808 out of 5,329 occupied properties. Forty-eight municipal houses had been erected between 1920 and 1922, and he suggested that the Council should deal with the overcrowding problem by building at least 50 further houses. These houses should be of brick or stone with a living room, three bedrooms, scullery and WC.

In 1928 Dr Milligan was still reminding the Health Committee of the deficiencies in housing:

> "We have at least 100 overcrowded houses, in one case we have two males and four females over ten years and seven males and two females under ten years, in all fifteen persons, occupying a house with two bedrooms and one living room, and a

back-to-back house into the bargain. The housing conditions of our town have been brought to the notice of the Council as long ago as 1924. I suggest now as an absolute minimum that the Council should build at once ten houses and build more in accordance with demand, dealing suitably with overcrowded houses."

As a result of an inspection carried out by a sub-committee of the Health Committee, a report was submitted that recommended 12 houses should be erected by the Corporation in the first instance under the Housing Act of 1924. Dr Milligan found a supporter in Alderman Doyle in the matters of conversion of pail toilets to water and in the push for more council houses to be built.

In addition to pressure being brought to bear on the Borough Council, informal action with private landlords brought about some improvement. Those who dragged their feet could be threatened with court action under one of the relevant Acts of Parliament.

The position was made worse by the Depression which brought mass unemployment to Glossop and Hadfield, and at a special meeting of the Council on 9th April 1930 a resolution was passed that no houses be erected until the financial position of the town improved. Dr Milligan was of the opinion that the Council should still erect the houses and that the matter should be reconsidered at the earliest possible date, and he gave an example where a father, mother and seven children were living in a house with two bedrooms. He therefore submitted that the building of 12 houses in the first instance should be proceeded with, as it could be provided without serious financial loss to the Corporation.

An inspection of houses revealed 2,813 with defects including slop sink pipes; leaky roofs; defective windows, drains, gutters and spouts; and ash-pits. The inspection found that 173 houses were in all respects not reasonably fit for human habitation.

It seemed that each inspection of schoolchildren revealed a problem. If our teeth were inspected, then a whole gang were off to the dental clinic. Similarly with eyes; suddenly it seemed that problems with eyesight were common. No doubt all this testing and treatment was beneficial but at times it seemed as if the good doctor had a mania for some particular condition each year.

One year almost every child was diagnosed with flat feet and put on a series of exercises to remedy this fearful condition. Teachers found themselves giving instructions on picking up pencils with one's toes and similar capers. The whole thing was an exercise in futility and was eventually allowed to fade away until the next condition was diagnosed.

The Sanitary Inspector, Mr Harry Dane, ensured that all the tips and sewage works were baited regularly with various poison baits. Many houses, shops, slaughterhouses, stables and farms were also dealt with, leading to a diminution in the number of rats. The general public had to be informed to notify the Sanitary Inspector when there was any reason to suspect the presence of rats and not wait until their premises were infested. No charge was made for the provision and laying down of poison baits.

The Medical Officer of Health's report of 23rd July 1937 shows that Dr Milligan was still beavering away. The death rate was by this date very low and the infant mortality rate was a record for the Borough. The death rate from pulmonary tuberculosis was also low, as was the death rate from infectious diseases. The largest killers were then diseases of the heart and blood vessels, respiratory diseases, cancer and nephritis. In Glossop, for instance, while all infectious diseases caused only five deaths, these devastators caused 192 deaths.

He went on to say:

"The Public Health Acts, even in their latest form, the Public Health Act of 1936, are largely behind the times. They deal with the conceptions we had of disease 60 years ago; but this is 1937; the old sanitary abuses have been largely abolished, we now have clean water supplies, water carriage system of sewage disposal and prompt

Hadfield Council Houses.

and a reasonably satisfactory method for disposal of refuse; housing is being improved, the milk supply is being carefully watched, and infectious diseases are adequately isolated; vast numbers are not now dying of smallpox.

...I may mention that more education of the public in the causes and prevention of these deaths is needed, more hospital accommodation is needed for diagnosing and treating them, more co-ordinated action and co-operation is required between the State, local authorities and the medical profession. We need far greater facilities and accommodation for the treatment of medical diseases, for instance pneumonia, diabetes, severe anaemias, rheumatism and arthritis, to mention a few."

Today we have become sceptical of official announcements, but there was a time when folks had confidence in the BBC News and similar sources. One piece of information that has been frequently disseminated is that we had a healthier diet during the Second World War than we have had since. This is demonstrably not so, merely from observing the great increase in height and weight of today's young people. Some of Dr Milligan's wartime work serves to illustrate this point. Between January and February 1941, and the same dates in the following year, he carried out a series of investigations.

He used a "Strength Machine" which consisted of a horizontal bar placed high enough to keep a boy's feet off the ground. The test consisted of seeing how long the child could hang on for, to give a measure of endurance. After the first series of tests the boys were given a course of pills and then retested. Half the subjects received a vitamin pill and the other half a placebo. His conclusions were:

1. The rates of growth in weight and height of 11-year-old Glossop boys had in 1941 become significantly reduced below the pre-war rates.
2. Growth had regained pre-war level during the 12 months to late October 1942, and to January–February 1943.
3. Though growth reached pre-war standard, the standard was a very low one, accompanied by a relative stunting in both weight and height growth and associated with family dietaries of a low nutritional level.

From early 1941 to early 1942 the children were found to have a significantly lower rate of growth than during the pre-war period. Their energy had been lowered, yet strength per body weight had increased.

The latest tests showed that from early 1942 to early 1943 growth in weight and height had almost become normal. Dr Milligan's next task was to find out when the improvement started and what was the probable cause while taking into account seasonal variation. The most obvious cause of the improved growth appeared to be the giving of vitamins, as 31 out of the 65 boys examined during a particular period had a multivitamin capsule given to them. The data of the 31 boys was separated but it was found there was no significant difference between the rates of growth of the vitamin and non-vitamin children. This did not mean that the giving of vitamins had no effect. The boys who had them showed higher resistance to fatigue.

The next possible cause was the school dinners, which had started in Glossop in April 1942. Of the 65 boys, 28 had the dinners. It was found that the gain in weight of the school dinner boys was significantly worse than that of the non-dinner ones and worse than the standard pre-war rate.

Dr Milligan also made telling comparisons between Glossop schoolchildren and those attending a public school. A survey was carried out in Glossop in the early summer of 1937. The amounts of animal protein and vitamin C consumed per person per day were near to what he found in January 1942 and again the rates of growth for children in 1942 and the pre-war period were not significantly different.

But was the pre-war standard a satisfactory one? It was not. In fact it was a poor one, for these Glossop boys were stunted in growth. For instance, Glossop's 11-year-old non-necessitous boys as compared with Christ's Hospital boys of the same age were 1.1 inches shorter and 9.63 lbs lighter than their public school colleagues. Glossop's necessitous children were 4 inches shorter and 16 lbs lighter.

In addition to his work as the local Medical Officer of Health, during World War II he worked for the Ministry of Health where he advised on the nutrition of the forces and interestingly, when Britain was being supplied from the USA with cargoes of potatoes and eggs, he came up with the suggestion that it would be more efficient to ship powdered eggs and potatoes and add the water after distribution, thus saving shipping space.

With his pioneering work, Dr Milligan certainly helped to put Glossop on the map. One of his activities outside the medical sphere was to co-author several successful radio plays with his son-in-law who was a solicitor. Perhaps not surprising since he came from an Irish literary family.

In his report of 18th May 1923, he made the following statement: "During the year efforts have been made to make the attractions of Glossop more widely known; it ought to have a great future as a residential town. The air is invigorating, the surroundings ideal, and there is ample ground for building; there are also facilities for manufacturers. Glossop can be a town of health and the 'Town Beautiful' if it but wills it."

He was correct in seeing Glossop becoming a residential town. What a pity he isn't still with us to press for adequate access to the town. Dr Milligan retired from his post at Glossop in 1946 and took up employment with the Ministry of Health.

It is regrettable that after a lifetime of service to the Community and the Health Service, Dr Milligan received no formal honours. Perhaps he stepped on too many official toes in his ceaseless struggles on our behalf. Certainly his comments on the heights and weights of children from poorer homes compared with middle-class children pointed out a disgraceful state of affairs, and his statistics on children during wartime give the lie to the propaganda that we were on a better diet during World War II.

Improvements in health care have continued in Glossop. In 2001 Dr John Oldham received the OBE and in 2003 was awarded a knighthood in recognition of his work.

13
EDUCATION IN GLOSSOPDALE

There were schools in Glossop from an early date. In 1494 Dr John Talbot was appointed Vicar at Glossop and it is possible that he started a school in the churchyard.

In 1670, 1671 and 1672 Daniel Leech received £10 per annum from the Lord of the Manor for teaching the Free School. In 1677 Nicholas Dernaley bequeathed £30 to the Free School. From 1738 to 1741 John Hadfield acknowledged half-yearly the moiety of the £10 as a gratuity for teaching the Glossop School.

Glossop Parish Church Magazine, June 1895, records that Rev Christopher Howe (1793–1849) established a day school which stood on the ground later used as the kitchen garden of the vicarage. In April 1896 the same writer, Rev A.P. Hamilton-Wilson, says that he believes that Mr Howe's first school was succeeded by one that stood where four cottages now stand on Castle Hill. Robert Hamnett tells us that in an old deed dated 1675 Thomas Twyford was schoolmaster at Glossop, and also that the school occupied numbers 8 to 14 Castle Hill.

Hague's Endowed School, Whitfield, opened for teaching on 22nd November 1778. There are two tablets inset in the wall, one with a carved relief of a beehive intended as a symbol of industry. The other tablet reads:

> "This school was erected by Joseph Hague, Esquire, as a testimony of gratitude to Almighty God for his favour and blessing through a life of years whereby he was enabled to accumulate an ample fortune and make plentiful provision for his numerous relations and dependants. Anno Domini 1779."

A likely explanation for choosing the site was that at the time Top Whitfield was the most populous part of the township. Furthermore, much of the land in Whitfield was freehold, whereas if he had built in Glossop, Hague would have had to pay ground rent and the land would only have been leased for a number of years. It could also be that a wealthy man like Joseph Hague wanted it to be known that he was not overawed by the Howards.

Hague's School was intended for the instruction of poor children within the Parish of Glossop in the English language, writing and arithmetic, and to teach such children the Church Catechism. The trustees had the power to dismiss the schoolmaster by simply placing a notice on the school door.

The school wage for teaching the English language only was one penny a week for each child; for teaching English and writing, twopence a week; and for teaching English, writing and arithmetic, threepence a week.

The first schoolmaster at the Endowed School was George Roberts. Born at Deepclough, he had previously taught at Tintwistle School. On the opening day there were 42 scholars. Mr Roberts seems to have been a man of exceptional abilities. He was a land surveyor, an

Above: Hague's School, Top Whitfield and right: the Plaque on Hague's School.

amateur lawyer and an accountant. He was of considerable wealth and made most of the local wills.

Mr Roberts resigned on 27th January 1800 and was succeeded by John Dearnaley, who came from Wedneshough Green School. Mr Dearnaley held the post until his death on 4th January 1843.

Mr James Bosley was appointed on 6th May 1843. He died on 29th May 1844. Mr John Ball succeeded Mr Bosley on 9th September 1844. He was dismissed on 29th June 1853, on account of his irregular conduct and neglecting his duties.

On 10th August 1853, Mr John Bardsley of Edale was elected, and held the post until he resigned; and on 4th March 1872 Mr George Ford was appointed. He died on 10th February 1878. Mr Noah Booker was appointed on 15th April 1878, and was apprehended on a charge of bigamy on 9th February 1881, serving six months for his offence. The last schoolmaster was Mr Walter Pedley Evason, who took possession on 25th March 1881 and occupied the position until he retired in February 1925.

When the school closed, the trustees converted the school into flats which, together with the master's house, were let and later sold and the proceeds invested. They obtained permission from the Board of Education to use this income to help children from the old Parish of Glossop with their secondary education. Grants are usually made at the beginning of the academic year, in October. They are made to assist anyone living in the ancient parish who has attended a school in which religious instruction in accordance with the doctrines of the Church of England is given.

The factory system forced the cotton operatives and their children to work long hours and so they got little chance of learning. The sons and daughters of farmers were better situated and the more affluent could send them to private schools. The teachers would charge a few pence per week, depending on the subjects taught, and often received payment in kind where that was the most convenient way to pay. A farmer might pay his school fees with potatoes, bacon, milk or butter, a tailor with clothing, and a fishmonger with herrings.

A remarkable initiative was started in Glossop by ordinary working folks. The date coincides with the growth of political awareness and such movements as Chartism which were to lead to an improvement in working conditions.

At one time it had been the practice for writing to be taught at Sunday Schools, but the custom had ceased. Realising that education was the route out of poverty, an attempt was made to persuade the Sunday Schools to return to the teaching of writing, but when this failed, a group banded together and started their own school in a building attached to the Norfolk Arms. This first school proved too small, so they set to build one of their own and chose a site which is now occupied by the Shopping Giant Supermarket.

This school was described in the *Manchester Guardian* as a plain but substantial school house, capable of accommodating 600 children, towards the expense of which the Lords of the Treasury had been pleased to make a grant of £225 out of the funds voted for the building of schools.

Many of the workers gave their support to the movement, as did some notable citizens. Amongst the subscribers were: Royal Foresters; Ancient Druids; Gardeners; Oddfellows; Mr Ellison; Robert Shepley; and the Co-operative Society. The annual sermons realised from £7 to £15. In 1836 they received £4, a gift from the magistrates, being part of a factory fine; they also received sums from 2s. 6d. to 10s. from fines on persons who had committed assaults or been caught poaching. The school was established on 21st July 1833, and flourished until the site was required for the railway station.

The workers' school may have been demolished to make way for the railway station but other schools opened to cater for the needs of the town's children. Around 1840 Edmund Potter started a day school for the children of his employees at his mill; in 1847 a Catholic Girls' School was built in Old Glossop; in 1850–1 the 13th Duke of Norfolk built Glossop's first Grammar School near the Parish Church. We still call it The Duke of Norfolk's School.

Further denominational schools were started throughout the remainder of the 19th century. A Church of England School was opened at Waterside in 1872; Saint Luke's was built in 1880. The Methodists and Independents did not intend to be left behind, Zion Methodist School opening in 1883 and Littlemoor Independent in 1886.

These schools made a valuable contribution but I will concentrate on Whitfield School because I was a pupil there for six years and can add something from personal experience.

The first Whitfield Church School opened on 6th May 1848, and the earliest Log Book still in existence was started in 1862 when the Master was Joseph Eckersley. Some of the entries made in the Log Book during the Cotton Famine have already been given, but there were lists of the staff and their qualifications and some of the more notable events. It is obvious that the number of qualified staff continued to grow until the Hadow Report of 1926 recommended the formation of schools for seniors over the age of 11.

After meetings of the Church authorities and L.E.A. in Glossop it was decided to transfer all senior children to the West End School and convert the Church Schools to Juniors and Infants.

The schools connected with churches and chapels had been built and financed in the first instance with funds collected by their congregations. Whitfield School was more fortunate than most in having had the financial backing of the Wood family. For example, in 1877 the Infant Room was built by Mr and Mrs Samuel Wood, thus making the Infants a separate department.

In April 1899, at Whitfield National School, the large mixed schoolroom had its new floor laid down in red deal at a cost of £32, towards which £25 came from the Voluntary Schools Aid Grant.

In August 1900 the Board of Education refused to further sanction the use of the large Sunday Schoolroom for Day School purposes. The Sunday School teachers and trustees therefore agreed to build new classrooms, the two upper rooms being set apart for the use of

Duke of Norfolk's
School.

Littlemoor School.

Mrs Wood's class and the senior young men's class, and the two lower rooms being leased to the Day School. Mr Joseph Howard executed plans, which were submitted to the Board of Education, the estimated cost being between £900 and £1,000. This sum was raised by holding a bazaar. Mrs Wood provided a stimulus by promising to double whatever sum was raised. The new classrooms were occupied for the first time on 5th May 1902.

On 1st May 1902 Frederick Herbert Morris started as headmaster. The hall had proved inadequate for both Day and Sunday Schools, so Mrs A.K. Wood promised to have four classrooms added. Mr Morris was to be responsible for a whole range of improvements; he arranged with the local Co-operative Society to sell a school badge and later a school cap became available. In May 1904 a field at the Hobroyd was rented for outdoor sports and pitches prepared so that Whitfield School had facilities for sports long before playing fields became the norm.

In 1913 the Junior Day School in Victoria Street was erected, the cost borne by Mrs A.K. Wood. The official opening was in September 1913 by the Mayor of Glossop. It was surrounded on three sides by very extensive gardens, the freehold of which was purchased by Sir Samuel Hill Wood, M.P., and was owned by the church and school authorities. These gardens were used to instruct the boys in gardening, yet another initiative of Mr Morris.

The Great War led to further entries:

January 1st 1915. The headmaster has been granted leave of absence from school duties during the progress of the War as he has received a commission in the 6th Battalion Cheshire Regiment.

March 5th 1915. Mr W. Harrop has been granted leave of absence during the War from school duties.

June 21st 1915. Miss Sutcliffe was granted leave of absence this afternoon in order to meet her brother in Manchester prior to his departure for the Front.

J.W.HOWARD,

Whitfield School 1902. Demolished 1981.

Whitfield Inft School
Class II.

Class at Whitfield Infants *c.*1920 with Miss Bradwell seated.

Whitfield School choir. Blackpool Music Festival, Winter Gardens, 1932. Back row: Teachers; Miss Wilde, Jessie Rowbottom, Maud Hampson, Miss Ashton: Pupils; George Beard, ?, ?, ?, Kathleen Needham, Sydney Clarke, Bernard Bowden, Lucy Tero, ?, Hallsworth, Alice Grant, ?, Aubrey Minshull. Middle row: Pupils; Joan McGowan, Eric Barker, ? Thornley, ?, ?, ?, Margaret Hallas, ?, Doris McCrone, Fred Walker, Gladys Reddington, George Bradley, Laura McCrone, Tom Harrison: Teachers; Miss Hadfield, ?, ?, Miss Thornley. Front row: Wilfred Pownall, ?, Middleton, Frank Hadfield, ?, Taylor, Victor Furniss (Headmaster), Enid Arrandale, Sydney Hand, ?, Norman "Curly" Bowden.

Whitfield School staff *c.*1935. Back row: Maud Hampson, Miss Harrison, Muriel Ashton (later Mrs Bird), Miss Fielding, Nellie Swindells, "Big" Miss Jessie Rowbottom. Front row: Miss Wild, "Little" Miss Ada Rowbottom, Miss Bradwell, Captain Victor Furniss, Miss Dearnley, Minnie Robinson, Miss Thornley.

One event which occurred early in the War did not merit a mention in the Log Book. West End School had one advantage over Whitfield in that it was equipped with a woodwork shop, and classes from Whitfield would use this facility. One morning, as the Whitfield boys were leaving, they were set upon by a gang of West End boys and being outnumbered they received something of a beating. As soon as these lads got back to Whitfield, the news spread through the school like wildfire and at the first break a small army surged out of Whitfield School heading for West End. On arrival a battle royal commenced in which considerable damage was done to the school windows, quite apart from damage inflicted on each other. As one of the combatants told me years later, "The grown-ups were having a war, so we thought we would have one as well."

Major Morris conducted a thorough investigation into this shocking affray, but strangely no one had any knowledge of the event.

In October 1930, Major Morris left Whitfield School to become Headmaster at West End School and Captain Victor Furniss became Head at Whitfield on 1st November. On 30th July 1937, Captain Furniss left to go to West End in place of Major Morris, who had retired, but on 30th August 1937 Captain Furniss died in Shanklin after a very short illness.

Major Morris died on 7th February 1938, a few months after his retirement. He had served Whitfield for many years, not only as Headmaster but as Secretary for many organisations, Churchwarden and Sidesman; in the town he was active as a leading member of the British Legion.

A feature of Whitfield School was the choir, which entered successfully in many contests. The walls of the school hall were lined with photographs of choirs from different years.

On 1st October 1937, Herbert A. Whitehead commenced as Headmaster at Whitfield. Mr Whitehead made numerous changes; one was to invest more teaching time in academic subjects instead of concentrating on the choir. I cannot speak for others but was glad to see the downgrading of the choir, much preferring to get my head into a book. Miss Jessie Rowbottom carried out tests to see whose voices were suitable for the choir and would walk along the rows of children. As she passed, I made the worst possible racket. I can still remember the look of horror on her face and my satisfaction at being rejected.

With the approach of World War II comments on Air Raid Precautions appeared in the Log Book:

October 19th 1938. Members of the staff attended ARP classes at 4.30 p.m.
September 12th. Gas mask drill and clearing of the school will be practised daily.
September 4th 1940. Children went to air raid shelter at 10.30. All clear went at 10.50.
April 16th 1942. Equipment received in connection with midday meals.

In 1943 the Whitfield Infants School was converted and became, for the period of the War, a Wartime Nursery, the infants being transferred to the Ashton Street Schools.

Whitfield Infant and Primary School is a subject where I can contribute something from personal experience. It is just over seventy years since I started at the Infant School in Victoria Street and, looking back after having been involved in various capacities with over twenty different establishments of learning in the interim, I can say with confidence that Whitfield School was among the best.

I started after the Easter holiday in 1934. I can still recall learning to write with a crayon and a slate.

"Don't spit on your slate and wipe it with your sleeve," the teacher would say. Since there was no other method provided for cleaning the slate, one soon learned to wait until the teacher was not looking before spitting on the slate.

On moving to the "Big School" I gained the impression that the staff felt that things were not what they once were. There were several factors which could have contributed to this belief. One was the loss of support from the school's great benefactor, Mrs A.K. Wood. The slump which affected Glossop so drastically caused an exodus from the town and there was a drop in the birth rate, which meant that the number on the roll decreased rapidly from 280 in 1930 to 180 in 1937.

That the Great War was still very much in the memory of the teachers was evidenced by the songs they liked to lead in the Christmas parties: 'Pack up your troubles' and 'It's a Long Way to Tipperary'. The children showed less enthusiasm, since it had happened before they were born.

Life was not easy in the 1930s, with many fathers unemployed and children undernourished. By no stretch of the imagination can the hardships which families have suffered during more recent times of unemployment be compared with the 1930s. One day the teacher asked a boy why he hadn't combed his hair that morning.

"Because we haven't got a comb."
"Your sister has managed to comb her hair. How did she manage?"
"She used a fork!"

On another occasion we were given a talk on the importance of regular brushing of teeth. The walls were festooned with diagrams showing the structure of teeth, and each child was given a toothbrush and a tin of Gibbs dentifrice – an excellent initiative which worked well until all the dentifrice was used up and the toothbrush worn out. Not everybody could afford replacements; a new pair of shoes might be more urgent.

There were still parents who regarded their children as an economic asset and were only waiting for the day when they could start in the mill and contribute to the family income. Some children were programmed to believe that school was a waste of time. The girls suffered most from this attitude.

"What's the use of a girl going to the Grammar School? She's only going to end up in the mill and then get married." Or, "All this study is no good for you, it softens the brain." Or, worst of all, "He's fourteen and we haven't had a penny out of him."

Despite all the difficulties, the teachers did a wonderful job. The most remarkable thing about them was their unquenchable enthusiasm. If there was a pupil who left Whitfield School who could not read and write, I was unaware of them. This enthusiasm was carried over into all subjects, from mathematics to physical training. There was no slacking; everybody was kept hard at work. There was a certain ethos about Whitfield School – you felt you belonged to something worthwhile. Other schools might be good but Whitfield was indefinably better. No doubt pupils who had attended the Duke of Norfolk's, Saint Mary's, Zion or Saint Luke's held similar opinions.

"Big" Miss Jessie Rowbottom did not get her sobriquet for nothing, but it did not prevent her tackling every task with enthusiasm, from teaching mathematics to leaping about as energetically as the youngsters in the yard doing exercises, to leading us on expeditions into the countryside. With teachers like her it was no wonder that Whitfield School students obtained so many scholarships to the Grammar School.

The testing time came when the children sat the scholarship exams which could give entrance to Glossop Grammar School. Whitfield School achieved consistently good results despite several factors militating against it. Some children were not allowed to sit the examination by their parents. Another factor affecting the parents' decision as to whether to allow their children to proceed to the Grammar School was the question of the expense of purchasing uniforms and equipment. They did not wish to be placed in the embarrassing position of not being able to pay. At the same time it should not be forgotten that West End was an excellent school and provided a better preparation for the world of work for a majority of pupils.

Glossop Grammar School

"In teaching there should be no class distinctions." Confucius.

On 4th January 1897 Sir Robert Ball gave a lecture in the Victoria Hall on "A Universe in Motion". Lord Howard presided and, at the close, said that the large audience showed that the people of Glossop took great interest in technical education. The building in which they were assembled was not erected for that branch of study, and it was inadequate for the purpose, and an idea had struck him some time ago that he should have pleasure in offering to the town of Glossop a building for a Technical School. He had been for some time talking the matter over with his agent, and he had already arranged where the building should be, and had gone so far as to appoint the architect.

Building operations commenced in November, and on 23rd March 1898 the Council formally accepted the gift. The Draft Deed of Gift was accepted on 3rd April 1901, and the Technical School formally handed over on the 11th. The basement was used for weaving and other trades. On the ground floor were laboratories, the secretaries' office and other rooms. The upper floor was mainly used for art teaching.

The reasoning behind setting up a technical school was concern that Glossop was falling behind neighbouring textile towns which already provided technical education in mechanics' institutes.

Over the main entrance is a plaque which reads as follows:

HAS * AEDES
ARTIBUS * TECHNIS * PROMOVENDIS
DICATAS
MUNICIPIO * GLOSSOPIENSI * DONAVIT
FRANCISCUS * GLOSSOPIENSIS
BARO * SECUNDUS
A * C * MDCCCXCIX

I have taken the precaution of consulting a Graeco-Roman scholar for a translation of the above. The inscription is not completely Latin, but includes Greek words such as *technis*. A literal translation would be: "Francis of Glossop, the second baron, gave these buildings dedicated to the advancement of the technical arts in the municipality of Glossop. AD 1899."

Oddly, the word *baro* is Latin for blockhead, hardly the way to describe the Second Baron Glossop. The title "baron" did not exist in Roman times and so a Latin translation had to be invented.

There can be no doubt that Lord Howard intended the new building for use as a Technical School, and in the main entrance is a rubber mat with the words Glossop Technical School moulded into it. It was both far-sighted and generous of Lord Howard to make this sensible provision, but his intentions were soon to be circumvented.

Lord Howard was certainly not a blockhead, but he failed to foresee that educationalists would be true to form and put their own interests first. Without exception they will use every stratagem to turn the institution in which they work into something they regard as more prestigious.

We have seen that the working class were seeking education when they formed the Workers' School in 1833. This initiative seems to have sparked the founding of a whole series of educational institutes over the next few years. The year 1841 saw the founding of the Littlemoor and Howardtown Mechanics' Institute, and the following year Robert Kershaw and others established the Glossop Mechanics' Institute at the Castle Hill Schools.

In 1848 Robert Kershaw started a night school in the Whitfield Church School. Ten years later he moved to a building in King Street which proved to be too small for his purposes, so he built the Kershaw Institute at his own expense of £400. The Institute opened in November 1859.

The question that remains unanswered is, why did not Glossop end up with both a Grammar School and a Technical School so that more careers could be catered for? The Junior Technical School in Ashton-under-Lyne was highly thought of by local companies and ex-pupils were virtually assured of employment. Surely some students would have found Technical Drawing or Accountancy of greater value than Latin.

The first headmaster at the Technical School was Ralph Herbert Dickenson, and by 1920 the Technical School had become Glossop Grammar School. Mr Dickenson retired in 1928 and was replaced by Mr C.H. Chambers, B.Sc., B.Eng. For some reason he was known as "Pa" Chambers.

The Grammar School system was loaded against the children of working-class parents. Such children who entered on the strength of a scholarship were generally exhorted by their parents to "work hard", which most of them did, quite unaware of the forces ranged against them. The effects of these forces become clear if you note the number of working-class children who started at Grammar Schools and then check to see how many stayed till the end of the fifth year to sit the School Certificate, or its later counterpart, O Levels. An examination of the sixth form would show that even fewer carried on to take the Higher School Certificate. Amongst those who did, a high percentage went to Teacher Training Colleges rather than University, the main obstacles being the cost and bad advice, or the total lack of it, in earlier years in the matter of subject choice.

The working-class child was faced with many difficulties: the cost of providing uniforms and sports kit; the need for the child's income in the case of large families; lack of support from parents; no easy provision for home study in a small terraced home. Girls in particular were at a disadvantage thanks to the notion that education didn't matter for women. Their parents generally had no clear idea of the paths that could be followed through the system and where it could lead to in the field of employment. Most children were no better informed about the possibilities and, even when preparing to leave school, only a few had decided on a future occupation. The upshot of this was that the working-class child was conscious of being on his own, having to make important decisions without having the necessary facts at his disposal. Simultaneously he felt he was surrounded with classmates who knew exactly where they were going.

The obvious place to obtain information should have been the school. The snag here was that most teachers knew precious little about life outside the system. Having gone from grammar school to university, and from university into teaching, they were hardly the ideal people to give advice on careers in accountancy, engineering, dentistry, management, and a host of other interesting and worthwhile occupations. Now, if on completing their degree they had spent six months in the slaughter hall at Wall's Meat Company, with giblets flying around, or working on a building site in all weathers, they might have had a better idea of what ordinary folks were doing to earn a living, and learned a spot of humility into the bargain.

Teachers as a group suffer from several delusions. The most ridiculous is the notion that, because a pupil doesn't perform well in academic subjects, then by some wonderful compensatory mechanism, he or she will be good with their hands.

Middle-class parents had a better understanding of the educational system and the "clout" to ensure that their children were in a position to make the most of their schooling. Around 1915, one girl who had decided upon a career as an industrial chemist was told by "Daddy" Dickenson that she could not take Physics and Chemistry, but would attend the Biology class with the other girls. Fortunately for the girl, her father was a high-ranking manager with a local company. He was round to see Mr Dickenson straight away, when it was found she could do Physics and Chemistry after all. On leaving the school she obtained employment with a firm of industrial chemists in Manchester.

Many of the children were aware of the "them and us" attitude where Grammar Schools were concerned and were determined not to have a bar of it. One man, whose father kept a public house in a tougher part of town, told me, "I knew none of my mates would be going to the Grammar School and I made sure that I failed the scholarship examination so that I could stay with them and play football in the street at night instead of sitting in doing homework." I am sure he was not alone in such subterfuges.

The idea common amongst ordinary citizens was that, to be regarded as suitable material to attend Glossop Grammar School, it was necessary to live on the correct side of the railway line, the reasoning being that North Road, Spire Hollin, Talbot Road and Fauvel Road were regarded as more affluent areas inhabited by folks who could afford to pay for their children to attend the Grammar School should they fail to gain entry by scholarship. The truth of the matter was that your entrance to and progress in Glossop Grammar School was to a considerable degree dependent on the employment of your father. Teacher, bank manager, station master, head of the boot and shoe section at the Co-op, were quite acceptable; labourers at Turn Lee Paper Mill or the Calico Printers Association were definitely not.

The children, for their part, remembered the fairness of their elementary school and were aware that they were being singled out for different treatment, even if they could not divine the reason. This is why several left without completing their education.

For a reasonably bright child who was prepared to conform to the expected pattern, and given the support of his parents, both financial and in the form of special tuition, Glossop Grammar School could be a straight road to university and one of the professions. Nevertheless, it hardly provided the type of education required by local manufacturers seeking skilled technical and management people, and it certainly wasn't what Lord Howard had in mind.

On the credit side, the school provided the opportunity to mix with students who had not been brainwashed into believing that school was a waste of time and who as a group were brighter than one's elementary schoolmates. Such an environment made for better academic progress.

On Mr Chambers' retirement in 1937 Mr Cecil Lord became headmaster, and when he first arrived was christened "Joe" by the pupils. He had several good points; he certainly did his best to establish the standards of discipline necessary in a school if teaching is to be possible; he also did his best to stamp out what vandalism there was and went to a lot of trouble to detect the culprits when there was the occasional theft. Students were certainly expected to look after the books that were issued free and these gave years of service.

Never having been in the sixth form, I am unable to comment on his teaching abilities at that level, but from the performances we saw each week in "Lord's Lesson", I would say he had no interest in the job of actually teaching. This was made abundantly clear by the fact that he was almost invariably late to start his class, and on a few blessed occasions never showed up at all. If he ever went to the trouble to prepare a lesson, I was unable to detect any signs of it.

I do not doubt that he was competent at timetabling staff, negotiating with the county authorities for extra accommodation, and similar administrative work. I don't know what the staff thought of him but I did note that on the occasions when he was absent, and Sammy Holt as Deputy Head took morning assembly, he always chose the same hymn from the school hymnal: "Number 146, Lord Of All Being Throned Afar". I leave you to form your own conclusions.

Derbyshire County Council and Glossop Borough Council were more generous than many authorities in providing scholarships to enable students to gain admission to Grammar Schools. I wonder why they should then appoint a man as headmaster who did his very best to negate this policy. Mr Lord judged his students not on their academic abilities but on their father's occupation; indeed he must have spent a lot of time investigating this matter because he went out of his way to give certain students a hard time from the moment they entered the school. He even had the gall to make such comments as "The sins of the father being visited on the son".

Mr Lord affected a hairstyle more suited to a Prussian Junker, and in consequence his nickname soon changed from "Joe" to "Gauleiter". He was overfond of ridiculing students from poorer homes but didn't like it when the tables were turned. He liked to ask questions and then dismiss the answers out of hand in a contemptuous way, even though the student might be correct.

We did learn a few things from the Gauleiter. Thanks to his fondness for hitting people, we became adept at ducking and weaving and learned how to ride a punch. Another useful skill was how to give an answer which took the wind out of his sails. The best example of this was, when asked why you had been absent, to say, "For domestic reasons". This could mean anything, but the true import was "Mind your own business".

Before leaving Mr Lord for the present I should point out that, when the war was going badly for Britain after Dunkirk, he and Mr Holt joined the Home Guard without hesitation. However, the rank of private was not quite to his liking, and it was not long before the school Air Training Corps was formed with himself as Commanding Officer and Mr Holt as his Second in Command.

Glossop Grammar School had many good points. Some of the staff were excellent and well on top of their subjects. I would give high marks to Miss Dorothy Greenwood who took Biology. She did not find it necessary to go round hitting people for the simple reason that her lessons were interesting and there was rarely occasion to reprimand pupils.

Charles Casey, the senior Chemistry teacher, knew his stuff and was not overawed by the Gauleiter. He might have been strict, but he was fair, and he was another who found it unnecessary to strike students. One day he went through my nature diary, and afterwards made the suggestion that I should consider writing a nature column for a newspaper. He was the only member of staff who ever offered any sort of careers advice.

Mr Bell, the Woodwork teacher, left at the end of my first term when he was called up into the forces. Younger students who were taught by him after the war tell me he was one of the best teachers in the place. He was replaced by Mr Gooch from Lowestoft. Mr Gooch was an Art and Handicraft teacher rather than a Woodwork teacher, but he showed us many interesting techniques including bookbinding and making lino prints.

In fairness to a number of the staff at Glossop Grammar School it should be pointed out that several of them were close to, or past, the age of retirement and but for the war would probably have retired. Despite this pupils managed to achieve some good results in externally marked examinations. With the cessation of hostilities younger members of staff started and this infusion of new blood brought about a considerable improvement.

Apart from personal likes and dislikes, staff must be judged on their abilities in the classroom. Mathematics and the sciences were taught well, as was Geography. History was a joke during the early years, and all that I can remember is that primitive men had receding foreheads and that Hammurabi made good laws. Despite the wealth of historical sites within easy walking distance of the school, the only expedition we ever went on was a trip to Edrotalia to see the remains of the Roman fort. Here was the chance to explain the reasons for choosing the site, explanations of the layout and the directions of the roads starting from the site. Alas, not a mention. During the last two years, while preparing for the School Certificate, a choice had to be made between History and Geography. I do not know which educated idiot was responsible for this decision since the two subjects are inexorably linked.

It was a toss-up which was the biggest waste of time, Religious Instruction or Physical Education. Why put a subject on the syllabus if there is no intention of teaching it? There was clearly no one at Glossop Grammar School capable of tackling Religious Instruction and I wonder why they didn't approach some local clergyman to do the job.

Physical Education was an absolute farce. Half the lesson was taken up with checking that your name was marked on your kit, that your kit was spotless and, most important of all, that your plimsolls were white. The remarkable thing was that the teacher's only change of dress was to don a distinctly off-white pullover which gave the impression that it had not been washed in years. The only time in five years that we actually learned anything in P.E. was the occasion when we arrived to find a climbing rope had been set up and we were shown the correct method of ascending.

We were saved from the endless inspections of white plimsolls by someone not usually regarded as a public benefactor. Adolf Hitler's policy of unrestricted submarine warfare meant that materials for sports equipment were not given priority on Atlantic convoys. The same fellow unwittingly helped in another way, by preventing educational visits to France, thus saving some the embarrassment of not being able to participate for financial reasons. It would have been better to have kicked P.E. and R.I. into touch and introduced a few subjects which would have come in useful later on.

No attempt at coaching was made in any area of athletics. The only throwing event was throwing the cricket ball, and this led to a display by Dennis Winterbottom, who was more gifted than most as an athlete. When it came to his turn to throw the cricket ball he suggested that he start from a point further back as otherwise the ball would land outside the field. The teacher would have none of this, so Dennis carried on, and sure enough the ball landed far beyond the confines of the Lord Street field, crashing onto the roof of a house in Fauvel Road.

At one stage we were taken to the Glossop Baths. I am still wondering what was the purpose of these outings as swimming instruction consisted of such comments as "Don't just stand there in the water, do something." Clearly nothing was going to be learned from this farce, so I went to the baths one Saturday afternoon and Hughie Goggins had me swimming a few strokes within half an hour. I wonder how he would have performed in Religious Instruction?

When the headmaster has a policy of streaming students according to their parents' occupation, it is only to be expected that some staff members will follow his lead. Children who had made good progress at elementary schools and never been in any serious trouble suddenly found themselves subjected to all sorts of unjustified remarks. "Where were you dragged up?" for example. Some had the audacity to tell children who they should associate with during their leisure hours.

As the years passed a definite pattern was established. The "A" stream tended to consist of those from the right side of the railway line, while the "B" stream consisted of the less academic and those Mr Lord considered of unsuitable parentage. Under these circumstances we were probably fortunate that none of our fathers were behind bars. The unfair aspect of this method of streaming was revealed from time to time. When Mr Holt came to mark the "mock" School Certificate mathematics papers, he was taken aback to discover that only two people had managed to solve a problem correctly, both from the "B" stream. Certain classes, Physics, for example, were made up of students from both streams. Surprise, surprise, the dunces turned out some good results in the School Certificate.

Children are soon aware of any sort of discrimination and the Gauleiter's streaming methods ensured that a group of disaffected anti-school-establishment pupils was set up. Time which would have been better spent on learning was used to concoct some pretty wild schemes by the anti-school group. A couple of examples spring to mind: the sabotaging of the heating system in the new huts; and connecting the gas and water taps with a length of rubber tubing, last thing on Friday afternoon, and turning both on before leaving.

Shortly before World War II a strapping youth, who had had enough of Mr Holt's clouts round the ear, stood up and laid him out. He then packed his bag and went home and stayed there. About six weeks later he received a letter to the effect that if he were to return, all would be forgiven. His father was the biggest operator in the town in his particular field.

One of the most disgraceful incidents occurred when Mr Holt noted that three lots of mathematics homework were identical, and wrong. Naturally he assumed that there had been some copying and immediately accused a boy at the front of the class of being the culprit. The boy denied that he had copied and was rewarded with a clout across the head. Mr Holt repeated the accusation and the boy continued to deny it and received a clout every time. When this had been going on for some time the Gauleiter entered and joined in the fun, handing out a few clouts of his own. This performance continued until the class finished at twelve o'clock.

After dinner Messrs Lord and Holt prepared to carry on handing out further punishment, but were to be thwarted when the lad produced a letter from his father to the effect that he had seen his son do his mathematics homework the previous evening. Cheated of his prey, the Gauleiter retreated to his study, hemming and hawing, while Mr Holt could only carry on with the lesson.

The significant thing about the whole incident was that not a word was said to the other two who had turned in the same wrong homework. The obvious difference was that they lived on the right side of the railway line whilst the victim's father had a labouring job. To make matters even worse, the boy who received the thumping was a far better mathematician than the others and was almost certainly the one who had actually done the homework.

Pupils soon rumbled that there was no chance of them being involved in sporting activities and so made no effort to obtain football boots. The Gauleiter had a gang of twenty or so of these bootless types lined up in the hall and went along asking the same question, "Why have you no football boots?"

Each time he received the same reply; "I cannot find any, sir."

The last boy in the line very definitely lived on the right side of the railway line and was therefore able to give the correct answer without fear of any comeback. "My parents have no intention whatsoever of wasting money on football boots, when I never get the opportunity to play." The Gauleiter disappeared into his office without a further word.

There were several effects of this policy of discrimination directed at those whose financial situation meant that there was little or no possibility of them proceeding to university. Students from wealthy homes probably never realised what was happening and may even have looked down on their less fortunate colleagues as being pupils of lower academic ability who shouldn't really have been at a Grammar School in the first place.

The response of those consigned to the "B" stream varied. Some kept out of trouble by keeping as low a profile as possible and waited patiently until they left the school and were able to blossom into worthwhile careers. Some of them showed considerable business acumen. Two became successful businesswomen, and one to my surprise became a millionaire property developer.

Others retaliated in an entirely predictable way and formed a hard core who liked nothing better than to disrupt school activities. Considerable pressure was put on boys to join the school Air Cadet Squadron, but these misfits had seen quite enough of the school during the course of the day. The Gauleiter took pleasure in arriving at the school gates at night to be greeted by a couple of lads in ATC uniform waiting to throw up a smart salute. On several occasions he was to be disappointed when he found the picket ducked down behind the wall, pinned down by sniper fire from catapults and air rifles, and on one occasion the picket had been abducted.

Lest you should think that my criticisms are part of a personal vendetta here are a few unsolicited opinions from former pupils:

"The young people of Glossop were ill-served by Glossop Grammar School": a girl who later ran a successful business despite being consigned to the "B' stream.

"The only people who were given any instruction in sports were those who already knew how to play. I would have loved to learn how to play cricket, but they never even showed me which end of the bat to hold": a boy who later ran a local company and was a director of at least two others in the area.

Another boy, in the opinion of one member of staff, was so stupid that he didn't know his ABC. Despite this handicap he ended as a specialist in his chosen field, whose services were called upon by several European governments.

And finally, "XYZ could do no wrong because her folks had a grocer's shop and the teachers could get those little extras off the ration."

The effects of changing the Technical School into a Grammar School were exposed when the cotton industry collapsed. The new industries that gradually saved the town from complete disaster were started by entrepreneurs from outside. Where were the products of the Technical School set up by Lord Howard to provide the technicians and managers so that Glossop could hold its own with neighbouring towns? Bank managers, schoolteachers and solicitors are all useful members of the community, but hardly the people to set up new industries.

It would be an interesting exercise to follow the careers of those who progressed to university. I suspect that relatively few ended up working in Glossop; certainly many ended up in Canada, South Africa, Australia, New Zealand and the USA – quite a loss of talent to the town.

Alderman Doyle became a governor of the Grammar School in 1922 and Chairman in December 1926, and remained a member of the governing body for many years. The following remarks have been attributed to him:

> "On matters educational, he hoped he would live to see the day when every child of proved capacity would be able to pass unhindered or unhampered by poverty or any other circumstance from the elementary school to the university. There should be closer union between industry and education and he was sure that the education committee and the factory owners and managers were doing all they might to spread technical education."

I can only assume that Alderman Doyle and other governors were unaware of what was happening under their very noses. What also of His Majesty's Inspectorate? If Religious Instruction was a compulsory subject, why did they not insist on it being treated with due seriousness?

In 1960 the new Grammar School buildings on Talbot Road were completed, staff and students moved en bloc to the new site and the old buildings were turned into the Adult Education Centre. In 1966 Mr Cecil Lord retired and was replaced by Mr Climo.

In 1965 a new era commenced when Glossop Grammar School, West End School and Castle School were amalgamated to form the new Glossop Comprehensive School. Comprehensive schools have the advantage that, with the greater numbers on the school roll, it is possible to provide a wider range of subjects and cater for the careers of the students. One disadvantage is that with such large numbers of students on the one campus it is almost impossible for the head to know every student. Another criticism made of comprehensive schools is that the standards of behaviour have fallen, but this is part of a general trend.

In 1971, a new comprehensive school opened in Hadfield, and in 1989 Hadfield and Glossop Comprehensive Schools merged to become one split-site school, which was later renamed Glossopdale Community College.

14
LOCAL BOUNDARIES
OVER THE CENTURIES

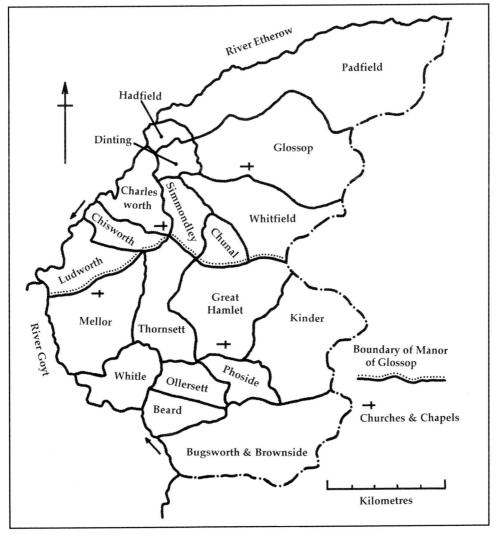

Map Nine: The Ancient Parish of Glossop.

Glossopdale was formerly divided into ten townships. These were the inner townships, Glossop, Whitfield, Chunal, Simmondley, Dinting, Hadfield, Padfield, and Charlesworth; and the outer townships, Chisworth and Ludworth. The fact that all ten townships have Anglo-Saxon names, as do others close by such as Hollingworth and Hayfield, suggests that they were established in Anglo-Saxon times, but it is likely that they superseded British settlements. The Celts had farmed the land previously and cleared some of the forest. It is entirely possible that their leaders built their halls on sites such as Lees, Simmondley and Hadfield Halls. The earliest map that shows the boundaries of the ancient townships is Sanderson's map of 1836, but they must have been established long before that date. All are listed in the Domesday Survey except Simmondley.

Most folks would not know where the boundaries of the old townships lie, but a hundred years ago inhabitants of the various townships knew where they were and it was a common practice to throw any young man from a neighbouring township into the local well. One of the tasks of the newly established police force was to stamp out this type of horseplay. There was even worse violence on Besthill Bridge, where youths from Charlesworth and Broadbottom fought pitched battles which led to the arrest of some combatants. The Rev Goodwin Purcell, in his book *Stone Upon Stone*, tells of how it was the practice of the natives of Charlesworth in the mid-19th century to throw stones at any stranger passing through. Township boundaries were delineated by streams, large rocks, watersheds, old tracks and ditches. Most of these markers were in position long before the townships came into existence.

The boundaries of Whitfield are marked by the Hurst and Glossop Brooks on the north side to where the Glossop Brook meets the Gnathole Brook near the Junction Inn. This boundary is marked by the boundary stone set into Victoria Bridge, and there was a similar stone set into the bridge near Hurst Mill until it was washed away in a flash flood. The Gnathole Brook marks out much of the rest as far as its source at the head of Whitethorn Clough. From the top of Whitethorn Clough the Whitfield boundary is completed by following the watershed to the summit of the Snake Pass, which is approximately the same as following the Pennine Way. Old inhabitants of Whitfield used to claim that Whitfield was an island because it was surrounded by water.

Chunal lies between Whitethorn Clough and Longshaw Clough. The southern boundary of Chunal follows the watershed until it crosses the A624 and carries on to Hollingworth Cross base which stands just off Monks Road at SK030904. At this point it makes a right-angled turn and crosses Monks Road until it reaches the Abbot's Chair. This sudden alteration in a township boundary is unusual, and as Hollingworth Cross base does not stand at a point typical for a wayside cross it is possible that it was once the base of Charlesworth Cross and was moved to this site to serve as a boundary marker. At the Abbot's Chair the boundary makes another right-angled turn and heads in a straight line north-west until it reaches SK016915 on Cown Edge. Where Longshaw stream passes under the road at the bottom of Chunal there is a boundary stone built into the bridge with the inscription "Townships of Simmondley and Whitfield". This is not strictly correct because it marks the boundary between Simmondley and Chunal. The explanation is that Whitfield and its smaller neighbour, Chunal, were often grouped together for administrative purposes.

The straight stretch from the Abbot's Chair to Cown Edge reveals something unusual. At SK022910, beside the track leading to Robin Hood's Picking Rods, stands a stone which is not the usual millstone grit of the region. At one time this stone had the letters LUDW carved into it to indicate that this was once the main route to Ludworth. Also the stone is rounded and shows no signs of being quarried. This is not the only example; at SK023909 is another piece of similar stone buried in the base of the wall beside the road to Rowarth, also exactly on the boundary.

Furthermore, on the boundary between Chisworth and Thornsett between SK013912 and

SK013910 there is a line of similar stones marking the boundary. I would suggest that the explanation is that these stones are glacial erratics which in medieval times were rolled to their present sites to mark out township boundaries. When fields were enclosed later, these stones were left in situ and built into the walls. The last stretch of the boundary leading up to SK016915 is marked by a ditch which is clearly artificial and almost certainly medieval.

The general position of the other township boundaries can be gleaned from Map Nine, and anyone interested in knowing their exact location should study Sanderson's map which is available in the Local Studies Section at Glossop Library.

There are various indicators to confirm other boundaries. The former site of Charlesworth Cross at the highest point on Monk's Road marks the divide between Simmondley and Charlesworth. The suitably named Boundary Cottage in Simmondley Lane marks the boundary between Simmondley and Dinting. Robin Hood's Picking Rods mark the point where Chisworth, Ludworth, Mellor and Thornsett meet. This ancient twin-shafted cross was in place long before these boundaries were set out. The rivers Etherow and Goyt serve as further boundaries.

Striking, oddly shaped rocks at the junction of Glossop, Padfield and Hope Woodlands are the Wain Stones, sometimes referred to as the Kissing Stones. The origin of the name is obscure; they certainly bear no resemblance to wagons. The surname Wain was formerly common in the Upper Derwent valley and they may have gained their name from a shepherd of that name. Another obvious feature which can be seen clearly from Cliff Road is the ditch along Peaknaze which defines the division between Glossop and Padfield. On the east side of the road, roughly opposite to Windy Harbour, is yet another glacial erratic which also lies on the boundary between Glossop and Padfield.

Now that Tintwistle has been transferred to Derbyshire its boundaries must be included. One boundary is the River Etherow. Tintwistle is divided from Hollingworth by the Hollingworth Brook and Ogden Clough, and to the east by Saltersbrook.

The Ancient Parish of Glossop was one of the most extensive in the north of England, stretching from Saltersbrook on the Yorkshire border in the east and to Marple Bridge in Cheshire in the west, a distance of twelve miles, and from Woodhead in the north to Chapel-en-le-Frith in the south, eleven and a half miles, the whole comprising no less than 49,960 acres. The rivers Etherow and Goyt formed its boundary on the north and west, while to the east it followed roughly the watershed along the summits of the moors. In addition to the ten townships it included Mellor, Thornsett, Whitle, Ollersett, Beard, Phoside, Bugsworth and Brownside, Kinder and Hayfield or Great Hamlet.

At one time it was the practice to Beat the Bounds at Rogation time. This was to make sure that people knew where the boundaries lay in the days before there were reliable maps and to check that none of the marker stones had been moved in an effort to claim the land of others. It also provided an opportunity for the priest to bless the fields and crops. I know of no record of the bounds of the Ancient Parish of Glossop being beaten. To traverse the circuit at one go would have been quite a feat.

The Manor of Glossop, held by the Talbots and Howards, formed the northern half of the Ancient Parish, consisting of the ten townships run from the vestry until the town received its charter.

On 23rd October 1866 Glossop's Charter of Incorporation arrived and a new era in the town's history commenced with the election of a Borough Council responsible for running its affairs. The Charter started by describing the boundaries of the new Borough of Glossop as intended in 1866. Basically, the boundary consisted of a circle of one mile radius centred on the Town Hall, running clockwise from Lane Head on the Woodhead Road, to where it met the Gamesley end of Dinting Arches. From that point it ran north-west until it met the Glossop Brook at Moodsbottom Bridge and then followed the Brook to its confluence with the Etherow at Woolley Bridge. From Woolley Bridge it followed the River Etherow upstream

Boundary Stone on
Saltersbrook Bridge,
now lost.

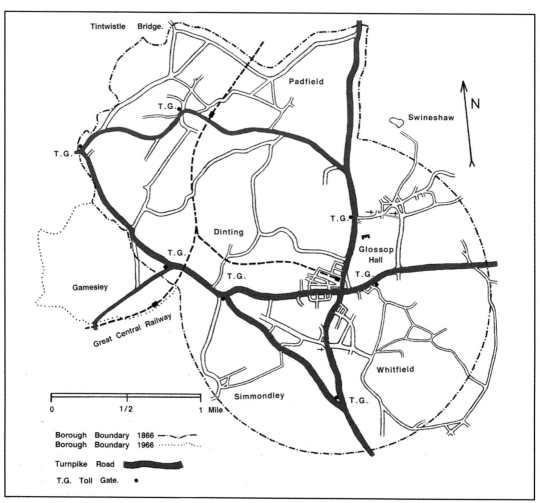

Map Ten: Boundaries of Borough of Glossop.

to Tintwistle Bridge, where it turned east and ran just north of Padfield Main Road until it met the Woodhead Road where it turned abruptly south until it reached Lane Head once more. In 1966 additional land at Gamesley was added to the Borough in connection with the sewage treatment plant.

The Charter next provided for a body corporate to consist of a mayor, six aldermen and eighteen councillors. The Borough was to be divided into three wards, namely All Saints' Ward, St James' Ward and Hadfield Ward. Each of the three wards was to return six councillors.

The first election of councillors for the Borough was held on 21st December 1866, and the aldermen were elected and assigned to their respective Wards on 26th December 1866; the Mayor was elected from among the aldermen and councillors on the same date. Finally, the boundaries of the three wards were delineated.

The Town Charter was kept in a glass case in the Town Hall, but was stolen on 20th January 1994 in the most brazen manner when it was wrenched off the wall. Fortunately, Mr Hamnett has left us a record of the details and anyone who wishes to examine them can do so in the Local Studies Section at Glossop Library or at the Heritage Centre.

It would be interesting to know why the one mile radius was chosen; perhaps the people of Charlesworth did not want to participate in the new Borough. There was certainly considerable opposition from the residents of Hadfield.

In 1894 the Parish Council Act was passed, and those portions of the hamlets of Simmondley, Chunal, Whitfield, Glossop, Hadfield and Padfield that were outside the Borough area were formed into Number Two Ward of the Parish of Charlesworth. Thus people are able to say that Charlesworth is larger than Glossop, and a glance at the map will show that this is so. This meant that Derbyshire Level and some of the properties in Woodcock Road above the Royal Oak were in Charlesworth, and the Charlesworth refuse cart had to make a special trip to these areas. The Borough Police were at one time limited to the Borough and folks just outside the boundary had to send to Charlesworth if they had problems. In 1952 the number of electoral wards was reduced to two with St James' Ward disappearing.

The possibility of overspill estates being built was first debated around 1954. Certainly there were plenty of brick terraced houses in Manchester which badly needed replacement and were inferior to the stone cottage houses in the poorer streets of Glossop. The first overspill estate was built at Hadfield in 1962 and in 1966 building work started on the larger estate at Gamesley. These new estates, where the houses had small gardens, parking spaces and open spaces for sports, had to be an improvement on the houses vacated in Manchester, some of which were thrown up with single brick walls. Public houses and a school were built on the Gamesley estate. On 12th September 1970, the Parish of St John, Charlesworth, opened a church in the Geoffrey Allen Centre on the estate.

Insufficient thought went into the planning as far as provision of employment or transport to work was concerned. When the Manchester to Sheffield line was under construction, there was a temporary station at Gamesley until the Dinting Viaduct and station had been completed. If a halt could be provided for the new estate at Hattersley, a little closer to Manchester, why not one at Gamesley? One could be excused for harbouring suspicions of the way rail transport has been dealt with in the area. If there is no station for passengers to board the train, then it is only to be expected that folks will look for an alternative mode of travel. The closure of the Woodhead line between two major industrial areas with inadequate roads joining them was another piece of peculiar logic. As recently as 1999, North West Trains announced that its train services from Glossop to Manchester were to be reduced from every twenty minutes to half hourly as passenger numbers had fallen, this at a time when the prospect of driving from Glossop to Manchester by road is a nightmare and a rapid transit system to Manchester ought to be a priority. There has even been a suggestion that Dinting Viaduct might be closed because of the cost of maintenance.

With the later reorganisation of county boundaries, there was discussion on the subject of whether Glossop would be better joined to Greater Manchester, but in 1972 Glossop people voted for Glossop to stay in Derbyshire as part of the High Peak rather than become part of Greater Manchester.

George Chatterton was the last Mayor of Glossop from 1973–74, after which Glossop officially became a part of the Borough of High Peak. Glossopians should note that the twin town signs on Chunal and Woodcock Road are located exactly on the Borough Boundary.

One obvious disadvantage of these new arrangements was that Glossop is at the extreme opposite end of the county to Derby, an arrangement which lent itself to suspicions that the town might be the last to benefit from improvements. For the town's representatives on the County Council it meant a long round trip, and even today, when car ownership is common, the trip to Derby and back can take up a large part of a day. The transfer of the County Offices from Derby to Smedley's Hydro at Matlock in 1955 was certainly a move in the right direction so far as High Peak was concerned.

One great advantage of a small town council was that aggrieved ratepayers could buttonhole their local councillor without difficulty. Local officials such as the Sanitary Inspector or Chief Constable were also well known.

With the steady erosion of the powers of local councils it might be thought that there would be little left for them to do, but these changes aimed at greater efficiency were almost inevitable as local councillors would have been overwhelmed by the seemingly endless flow of new legislation. The position of councillor had become much more time-consuming when compared with the days when men like the Woods and Sidebottoms could act in this capacity in addition to running large industrial concerns.

In 1982 the Gamesley and Hadfield overspill estates were taken over by High Peak Borough Council.

It is hard to imagine that, in the days when cotton was king, Glossop Council would have allowed the closure of the Woodhead railway line, or the building of an excessive number of residential properties, many on unsuitable sites, without ensuring there was adequate infrastructure to provide for the additional population.

15
A FEW FINAL COMMENTS

I hope I have cast some light on subjects either forgotten, or not previously mentioned. It has been said that those who do not learn from history are destined to repeat it. This can be true at all levels and there are some useful lessons to be learned from local people and events that can be used to our advantage. One example that springs immediately to mind is the way the Wood family knew when it was time to leave the textile industry.

We have seen that history and geography are closely connected, and how the climate situation, water supply, and existence of a home textile industry contributed to the growth of the town. The construction of roads and later a railway interconnecting two large industrial centres encouraged this growth. The existence of a large landowner with the foresight and capital to make the most of the opportunities was another important factor.

There may be some who regret the passing of past glories when the town was run by the Lord of the Manor and the Cottonocracy, but we have much to be thankful for. Glossop no longer suffers from a pall of smoke as in the days when dozens of mill chimneys belched their filth into the atmosphere. There was a time when the air was only clear during Wakes Week. Birds and sheep are much cleaner, streams are far less polluted and trout have returned. People are healthier, better housed, educated and clothed. In 1901 people in the upper class could expect to live for nearly 60 years, but those at the very lowest level for only 30. The manner in which way folks displaced in wartime integrated into the community is remarkable.

On the debit side of the ledger I would put the failure to provide adequate roads and rail services to cater for the needs of a commuter town at the top of the list. It is still the case that many ambitious young people have to leave the town in order to further their careers.

In the days before the Great War there was a whole range of social activities associated with churches and chapels ranging from sports clubs to bands, and dramatic societies all of which contributed to a sense of community. These activities never really recovered after the war, partly due to the loss of so many young men. At the risk of upsetting people of a religious bent I would suggest that some attended their place of worship so as to be eligible for the football team rather than to hear the sermon.

It has proved impossible to compress the events of centuries into so small a compass and I would have liked to have included so much more. The history of our churches and chapels certainly deserves a mention as does the remarkable progress of Roman Catholics, particularly in the field of education.

The trials and tribulations of folks on the new overspill estates is another topic worthy of a chapter. It is now a common sight to see Gamesley folks loading their shopping into a taxi outside a supermarket, a far cry from the days when the only time ordinary people rode in a taxi was at a funeral.

INDEX